BURY THE HOT

A childhood lost hiding from Hitler

A lifetime intent on escaping the memories

BURY THE HOT

A true story

Dear Bernadette,
Richard, Rufs & Theo —
To life. To friendship...
always
DL

Deb Levy

Grateful acknowledgement is made to Elie Wiesel for his words from his Nobel lecture
in 1986 and the book *Night*, and to Yeshiva University archives, Rescue Chidren, Inc.
collection for the cover photo.

ISBN 978-1484068632

For David

Of course we could try to forget the past.
Why not?
Is it not natural for a human being to repress what causes him pain,
what causes him shame?

Like the body, memory protects its wounds.

~ Elie Wiesel, *Nobel Lecture*, 1986

Szulim Wajnberg / Sal Wainberg's Family Tree

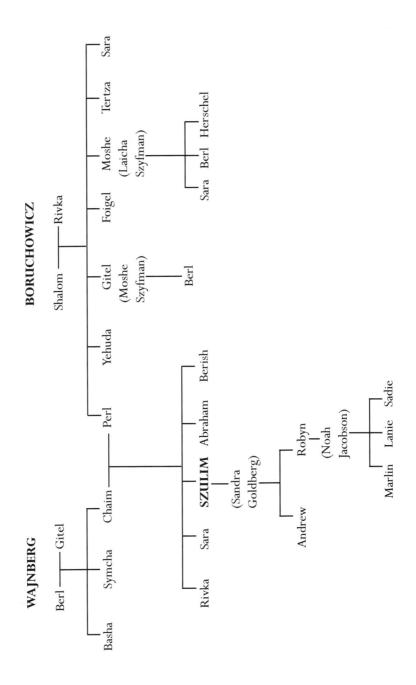

PROLOGUE

He doesn't have a number.

Yet still they ask. The curious, the skeptical, the ones who know all they need to know. When he speaks now of his past, they eye his forearm searching for that telltale proof. "Where's your number?" But Sal never went to a concentration camp. He is a survivor without a number.

I've known Sal Wainberg for as long as I've known my own parents - he a quiet presence at weddings and Bar Mitzvahs, the lighting of a menorah, the building of a *sukkah*. A lifetime of familial milestones and casual gatherings are the backdrop of our shared past in Miami. Sal and his wife Sandy are dear friends of my mom and dad, their children my playmates from long ago. Yet I knew nothing of his life from before. I didn't know that he could have had a number, or might not have been here at all. That he was once a boy named Szulim living in a Polish shtetl. But I have learned that what he doesn't have branded on his skin, he carries deep inside. An invisible barbed wire wrapping around him.

So he doesn't have a number; just a narrative. And he wants me to write it.

It started with a post-it note. Actually, if one were to be truly accurate, it could be argued that it was an ill-fated bullet fired at an archduke, or even a nail hammered into a plank of wood under the Middle Eastern sun. But for me, it was the small yellow square of paper stuck to the kitchen table in the spring of 2009 – rising on one end like a sail, beckoning – that took me by surprise.

"Sal Wainberg called," it read, and underneath his name, a phone number jotted down in my husband's barely legible scrawl. For a brief second, I panicked; did something happen to my parents? But that thought quickly dissolved, because it wouldn't be Sal who'd deliver bad news. Sandy, maybe. She's the one with an engaging energy, a bubbly spirit, the mom-figure with the *coochie coos*. I recalled being in 6th grade, contemplating training bras along with their daughter Robyn. "Booblets," Sandy had dubbed the non-existent breasts we were hoping to grow. And it was Sandy who lovingly and calmly cleaned up the mess I had made in their bathroom when, at age 10, I gorged on all of my candy at Robyn's Halloween sleepover party.

Sal? He was the one with a tentative smile, sitting just off to the side.

Curious as to why Sal would be calling me after 20 years of not living in the same city, after not seeing each other for two decades - save for a funeral or 60th birthday celebration - I picked up the phone and dialed their number. Sandy answered and immediately asked Sal to get on the call.

"Hi, Debbie?" he said without introductions or formalities you'd expect from a lifetime friend who you haven't spoken to in a lifetime. "Do you know my story?"

I was silent for a moment, racking my brain, trying to remember if my mother had said anything recently that stood out.

"Did you know I'm a Survivor?"

"I think I knew you weren't from here," I stammered. After all, he did have an accent. But how could the fact of a family friend suffering through the Holocaust not resonate somehow, not etch itself into my memory? I flushed, worrying that I might have been an incredibly self-centered teenager.

"I kept quiet most of my life because I didn't think people wanted to hear about it," he said. "I felt shame. Shame at not fighting back, shame at not knowing the things that everyone around me seemed to know. So I suppressed it. Not forgotten. Just compartmentalized."

My mind reeled as I remembered New Year's Eve 1980, dancing among a pack of kids in front of Sandy and Sal's house at midnight, singing *Ce-le-brate good times!* at the top of our lungs. I was curious to hear how Sal escaped. But even more, I wanted to know how he could have been a child who had experienced the horrible things that I had only read about and seen in movies, and then grown up to become a man who would play Kool and the Gang on his home stereo.

"I want you to write my story," he said into the silence of the phone. Sandy chimed in. "It's truly unbelievable."

And that is why it has remained untold for all these years. After everything Sal had been through, he was afraid to be doubted. "But everything I'm about to tell you is true," he said. "And I don't want you to embellish it. I don't want you to write some Hollywood version or make me into a hero. I just want the truth."

Sal couldn't make it up if he tried. Nor erase it, that he has tried. Nothing goes

away completely. It all comes back - and then some. He has wanted to write his story for a long time; he's just a lost soul, or so he tells me, when it comes to putting pen to paper. Seeing the written testimony is the final step he needs in the five stages of grief. He needs to know he's left his legacy.

We agreed upon a date for the first of what would be dozens of three-hour-long phone calls. Conversations where I would pepper him with questions I was terrified to ask, and he'd recall events with a level of detail that astounded me. All the while, Sandy would sit on the line, a silent listener, save for the times she and I spoke privately. As it turns out, there was a reason I didn't know his story.

"*Her tzich*," Sal said. Listen. "I think I'm ready to tell it now."

LIVING

Zelechow, Poland

September 1, 1939

Szulim didn't know, on the 17ᵗʰ of *Elul*, how a single day could divide before from after so completely. Even though the Jews of Zelechow welcomed the Sabbath bride every Friday as three stars rose in the sky, reflecting on the past week's events and ushering in a fresh start; and even though every fall, they celebrated the Jewish New Year, atoning for past sins and praying to be inscribed into the book of life - these rituals, drawing clear lines of distinction between before and after, weren't pivotal. Life in Szulim's *shtetl* went on in the same way. Old people died, babies were born, the occasional *samochod* rattled through town with creaky wheels, loudly announcing its beaten-up arrival from blocks away. But this day, the day known everywhere else as the first of September, was different. Szulim wouldn't know then, couldn't know then, the impact of a single day. Even a grown up could never have imagined how different the after would be from before.

Szulim was so excited to get his new clothes for Rosh Hashanah. The short black satin pants and matching vest, the white shirt, all hand made by Itzchok Witman, the village tailor. Next year at this time, he would get another new outfit, as would Rivka, his oldest sister. Rivka's clothes would go to his other sister Sara, Szulim's to his baby brother Abraham. Even though Rosh Hashanah was almost two weeks away, he put on the new clothes all by himself, and ran outside to show his friends.

"Don't get *schmutzy*!" Havah called.

He turned his back on the maid and began drawing in the dirt. With his stick, he could almost trace the letters of the *aleph beis*. He straightened his legs, rising from the crouch that kept his pants from touching the dusty, cool earth. Szulim wiped some soil off of his new Rosh Hashanah shoes and smoothed out his suit, hoping his friends from the neighborhood weren't hiding like the dim autumn sun. He wanted them to walk by and take notice of his new clothes.

He found his metal ring leaning against the side of the house and rolled it, prodding it along with the stick. He was thrilled the day his older cousin Herschel presented him with the bicycle rim. Exactly how Herschel got it, Szulim never knew. Herschel had his ways.

As he pushed the ring back and forth in front of his house, Szulim heard what sounded like a thousand samochods, ten thousand, and the overcast sky grew suddenly dark. He looked up. The 5,000 residents of Zelechow — women in *babushkas* plucking feathers from *Shabbos* chickens, bakers sliding challahs in the oven to rise, shopkeepers who would close their stores early in order to open their prayer books, the old man with the yoke across his shoulder carrying buckets of water for sale — they all looked up at the same moment towards the sky.

Szulim's jaw dropped. He had never seen anything like it. Machines, loud machines with wings, flying lower than the clouds. It was absolutely spectacular. *These must be what little Berleh calls airplanes*, Szulim thought. His three-year-old cousin, younger than Szulim by six months but wiser by far, knew of these strange metal birds from picture books he had seen at home, and he shared his knowledge with Szulim whenever they got together for holidays or the Sabbath. Szulim felt the ground vibrate as the strange thunder filled the sky. He listened to the long, slow whistle that seemed to come from the heavens and sink down to the earth.

"Szulim!" Havah came running out of the front door towards him. "Get inside!" At the same moment, his mother rushed from the family's store across the street and grabbed his arm, dragging him towards their one-story wood and brick house.

Szulim tried pulling from his mother's grasp. He didn't want to go inside. He stood mesmerized. Nothing in his three-and-a-half years had come close to this kind of excitement. Both his mother and Havah dragged him towards shelter. They didn't say why.

Inside the house, his father seemed excited too, rushing around shutting doors and windows while Sara and Rivka, sitting at the dining room table, seemed not to notice at all. Sara, at age four, played with her doll; Rivka nearly seven, practiced her letters. Why didn't anyone want to look at the sky?

Szulim heard the sound in his mother's voice. Did Abraham break something again? "This one's a *lobus!*" his *Mimeh* Tertza often said with a smile. She and the other aunts frequently commented on the impish nature of their youngest nephew. At two years old, Abraham was usually getting into some trouble or other, looking over his shoulder at wagging fingers with a mischievous grin.

"Did Abraham smash Mama's dish?" Szulim asked Rivka who just shook her head and continued with her writing.

Perhaps Rivka hadn't seen. Because certainly from the way his mother acted now, it must have been one of his *bubbe's* dishes that got broken. Szulim had never met his maternal grandmother; she died when his mother was still a girl. His oldest sister had been named after her.

"Chaim, the war has started!" His mother pressed her hand against her forehead. His father held onto the corner of the table, silent. Szulim didn't understand. What is war? All he knew was that he needed to get back outside.

Then, as suddenly as the noise circling above Zelechow began, it stopped. The villagers stepped nervously out of their homes, gathering in the street and wringing their hands as they looked up towards the east at the disappearing planes. The sky cleared to a light gray once again.

Back inside the house, preparations for Shabbat continued. But Szulim could see that everyone moved slower. Heavier. There must have been a lot of broken dishes, he guessed, grateful that he wasn't the one who caused the damage this time. He hoped he wouldn't be blamed anyway. He didn't want his father to punish him and pull out the *gartl*, the braided black rope Pop wore around his waist when he prayed, separating the upper, holy part of his body from the lower. Though lately, Szulim just laughed after the gartl smacked across his *tuchas*. Pop didn't laugh. He never laughed when he punished his sons. His shoulders would drop and he'd turn away, throwing the gartl on top of the armoire in his bedroom. Szulim and Abraham often waited until Pop left the room, then climbed on their parents' bed, reached for the gartl and hid it. Somehow, Pop would always find it again.

But Pop didn't pull out the gartl now. Feeling more confident that his parents weren't mad at him, Szulim went out back to the patio and saw a chicken feather lying on the ground. He picked it up and slowly traced from his wrist to his elbow, pleased as the hairs on his arm stood up in a tickle. He smiled, thinking about Abraham chasing after the chicken earlier in the day.

MAMA AND POP had left for the store just as Szulim woke up that morning, so Havah had gotten him dressed and made him a little bread and butter. When Szulim finished eating, Havah helped him catch the chickens that had been running around their patio since market day. Szulim's mother had gotten two birds from the marketplace on Tuesday which meant they'd be ushering in the Sabbath with all of his aunts — Mimeh Tertza, Mimeh Sara and Mimeh Foigel, along with Mimeh Gitel, her husband Feter Moshe Szyfman and their son Berl. Szulim loved when his little cousin came over for the Sabbath.

Szulim had felt much bigger than his almost four years when he and Sara carried the live chickens to the *shochet* for the ritual slaughter that morning. They held the chickens by their legs and tucked the feathered bodies under their arms.

"I go too! I go with Szulim." Havah sighed and had let Abraham accompany his big brother and sister.

Joisif Szlachter used a special knife and a contraption made of tin that looked like half of a funnel with a can attached. One at a time, he had carried the chickens behind his house and gently peeled back the feathers under their necks, cleaning their *gorgols* just so. "Oh God and God of our fathers," Szulim whispered to himself as he always did when the shochet recited the *brucha*, "please don't let this hurt the chicken too badly."

Working fast, Joisif Szlachter made a quick, clean cut of the throat without slicing the neck completely in two, as was prescribed by the laws of *kashrut,* and placed the chicken's head down into the funnel. The chicken didn't die immediately, but kicked until all the blood ran out and into the can, some of it spilling onto the ground. Szulim had waited patiently, reciting in his head the aleph beis, the *v'ahavta* and whatever other prayers he had learned that week in *cheder* in order to pass the time. Finally, the shochet tucked the dangling head under the wing and began on the second chicken. But this time, he accidentally dropped the bleeding animal. In a spastic quest for life, the bird had run circles around the yard. Szulim jumped back, but Abraham had run after the chicken laughing.

THE TRIP TO the shochet seemed so long ago, even though it had only been that morning. Now, it was nearly dusk; almost time to leave for *shtiebl*, the center of prayer established in their neighbor's living room. Szulim sat on the patio with the chicken feather and hunched into his jacket, feeling not just the cold that came with the season's setting sun, but something more. There were no broken dishes. But his parents' reaction to the noise from the clouds told him there was a problem. Abraham, meanwhile, ran around the house and yard as if nothing had happened. As if the sky grew dark with airplanes all the time. Szulim wondered how his brother could be younger than him, over a year younger, yet braver. He didn't understand what it all meant. But he knew it was something he'd remember forever.

FALL 1939

SZULIM WOKE UP on Tuesday morning, just four days after the airplanes cast a shadow on his shtetl; a shadow that remained long after the flying machines disappeared past the horizon. It was market day and Szulim couldn't wait to see the entire village gather at the big open plaza in the center of town - schoolmates from cheder, Pop's friends from shtiebl, farmers from the outskirts of the shtetl who came to sell their crops and buy things at his parents' store. Hundreds, thousands, would gather, Jews and gentiles alike, circling each other with civility, engaging in commerce.

He skipped from table to table, walking carefully around blankets laid out to display the wares, taking in the colors of the vegetables on the farmers' carts, the smells of the *cykoria* root ground up and ready to be brewed into a thick, dark liquid. He ran his hands over the bolts of fabrics when his mother wasn't looking, his fingers tracing mountains of smooth and rough. Each shopkeeper specialized in one type of product, bartering for services, attempting agreement towards a fair price. Jewish women in modest dress, their heads covered with scarves, rubbed elbows with the less pious, intellectual Jews who wore colorful clothes patterned with florals. *Chossid* men wore vests and dark coats, always hats, not *yarmulkes*, so as not to call too much attention. Though it was quite obvious who was who. Normally, the non-Jewish population of Zelechow was very small. But on Tuesdays, Szulim never saw so many *goyim*.

"Stop staring, Szulimel." His mother yanked his arm as she continued with her shopping. He couldn't help it. They looked different somehow.

Szulim could see the synagogue at one corner of the marketplace while a huge church with a tall steeple marked the other side of the square, along with the public school. Szulim's aunts had gone to the Polish school when they were younger, but his mother only learned to read and write Yiddish from the *Trine*, the women's prayer book. Her schooling ended at age 11 when her mother died and she, being the oldest daughter, had to care for her siblings.

Szulim followed his mother to the chicken man. "Mama, get that white one!"

She looked around the squawking cluster of feathers. She didn't need to lift the birds to know which was the plumpest. She could just tell. Szulim sighed when she selected a brown hen, holding the chicken under her arm that would provide enough meat to feed their family of six, plus Havah, plus the *oirech* Pop was bound to bring home from Shabbat services. Mama always made extra to feed the lonely men without family or food.

Szulim prayed silently. *Please let there be an unlaid egg when Mama cuts it open on Friday!* He loved when the hens gave him that Shabbos treat, a soft and creamy yolk without a shell.

They hurried back home and let the chicken flap its way around the patio. Mama rushed across the street to the store while Havah fed him and Abraham lunch. Even though his parents' store was open every day except Saturday, Tuesdays were especially busy with all the farmers and people from nearby smaller villages coming to town for market day. Mimeh Tertza and Mimeh Gitel worked in the store all the time, along with Mama and Pop selling various dry goods and household necessities. The store had been in Mama's family for generations, and it was only when Mama's father died, shortly after she and Pop got married, that Pop took over running the business. Mimeh Tertza didn't go to school like Mimeh Foigel or Mimeh Sara. But even Foigel and Sara could be found working behind the shelves on Tuesdays. They worked hard, yet always had time for a kiss.

"Why doesn't Abraham go to cheder?" Szulim asked Havah as he finished lunch and put on his jacket.

"He will, soon. You were just a bit older than your brother when you started studying."

Szulim walked by himself to his tiny school which, being a Tuesday, began later than usual. Mendl, a bigger boy of four, waved to him as they each approached the *rebbe's* house and the two youngsters headed down a few steps into the dark room, lit only by a single candle. Rouwen and Aaron were already sitting on the little wooden bench in the basement. Lessons hadn't even begun, but already Szulim counted the hours until the four boys could emerge back into the daylight and play.

"*Git morgon*, rebbe." Szulim sat next to the others and greeted his teacher. There were other rebbes in Zelechow, as there were other cheders. But this rebbe had been teaching young boys the Hebrew letters for years. He was very old, nearly ancient, *like the men in the bible* Szulim thought. Thick glasses rested upon his brow, his poor eyesight the result of straining in such dim light. A full beard hid the rebbe's face, and soot from the candles covered his hands and clothes. Apparently even the *mikvah* couldn't wash away the black. Szulim wondered if he had even stepped outside to see the airplanes the week before.

"Kometz aleph…" The rebbe sat at the head of the table clutching his wooden stick and pointing to the first letter of the alphabet in their *siddurs*.

"Ah," the boys recited, looking down into their prayer books.

"*Kometz beis…*"

"Ouch!" Rouwen's cry interrupted their recitations as the rebbe's stick rapped on his fingers. He sat up straight and stared at the words on the page. Szulim never forgot his lessons and he worked hard to pay attention, sitting very still, repeating exactly as he was told. The rebbe continued in his dusty voice. *Kometz beis, kometz veis* … four boys in little hats reciting the Hebrew consonants with their vowel sounds over and over, following dutifully in the siddur. Soon they would know all of their letters and could start putting them together to make words. Szulim looked forward to being able to read on his own like his sister Rivka. At age seven, she was already quite a student, having learned at *Bais Yaakov*, the girls' school.

SZULIM, ROUWEN, MENDL and Aaron walked up the few steps and out of the cellar at the end of class. They scanned the street, looking for other kids who lived nearby. Summer was over, but there was still enough light and warmth to run around outside. "Let's play *Comme Comme Tir*," Mendl said, running away from the boys. "I'll be 'it.'"

Mendl called to Szulim. "Come to the door?"

Szulim didn't have the secret; so he answered *Gai tzi an andre tir!* "Go to another door!" The entire neighborhood was their playground. They picked up pebbles from the dirt road and tossed them at each other's feet. Szulim ran into his house to get his slingshot. Havah had helped him fashion it together from a birch branch and the stretchy band his mother fished through her underwear with a safety pin. His mother didn't mind; she had extra pieces of elastic. Szulim and the boys took turns aiming small stones towards the giant yew that stood between his house and the neighbors.

Szulim noticed Havah watching him. Usually she stayed in the house with Abraham, doing some chore or another. But today she peered from the doorway, a silent figure in a gray blouse and black skirt, keeping a close eye. He wasn't doing anything wrong. He tilted his head and looked at her. She waved, and after too long of a pause smiled, as if for a moment she had forgotten how. Havah was younger than his mother, but taller. When Szulim was a baby, he snuggled into Havah, sucking his fingers and playing with her long, curly dark hair. Now Abraham got the cuddles.

Not many families in Zelechow had a maid. Then again, not many mothers worked outside the home. Mama needed the help and told Havah what to do. But in three years, when Mama would beg Havah to hide with them, Havah would choose her own family who lived in a nearby village. Szulim never really knew the people who loved Havah long before he did.

———

THE NEXT DAY, after spending the morning in the dark basement practicing his letters, Szulim wandered around looking for someone to play with. None of the other kids were outside, just a couple of soldiers in dirty green pants pointing every now and then at the bigger homes. He had noticed them more and more, these Germans, as his parents called them. Szulim ignored them and walked across the street to the store. He strolled past the barrels on either side of the door, pickles on the left and whole herrings on the right. Mimeh Tertza stood in front of the long counter that ran halfway down the entire length of the room. She pulled cartons of sugar cubes and chocolate out of large wooden crates and stacked them neatly on the shelves under the counter. When she saw Szulim, she pulled a sugar cube loose from a box and handed it to her nephew, putting a finger over her lips.

"Don't tell your mother!" Mimeh Tertza could always be counted on to give him a little something special. Szulim sucked on the treat and sank into Tertza's open arms, allowing her to plant several kisses on top of his *keppeleh*. She turned back to her restocking as Ester Nachman walked in and breathlessly greeted his mother, who was standing behind the counter. "Hello, Perl. I haven't heard word from my sister in Sobolew. Mind if I make a call?"

Szulim's mother, a short woman with enough girth so that hugging her was an act of great pleasure, nodded. "Of course!" She motioned with the back of her hand to the phone. Ester picked up the earpiece and turned the crank handle of the telephone that hung on the wall above the pickle barrel. She leaned towards the protruding black cup that looked to Szulim like the bottom of a clarinet.

"Hello, operator? I'm looking for the family of Bela Mynowski in Sobolew. Can you put me through to the bakery?"

Szulim wandered amongst the floor-to-ceiling shelves of powdered sugar, cigars and cigarettes, candy, rice and flour. He couldn't believe how many different kinds of flour there were. No clothes. Nobody bought clothes in Zelechow. Mama made the family's clothes, and what she couldn't fashion, Itzchok the tailor sewed. Szulim breathed in the smell of the soaps and the candles. His parents were lucky. No one else in the entire Garwolinska region sold cigarettes, salt and herring. And no one else in Zelechow had a phone, except for the fire department, the police and city hall. Then again, most anything that needed to be spoken of could be done face to face.

"Give me the charges please." Szulim listened as Ester argued with the operator. "It can't be that much! I didn't talk that long!" She hung up the phone and turned to Szulim's mother.

"*Veyismere*, Perl. Can you believe three *zlotys* for just a few seconds?" Ester slid the payment across the counter. "But thanks God, they're okay."

"Thanks God." His mother dropped the coins into a small wooden box. His parents didn't charge their neighbors and friends a fee for occasional use of the phone. It was simply a convenience for the community. But long distance phone service was expensive and people were honest, so they paid the charges right as they hung up. Most people in Zelechow sent telegrams to relations who lived in other shtetls. It was much cheaper.

Szulim stood right next to the phone as it rang, but he knew not to answer it. He listened as his father picked up the earpiece and a moment later shouted "*Mazel Tov!*"

Pop carefully wrote down the message and handed Tertza the scrap of paper. "Can you bring this to Mordche and Menuche Perkal? Their Tojbe had a baby boy."

"Oy, finally some good news," Szulim's mother said turning away from the back shelves. "Though God knows what kind of world this baby is being born into."

Mimeh Tertza ran to deliver the message to the grandparents. They'd need to make arrangements to attend the *bris* in Maciejowice. Even if his father hadn't offered his congratulations, Szulim knew the phone call brought good tidings. If the call brought word of a death, Pop would go himself to notify the family, but only if there were funeral arrangements and a need for imminent travel. Otherwise Pop would wait until he ran into the person sometime later in the week. No good could come from rushing bad news.

Szulim's head barely reached the top of the long countertop, but he could see the pencil in his mother's hand flying across the scrap paper, her lips moving as she added up the purchases. The customers stayed in the front of the store, never going behind the burlap curtain that separated the storage area from the products for sale. Szulim breathed in and took comfort from the earthy smell of the dirt floor. He watched the specks of dust dance in the sunlight that streamed in from the front windows. In the summer, his parents would close for the night when it grew dark, long after dinner. But soon, with the days beginning to grow shorter,

Pop would turn on the carbide lamps in the late afternoon, casting a blue glow across the large bags of sugar, kasha and flour. And soon it would be too cold for Szulim to spend time hanging around a place with no heat.

———

NORMALLY SIX CHAIRS of the same honey-colored mahogany marked the family's places around the table. Mama and Pop at the heads, two girls on one side, the two boys on the other. But on Friday nights and Saturdays, the table would open to seat thirteen. Mama, Pop, Szulim and his three siblings; Mimehs Tertza, Foigel and Sara; Feter Moshe Szyfman, Mimeh Gitel and their son Berl. And of course, an *oirech*. There was always room at their table for a hungry stranger. Szulim loved how the table could grow and shrink, and had once counted twenty chairs surrounding it.

Szulim had another uncle Moshe, his mother's brother Feter Moshe Boruchowicz. Big Feter Moshe Boruchowicz was as different from thin Feter Moshe Szyfman as night from day. Szulim preferred Feter Moshe Boruchowicz, but the big uncle who always had an extra sweet in his pocket usually spent the holidays with his wife Laicha's family. Feter Moshe Szyfman, who happened to be Laicha's brother, always came to Szulim's house with Mimeh Gitel and little Berl.

Even though the Szyfman's lived across the street in the apartment behind Gedalia Yosef's bakery, right next to Szulim's parents' store, little Berl rarely played outside. So Szulim loved spending Shabbat with his younger cousin. It was because of Berl that Szulim knew the flying samochods from two weeks ago were called airplanes. Feter Moshe Szyfman didn't work at the store like Mimeh Gitel. He stayed home with his ailments and spent time talking to Berl and teaching him things. Moshe was spindly, pale, and always sniveled like he had a cold or was frightened. Szulim thought it strange that a grown man would be scared. Pop was never scared. Pop was also stronger than Feter Moshe. But he didn't tell these things to Berl. And for sure he didn't discuss it with his parents. *Dzietzy i ribi glosi nie mayem.* Children and fish do not have a voice.

Mimeh Gitel spooned some pickles onto Berl's plate – no horseradish for the kids – and passed the bowl to her sisters. "How much longer, you think, before our army pushes back on Hitler?" Feter Moshe Szyfman asked before sipping his wine.

"*Oy gut*, I'm so sick of hearing talk of Hitler," said Mimeh Gitel as she cut Berl's kugel.

Szulim's mother tilted her head towards the three boys, and then across the table to his sisters. He watched as the grown ups all gave a slight nod. Years later, he would learn what the adults at that table already knew. Just a few days before, Germans had marched into town, seizing and killing a dozen villagers, setting homes on fire and taking prominent members of the shtetl as hostages for 24 hours. Actions like this were nothing new, but now, the pogroms were raged by foreigners.

One of Szulim's aunts cleared her throat as the talk resumed. "We're just lucky Zelechow's a small village," said Mimeh Foigel. "We didn't get the bombs like Sobolew."

"Well, they have the train station." Pop read the newspaper at the marketplace whenever he could, and so he knew important things. "But it shouldn't be as bad here as it is in Germany. We have our own government."

"Was that a sniffle?" Mimeh Gitel came at Berl with a handkerchief prepared to wipe away tears or mucus, though Szulim could see neither. The Szyfman family always seemed to have a handkerchief, along with a fear of actually needing it. Szulim wasn't afraid to get sick. That's when Mama and Pop loved him more.

"Play time is over," Pop said, addressing the children. *What? They hadn't even gone outside yet! Surely it wouldn't get dark so early in the day.* Szulim looked out the window but the sun was still shining.

"We don't know what will happen with this war," Pop continued, "but we have to be afraid." He looked from Rivka to Sara; at Berl, Szulim and Abraham. Abraham just giggled and bounced in his seat.

His father was talking about the Germans. They must have *gartls*, too, otherwise why should the kids be afraid? Szulim wondered if he and Abraham would laugh at the Germans and their silk cords, like they laughed at their father when he threatened to punish them. Maybe, unlike his father, these Germans would actually like hitting him across the tuchas. This must be why, just before Rosh Hashanah one year before, *Zayde* had said he was glad about dying.

SZULIM HAD BEEN just a little kid, not much older than Abraham now, but he remembered clearly his one and only visit with his paternal grandfather. It had been summer's end last year when Pop chose Szulim to accompany him to Maciejowice to see Zayde. Szulim had never before left Zelechow and was thrilled. A journey! With Pop all to himself! The train didn't run to either village, Zelechow or Maciejowice, so they took a *droshky*, an open wagon pulled by horses. Szulim was amazed at the rubber tires that made very little noise, unlike the squeaks he was used to hearing when the metal wheels of other droshkies screeched along the dirt and cobblestone streets of his town once or twice a day. For four hours, Szulim had jumped from bench to bench on the rocking wooden platform, occasionally looking out at the passing farmlands or copse of trees. They were the only passengers traveling to that tiny village.

When they finally arrived in the other shtetl, Pop helped Szulim down from the carriage and grabbed their small cardboard suitcase. They held hands and walked across the street to an unfamiliar house. Pop seemed to know exactly where he was going.

"Chaim! Szulim!" An old lady opened the door and Pop took her into his arms. Even though she was much shorter than Pop, Szulim noticed that she grabbed his father's head and slobbered kisses on his cheek, just like Mama and his aunts did to him. She let go of his father and turned to him. "My sweet Szulimel! What a big boy you've become!"

"That's my mama, Szulim. Give your Bubbe a hug."

They walked into the house and a man who looked like his father stood up from a chair. "Symcha!" Szulim's father grabbed this man and they squeezed each other's shoulders and kissed each other's cheeks. "Szulim, this is your Feter Symcha, my brother. He last saw you when you were just a tiny baby."

"Is that Chaim?" A woman had rushed out of the kitchen, wiping her hands on an apron. She hugged his father and pulled back, wiping her eyes. She bent down to Szulim and scooped him up into her arms. "I'm Mimeh Basha! Your Pop's sister, just like Sara and Rivka are your sisters."

Szulim was confused trying to sort it all out. He thought only Mama had a brother and sisters, while Pop just had Mama. Now, here were all these people laying claim on his father. During the short time he spent in Maciejowice, he endured hugs and pinches from his bubbe, tickles under the chin from Feter Symcha, doting from his Mimeh Basha. His Zayde, however, lay in bed, quiet and drawn. Zayde was the same size as Pop and had the same yellowish-reddish beard. But he was much skinnier, and his cheeks were pale, not pink like Pop's. He lifted his fingers, beckoning Szulim to come closer. Szulim stepped back, trying to hide behind his father, but Pop nudged him towards the bed.

"Give Zayde a kiss."

Szulim sat in a tall wooden chair next to the bed and placed his small hand into Zayde's. Wavy lines extended out from his grandfather's bony fingers, like plowed rye fields forming bumps along a cracked earth. The old man's eyes fluttered open, taking in for a moment the sight of his grandson before searching the room and finally resting his eyes on Szulim's father. Zayde's eyes grew wide and his mouth opened and closed silently, as if working up the energy it would take to speak. Finally, a whisper emerged in words that Szulim could not understand, uttering sentiments in a combination of Hebrew and Yiddish, the Holy Language.

"*Shomer*," he whispered. "So you shouldn't be seen."

The ride back to Zelechow was no different than the ride to Maciejowice; long, bumpy. But Pop was different. He sat quietly, his back rounder than usual. Szulim stopped bouncing among the three benches and nestled into his father, playing with the *tzitzit*, the fringe of his father's prayer shawl that lay hidden under his jacket and vest.

"What did Zayde say?" Szulim asked.

His father sighed and explained that Zayde was very sick. Szulim figured as much, since he was in bed the whole time. "But Zayde's not sad because he knows life will be much worse after he's gone. When there's a war."

Szulim didn't know what was war, but according to Zayde, it meant hard times were coming. What could be harder than lying in bed not feeling well? Pop had gone on to say that Zayde gave him a warning. "When the war comes," Pop said, "I should try not to be visible. That's how we'll survive."

A few months later, Pop had gotten word and went back to Maciejowice, alone. When he returned, he uttered a prayer Szulim had never heard before, his voice strained and cracking.

Now, SITTING AROUND the table with his siblings and cousin, the look on Pop's face reminded Szulim of that droshky ride a year before. But Pop's shoulders weren't round. They stood out, pointed. And his voice was sure. It wasn't just the children who paid close attention. Mama, all his Mimehs, Feter Moshe; they looked to Pop, too, searching his face for strength they could borrow. Szulim listened as the grown ups talked of this thing called war. The only detail he understood was that he needed to obey his parents or else. He'd try. Even when he couldn't listen very well, he always did try.

Szulim didn't know who or what Hitler was. But from the way he had been hearing the grown ups talk ever since the airplanes flew through the sky, he knew he disliked the way it sounded. Sharp, angry. It must be a person he didn't know, someone not from Zelechow. Definitely not Jewish.

———

SZULIM'S FAMILY GATHERED on the patio where the chickens were squawking around. Normally there'd only be one or two birds, but because tonight was the start of *Yom Kippur*, the custom of *shlogin kaports* called for each person to have his own rooster or hen. Earlier that week, when Szulim had gone with his mother and Havah to pick out the chickens at the marketplace, Mama had quizzed him.

"How many roosters, Szulim?" Mama asked.

Szulim counted on his fingers — Pop, himself and Abraham. "Three!"

"Very good. And how many chickens?"

That was easy. The same number. Szulim loved that his family was perfectly balanced, though he thought it horribly unfair that the girls got laying hens on the eve of *Yom Kippur*. *What good is a rooster?* No matter how hard he prayed this week, no boy chicken was going to provide that delicious unlaid egg; everyone knew that. Yet he didn't complain. The poorer families got only one rooster or chicken, even if they had five or six kids. Szulim knew he was lucky.

Pop grabbed a hen and handed it to his eldest daughter. Rivka took it by its legs and swung it over her head. Three times, the hen circled above Rivka as she recited, "This is my exchange, my substitute, my atonement; this hen shall go to its death, but I shall go to a good, long life, and to peace."

Mama took Rivka's hen and tied a piece of string around its leg; each person had to eat from the bird that swung over his or her head. Pop grabbed another hen and Sara, being the second oldest, went next – straining to hold the chicken aloft and look up past her eyebrows at the squawking, flapping bird while asking God to transfer her sins onto the swinging animal. Szulim looked around at his family. He couldn't remember a single time that any of them had left food on their plates, so he wasn't sure what sins they had to atone for. But he kept his thoughts to himself.

"Abraham! Shh!" Mama waved her free hand at Szulim's brother who was laughing and flapping after the chickens while she swung a bird over Szulim. Pop spoke the Hebrew words for Szulim to repeat, the same words his sisters had recited on their own. After Mama and Pop each swung a bird over their own heads, they all went together to bring the fowl to slaughter.

The shochet was even busier than the prior week, swinging his knife and saying the brucha so fast as to be unrecognizable. He cut a section off of each bird, wrapping the pieces separately and handing the package to Mama. Szulim wondered how the poor ate on other days, when it wasn't customary to give part of your chickens for *tzedakah*.

Together, they carried the lifeless birds home where the kids helped Havah pluck the feathers. Though hot water would have made the job easier, the laws of *kashrut* forbade it. Szulim, Sara and Rivka worked silently, removing the feathers one by one from the six chickens, picking each bird clean. Szulim watched as Havah lit some paper and used it to singe the skin, ridding the birds of the bits of feather that they couldn't pull out.

Havah brought the plucked chickens into the kitchen where Szulim's mother removed the head and the toenails, then cut the birds into smaller parts, still taking care to mark them so each member of the family could partake of their own. In order to make the meat kosher, Mama soaked the chicken in water for 30 minutes, then rubbed the flesh with kosher salt and let it sit for an hour before rinsing. Sometimes, when no one was looking, Szulim would reach into the salt bowl and pinch a tiny, milky white pebble to place on his tongue, enjoying the sharp tang that would make his mouth fill up with spit.

———

BECAUSE *KOL NIDRE*, the start of Yom Kippur, fell on a Friday this year, the Shabbat meal could not wait for sundown. Three stars in the sky would mark the start of the Sabbath *and* the fast, so dinner had to be eaten while it was still light. Pop closed the store earlier than usual for a Friday afternoon in order to go to the *mikvah* where all the men washed their bodies for the Sabbath. Mama would go afterwards with the women.

Meanwhile, Havah enlisted the help of Rivka, Sara and Szulim to polish the silver. Six candlesticks, two tall and four smaller ones for the children, graced the table each week. Szulim loved how the flames from the candles danced across the shiny surfaces of the silver tray upon which they stood, the sterling forks and spoons placed neatly around the settings. There was a comfort to the way candlelight flickered across the children's faces as they listened quietly to the grown ups' conversation. Szulim and his siblings knew the rules. Children didn't talk at dinner; they simply ate. Havah dined alone in the kitchen. The long, thick candles would provide the only light in the house and last until all songs were sung, food was savored, and stories were shared.

Szulim concentrated on his job, rubbing his candlestick, inspecting for fingerprints. Abraham stood on the chair, sucking his thumb and watching. As soon as Szulim was satisfied, the toddler grabbed the candlestick, giggling as he left a streak of saliva on the stem.

"Abraham!" Szulim slugged his little brother for ruining his hard work; Abraham only laughed and slugged back.

Soon they were on the floor, rolling and pulling and smacking. Rivka and Sara continued with their chores; they were used to the brawls. Mama, no stranger to the ways of young boys, ran in from the kitchen, grabbed their arms, yanked them to a standing position and pinched each child on his tuchas. *Wart ve der tate vet ahaim cumen!* "Just wait until your father gets home!"

Abraham and Szulim rubbed their bottoms. Would Pop really reach for the gartl on Kol Nidre, just as he was preparing to account for his sins? Most likely he'd sigh, saying *zeit broigis ain tog*. "Do me a favor and don't talk to each other for the rest of the night." That was the worst punishment for the two brothers. And utterly impossible.

Even though tonight was Shabbat, the meal would be a simple one - a little soup with some *locshen* or noodles, and Mama's gefilte fish, which she had made the night before from a carp Pop brought home and killed in the kitchen. Mama cooked the carp in *yuch,* a delicious fishy broth. "No spices, Rivkaleh and Saraleh," Mama said, teaching Szulim's sisters the right way to prepare a Kol Nidre meal.

"Too much salt makes you thirsty, and God forbid you drink on Yom Kippur." Szulim loved the sweet, sharp taste of Mama's gefilte fish made with generous amounts of sugar and pepper, though tonight's fish might not be so peppery. Still, Szulim's mouth watered at the thought of it all — challah, gefilte fish, chicken. And for sure some compote after they finished everything on their plates.

————

THE CHICKENS HAD been blessed, slaughtered, plucked, salted and soaked. Szulim watched as his mother chopped the carrots, onions and turnips and slid them into the giant pot along with the pieces of chicken. Once the chicken soup got going, that warm, yellow aroma would fill the house. It was the smell of family. And on the days when Mama worked longer than usual in the store, Szulim would press his nose into his sleeve and breathe deep. Sometimes, if he was lucky, he could still inhale brothy traces as late as Tuesday or Wednesday. Later, when he was six or seven, he would bury his head in his arm, desperate for that comforting aroma. Abraham would watch and think Szulim was trying to hide tears. But for those two years, he couldn't hide anything. Besides, there'd be no shame in crying then. Not when foul odors replaced pleasant memories.

Mama set the candles in their holders as Szulim and his siblings washed their hands and faces and dressed in their nicer clothes. Carefully, he put on his new outfit, the same short black pants, vest and white shirt he had tried on over two weeks before. Szulim thought about what happened the last time he put on the special clothes; he looked out the window towards the sky. It looked clear. But still, his parents seemed different ever since that day. He put on his shoes and came to the dining room. Szulim knew what would happen if he didn't sit respectfully. He'd be forced to leave the table. Szulim always sat dutifully and ate. They all did. That's what was expected of them.

The children weren't the only ones who dressed up for the doubly special occasion. Mama had taken off her babushka and replaced it with her *sheitel*. Though she owned two wigs of perfectly coiffed dark hair, Szulim only ever saw one. Mostly resting on the head-shaped stand in her and Pop's bedroom, or on her head when she went to shul. While one was in use, the other went to Leah Gothelf to be fixed. Years later, he'd find Leah Gothelf in Paris, working in a shop that sold fancy wigs to women who kept their heads covered for reasons other than modesty. Szulim would look around the store, his mouth agape, staring at all the hair without bodies, and he'd wonder what happened to the sheitels in his small Polish village. But now, Szulim simply eyed the wig on the stand in his home. God forbid he ever touched it. It was too expensive.

Szulim loved watching the transformation of his parents on Friday afternoons. They'd come back from the mikvah smelling clean. Not so much from the bath itself, but the soaping off they did before immersing in the waters of purity. Then they'd change from their normal work attire into special clothes. Szulim stood at the door of his parents' room and observed as they decorated themselves.

Pop put on a pocket watch, the chain peeking out from his vest. But what fascinated Szulim was Mama's jewelry. The gold wedding band was nothing out of the ordinary; Mama wore that everyday. It was the strand of shimmering white beads around her neck, the gold earrings adorning her earlobes, the gold watch just for show – "I know the time like I know my knuckles. So what it doesn't work? *Feh*." – all magically appearing on special occasions that made Szulim stare. He and Abraham had spent hours searching the closet for the secret place where Mama kept her valuables. But items of worth were kept in his parents' store across the street. Szulim would learn about the hole in the wall of the store when there was no longer a store. When needs became wants, and adornments were of another lifetime altogether.

NORMALLY SZULIM ACCOMPANIED Pop to shtiebl before dinner, but tonight they'd eat before walking to shul. Mama and Pop placed their hands atop each child's head, and one by one whispered the parents' blessing to the children. *Ye'simcha Elohim ke-Ephraim ve'chi-Menashe*. May God make you like Ephraim and Menashe, role models for the Jewish people. The girls were to be like Sara, Rivka, Rachel and Leah. Szulim couldn't understand how Sara and Rivka weren't already like themselves. Mama lit the candles as they blessed the Sabbath, the wine, and then washed their hands and blessed the challah. "*Aveynu shalom, Aleichem!*" Pop led the *zmirot*, everyone joining in song as they ate.

After the meal was finished, Havah came out of the kitchen to clean up. Szulim buttoned his coat and stood on the front step of his house, staring up at the heavens. So many stars began to shine at once. Good thing Pop had a calendar that told him exactly when the first three stars would appear every Friday. Especially tonight, when they had to be finished eating before then. Szulim didn't fast, nor did his siblings. "Not until you become a *Bar Mitzvah*," Pop always said. He watched his mother and father closely during that 24-hour period, listening to the rumblings in their bellies. The smell of Pop's breath as he davened and chanted the *Avinu Malkeinu* made Szulim's nose crinkle. No food for a whole day! He both feared and longed for the time when he could honor that tradition.

Winter 1939 – Spring 1940

The cold came with a force. Winter may have brought the drop in temperature, but another shadow altogether blocked the sun. Soldiers patrolling the shtetl wore stone faces that chilled the air around them. Except for the sputter and roar of unfamiliar motorized vehicles, the streets were strangely quiet. Children stayed indoors. Laughter subdued. Modest dwellings became even smaller as families moved in together, as German soldiers pushed aside lace curtains with their batons and defiled kosher kitchens with their *traif*. The military turned houses into billets or headquarters, and tossed out the people who, for generations, had made them homes.

Szulim stood in front of his house and shivered. He looked to the end of his block. Not the corner that met up with the marketplace, but the other end, where the woods began. The end he was no longer allowed to walk towards.

"But why?"

Szulim's mother had given him a look and that was that. It was a worse look than the kind that normally followed with, "Just wait until your Pop gets home!" Szulim saw this look and knew he had no choice but to obey. Mama had grown stricter. He still didn't understand why his parents were so mad when he came in for dinner the day before.

"Don't ever do that again!" his mother said. "Do you hear?"

He didn't know what he did. But the next day, Pop took his hand and walked him almost to the end of the block, towards the woods.

"You see that house, Szulim?" They stood across the street from where the Ryfmans used to live, before men with bayonets moved in and slept in Jewish beds. "You are never, ever to walk as far as that house."

Szulim nodded. He thought his parents were acting an awful lot like Feter

Moshe and Mimeh Gitel who never let Berl out of their sight. Maybe Mama and Pop were worried that he'd catch cold, like his younger cousin. Was there sickness in the woods?

———

"I KNOW HOW to get there myself," Szulim muttered into his scarf.

Havah walked him to cheder, the two of them taking hurried steps. It wasn't just the cold that made them move quickly. They hoped to arrive at the small house without passing a German soldier. Szulim had been told to stay away from them, to cross the street if they walked his way.

For weeks, Szulim had been noticing the change in the soldiers' appearance. Army pants once dirty and worn were now pressed and clean, tucked into high black boots almost as shiny as the candlesticks he polished for Shabbat. The visors on their hats, standing up so stiff and so strong; they were dark and shiny, too. Even the nightsticks they carried under their arms. All of it stood at such stark contrast to the filthy carbines with the bayonets poking from the tops, and the drab uniforms he had seen strolling around Zelechow for months already. Szulim was in awe of these new soldiers. He couldn't understand why his parents warned him to stay away.

"When you see the shiny boots, Szulim, you run right home." His mother cupped his chin and held his gaze before planting a kiss on his head. His parents voices were choppier, their bodies stiffer. Yet they seemed to love him more now, stopping to give him and his siblings an extra hug before running across to the store. Coming home more often for lunch. All those kisses on the *keppe*.

Szulim knew he was supposed to be afraid of the shiny soldiers, but he loved watching them ride around in their motorcycles and sidecars. When Havah wasn't looking, he'd march around the patio trying to lift his knees as high as he could. In time, he'd understand what his parents meant by their warnings of "they'll punish you."

AFTER SEVERAL HOURS of lessons, the rebbe closed his siddur and nodded to the boys who scrambled up the steps and into the daylight. It was a warm day for the month of *Kislev*, a welcome respite from the cold that began biting with greater frequency. "Look, Havah! The sun came out to play," Szulim said when he saw the maid waiting for him outside his class. But none of his friends could join him. They all walked home with their mothers or older sisters.

Szulim stood in his front yard and flicked his stick, tapping the bicycle rim up and down the street. He wandered, looking for someone, anyone to play with.

Abraham was still too much of a baby.

"Szulim!" Havah called from the doorstep. "Stay in front of the house."

She was always yelling at him now. Didn't she know he wouldn't get lost? He turned his back and wandered across the street to his parents' store. He ran through the front door, past the giant barrel of pickles and right into Mimeh Foigel's arms. Szulim sank into her softness. Dark curls peeked out from under her babushka as she squeezed his tuchas, kissing his neck loudly.

"Don't go back to Warsaw," Szulim said, pulling away from his aunt who was as squishy as his mother.

"Could I leave you, my Szulimel?" She couldn't. Mimeh Foigel had applied for a visa to the United States while studying in Warsaw. She waited a long time for her papers, which finally came at the end of summer. But she couldn't board the train from Warsaw to Gdansk, nor the boat headed to America, without visiting Zelechow one last time to kiss her sisters goodbye. She could never just leave her family like that. So she took a quick break from her studies, postponed her trip abroad and returned to her home village. The boat left without her. Normally there'd be other boats, but not after the planes darkened the Polish sky. That boat had been the last to leave Poland.

———

THE SUN DIPPED from the horizon, but it would be hours before any of the children were ready for bed, so Pop filled the two carbide lamps with water from the tank in the kitchen and turned the knob. The gas caught and cast a blue glow around the house. Szulim used to love that blue. It made him think of Hanukah, of walking home from shtiebl and seeing *menorahs* in every window with candles lighting blue paths in the snow to welcome him home. It was the color of opening the front door and stepping from the cold into the smell of fried potato *latkes*, the sound of laughter and the promise of a game of *dreidl*. Now, that blue was the color of faces that didn't smile as often as they used to.

Havah and Mama were preparing dinner when a tall man came to the door. Szulim had seen this man before; he remembered Pop shaking the man's hand at *shul* and saying, "Good *yontif*, Mr. Engel." The tall man didn't smile then, but today he had a big smile for Pop.

"Szulim, go play in your room." Mama squeezed his shoulder and pushed him towards the room he would soon share with his little brother. "Take Abraham."

Szulim looked over his shoulder and saw his father shaking his head. He tried to hear. The men spoke words that sounded important. It wasn't the first time this tall man named Israel Mordecai Engel had come. Szulim overheard his father say something about wanting five people. Szulim counted his fingers: Mama, Rivka, Sara, himself, Abraham. Satisfied, he lifted the cover off of his bed, making a tent for he and Abraham to play under.

After a few moments, Szulim heard the front door close and his parents' voices coming from the dining room.

"Chaim, why do you say no?" Mama asked.

"I just keep thinking about what my father said last time I saw him." Pop cleared his nose loudly into his handkerchief.

"He was delirious. It was before. What could he have known?"

"He knew, Perl. 'Shomer,' he told me. 'Watch yourself so that you're not seen.'"

Szulim wondered how you could watch yourself and at the same time, not see yourself. He tried looking at his own face but couldn't see anything other than a faint, pink blur.

———

SZULIM FELT PROUD walking into the shtiebl with his father on Saturday morning. So many men knew Pop. It used to be that the men shook hands, clapping each other on the shoulders and smiling with their declarations of "Good Shabbos!" Now, these hands grasped one another and held tight, as if leaning on each other for support. The men held gazes with eyes that were empty and full at the same time.

Though the shul in the center of town was much fancier than the crowded rooms Szulim and his father prayed in every weekend, Szulim preferred the shtiebls. Nestled throughout Zelechow, with arks and Torahs and a table to read from, the shtiebls were cozier, more relaxed. And while a cantor davened amongst the two-dozen men, chanting the prayers they all knew by heart, Szulim could play quietly with his friends.

"How's my little Szulimel?" Big Feter Moshe Boruchowicz got down on one knee. Szulim ran to him and gave him a kiss in exchange for a sweet. He wondered if it was the same kind of candy Feter Moshe was chewing. Big Feter Moshe always had something in his mouth, his tongue working over a snack of some kind.

"Go look for Herschel and Berl. Your older cousins are here somewhere." Feter Moshe patted Szulim's head and turned to the small sea of black coats, davening and chanting. But Szulim wasn't ready to leave his father.

"Chaim!" A thin man with rumpled clothes approached Pop. Szulim tightened his grasp on his father's hand as the crowd grew. He didn't recognize the man; he hadn't seen him before at Shabbat services. The thin man looked down at Szulim and smiled. "A beautiful boy, you have." Szulim looked up at the man, noticed his missing teeth and knew he would be the afternoon's oirech, the poor man who had nowhere else to go on the Sabbath.

The *gabbai* lifted the siddur onto the small table and opened the book to the proper *Parshah* as the crowd grew quiet in anticipation of that week's Torah reading. Szulim looked around the room. He saw a large man with lips too big to close neatly over his teeth. They puckered, revealing a pink moistened with saliva. It's not that the man was so fat; his belly didn't poke out. But it was as if someone had taken his belly fat and pushed it upwards and out across the shoulders. Pop nodded to the man with the lips and said, "Good Shabbos, Mylech." Szulim noticed that Pop didn't shake his hand, and recognized this man as Mr. Szarfartz. He had seen him at the marketplace earlier that week with Mr. Engel, the tall man who had come to the house on several occasions with smiles for Pop. The two men – Mr. Szarfartz with puffy lips and tall Mr. Engel - had shaken hands then at the marketplace, and Szulim had seen Mr. Engel give Mylech Szarfartz a big smile. But when Mr. Engel had run into Pop last Tuesday, he simply tipped his hat and wished him a good day. Szulim hadn't seen him at the house after that.

After the parshah, Mylech Szarfartz walked through the crowded shtiebl to the front of the room where the gabbai stood. His puffy lips whispered something to the leader of the services and the gabbai stepped aside.

"Come Monday," Szarfartz announced, "there will be new regulations. Make sure to go to the marketplace and read the postings from the *Judenrat*." Pop looked down at Szulim and nodded; Szulim could go look for his friends now that the prayers were over. Pop and all the other grown men had to listen to the announcements.

Herschel's hands were waving madly as he regaled his younger cousin with one of his stories. Herschel always had great stories, though Szulim seemed to be the only one interested in them. Pop came over, squeezed Herschel's shoulders and then put his arm around Szulim. "Ready to go, bubbeleh?" He gave Szulim a small piece of sponge cake from the *Kiddish*, the light meal after services. Szulim could smell the sweet wine and herring on Pop's breath.

Sure enough, the thin man with the missing tooth walked with them towards home. Szulim's stomach growled. All he had eaten that morning was a piece of pumpernickel bread and butter. He had been upset that there wasn't enough challah leftover for breakfast. But Mama made him some hot chocolate, stirring a little cocoa powder into water that had been left warmed overnight. Now, Szulim was anxious to get home, wash his hands, and make *motzi* before tearing off a hunk of challah and starting the meal. He skipped along thinking of his mother's egg salad and the leftover gefilte fish from last night's Shabbos dinner.

After the prayers were sung, they sat down to eat. The oirech sat at the head of the table next to Szulim's father. "That big house we walked by, the one across from the marketplace? That their headquarters?" The oirech turned to Pop, stabbing his fork in the air as if the big house were right in front of him.

"Yes."

"Thought so. I've never smelled bacon coming from a home with a *mezuzah* on the doorpost."

"I tried to hold my breath." Pop smiled softly and took another bite.

"That Szarfartz guy part of the Judenrat?" The oirech could barely talk between bites of food. Mama looked at Pop who met her gaze before lowering his eyes, then she turned to Sara and quietly offered her more kugel.

"No," Pop answered. "Engel heads the Judenrat. Szarfartz is the Chief of Police, the Jewish police."

"I still don't understand the point of these Germans forming a group of Jews who have to carry out their dirty work." Szulim had been hearing this word, Judenrat, but didn't understand. In a few years, when he'd have nothing to do *but* try and understand, he'd learn that the Judenrat was a governing body made up of activists from Zionist parties, members of merchant and craftsmen associations, Chossids like the men from shtiebl, and a lone communist. But now, the oirech kept saying this strange word and shoveling in the food; Szulim was worried there would be none left. "If they want to tell us what to do, why can't they just tell us? This Judenrat, ach! We need to demean our own?"

"Who can make sense of anything that they do now?"

"Well, you mark my words. The Chief of Police will be a rich man, if you know what I mean." The oirech rubbed his fingers together.

"Ach, that whole business of bribes. It's not for me," Pop said.

Szulim had never seen a bribe. He was pretty sure his parents didn't sell them in their store. He was trying to recall what little he heard of the parshah that morning. He didn't remember the words 'Judenrat' or 'bribe' being in the Torah.

———

As Szulim prepared to go with his mother and Rivka to the marketplace, he looked down and buttoned the star to the front of his vest. It was a yellow star, crudely formed, with the word "Jude" crocheted in the center. A star that resembled the six-pointed stars he had seen at shul. The star of David, his father called it, and Szulim wondered, *Who's David?* Now Szulim had his own star, as did his brother and sisters. His parents, aunts and uncles, the cousins, Havah. Stars sewn to elastic bands emblazoned arms and chests throughout the village.

At first, Szulim thought they were for Hanukah, little gifts to go along with the *gelt* he'd normally receive, the handful of coins he'd use to play dreidl.

But the yellow star had nothing to do with celebration.

"Szulim, you are never, ever to take off this star." His mother had held his chin and stared at his face after buttoning it to his jacket the first time. "Do you understand? You cannot be seen without it. The Germans will punish you."

"But why?" Szulim wondered if the Germans would march him to the woods, too, like he had seen them do last week to a group of young men, before Havah pulled him back inside the house.

"So they can know who's Jewish."

It didn't make sense. How could these men, soldiers who get to march around in shiny boots yelling at people, be so stupid? Even Szulim could tell the difference between Jews and goyim. But he knew better than to voice his thoughts out loud.

One by one, his mother had stared into the faces of his brother and sisters and given the same warnings. Even if they only walked out front to play in the sand, they must wear the star. The armband was easier to put on, but could easily fall off. So he and his siblings wore their stars buttoned to their shirts. Just to be safe.

Now, everywhere Szulim looked around the swarming marketplace, he saw yellow stars. Shiny boots and yellow stars.

"Szulim, stay here with Rivka and hold her hand." Mama left the kids on the perimeter of the square and pushed her way into the crowd gathering in the center. Abraham was home with Havah, and Sara was playing at a friend's house. Szulim and Rivka had wrapped their coats around themselves tightly and accompanied their mother to the marketplace since it was a Tuesday and they'd need to help carry the sacks of potatoes, not to mention a chicken or two.

Szulim stomped his feet to keep warm and craned his neck above and around the masses of people. He could see the wooden monument rising above the black hats and babushkas, like a pole that started out really fat and got thinner as it grew taller. Posters and sheets of newspaper covered the structure, and on market day there was always a rush to read the weeks' news and the latest announcements, directives from the Gestapo that the Judenrat translated into Yiddish and printed on large sheets of paper.

Szulim watched people emerge from the crowd, their hands fluttering to their mouths, arms pleading with the sky. He could tell the news was not good. Not that there had been any good news as of late coming from the announcement board at the center of the marketplace. He saw his mother push her way back towards them, wiping the corner of her eye. When she saw the kids, she put on a smile that Szulim knew did not come from inside her.

"What did it say, Mama?" Szulim was glad Rivka asked.

"The Germans need your school. You don't have school anymore."

———

MAMA NEEDED TO get to the store, so she rushed Szulim to get ready. She would walk him to cheder before going to work.

"You mean 'playing at my friend's,'" Szulim reminded her. He had to leave his siddur at cheder now. He'd get in trouble if the soldiers caught him carrying a prayer book.

AFTER HIS LESSONS, Szulim noticed the crocuses that were beginning to push up from the earth as he and Havah walked home from the rebbe's basement. He thought it was amazing to see tiny purple buds popping out of the still melting snow. He hoped Havah would notice the small flowers and let him play outside. Ever since the kindergarten was established in the front room of his house, he and Abraham had little space to play.

Mimeh Sara used to teach in the public school, but when the Gestapo forbade the Jews from formal education, and then took over the building when they needed bigger headquarters, Sara suggested they hold classes secretly in various homes throughout Zelechow. Mama immediately offered room, and Pop found some rolled brown paper from the backroom of the store and taped it up in the windows at the front of the house.

Mimeh Sara would come in the morning, just as Szulim prepared to leave for cheder. On the way to his lessons, he'd pass children walking towards him with their mothers. One by one, a child would walk into his house. In a space once meant for play, a dozen children filled the room with letters and numbers and questions. Throughout Zelechow, brown paper covered the windows of many Jewish homes as living rooms transformed into kindergartens.

No paper covered the windows of the school in the marketplace; Szulim could see inside. The downstairs classrooms had been turned into Gestapo offices, and upstairs was where the soldiers with shiny boots ate their meals. Perhaps some slept there as well, though most of the Germans now slept in the nicest homes in town.

———

SZULIM COULD NOT fall asleep. Outside of his bedroom, his parents sat at the dining room table, speaking in their stilted Polish. His parents usually spoke Yiddish – like all of the observant Jews in Zelechow – reserving the foreign tongue, native to their gentile neighbors, for when they didn't want the kids to hear what they were saying. But more and more, his parents tried making attempts at private conversation. From the warmth of his bed, Szulim strained to hear the words his parents fumbled over, words he did not understand, and thought they must be talking about his clothes. Just as he got a new outfit for Rosh Hashanah, Szulim and Rivka got new clothes and shoes at *Pesach*. This celebration, commemorating the Israelite's freedom from slavery and the arrival of spring, was less than a week away. Szulim had already decided that when he got his new clothes, he wouldn't put them on ahead of time and go outside to show off. He didn't want to attract any more airplanes.

His Bubbe had sent word earlier that week. She would travel from Maciejowice to be with Szulim's family for the holiday. Havah and his mother had been cleaning the house for days now. Sweeping every corner, brushing the cabinet that held their food, washing and stacking their everyday dishes into a box that would go in the crawl space above the kitchen ceiling, taking the space that the Passover dishes normally occupied.

Gedalia Yosef, Mama's distant cousin and a baker, had been busy cleaning his ovens of *chametz*, removing any traces of leavened breadcrumbs from his bakery and preparing the matzah that the villagers would subsist on for the week. These unleavened cakes served to remind Jews everywhere how their ancestors fleeing the bonds of slavery did not have time to wait for their bread to rise. What did rise, unbeknownst to Szulim and his siblings, was the Blood Libel, the rumor perpetuated this time every year through churches across Poland; as Jews quietly prepared for the holiday, preachers warned of Jewish kidnappers stealing gentile babies and using their blood to bake the flat bread.

Havah cleaned up the breakfast dishes as Szulim's mother helped him get dressed. "When you come back from cheder, stop at Gedalia Yosef's." His mother adjusted his hat and kissed him on his cheeks. "Yehudith has a package for you."

"Matzah!" Szulim jumped up and down.

Havah caught him before he knocked into any of the dishes that hadn't yet been put away. "Will you help me make matzah meal when it's time?"

Szulim and Abraham looked at each other and nodded. Szulim pursed his lips and made a rumbling sound. "We can be tanks, Abraham, and run it over!" He held his hands up and pretended to smash the unleavened bread with great sound effects. Sara and Rivka looked at each other and rolled their eyes.

"There are no tanks in this house," his mother said. "I am raising *mensches*. Not German soldiers."

Szulim lowered his eyes. He looked at Abraham and the two boys suppressed a giggle.

———

SZULIM WALKED UP the steps from the rebbe's dark cellar and saw Havah and his brother waiting for him. His sisters were still at school. Or rather, still studying their lessons in the home of a neighbor. Szulim, Abraham and Havah walked slower than usual, enjoying the kiss of the sun that had softened winter's chill. They didn't need to pull their coats so tightly around their bodies, their arms freer to swing at their sides. But the soldiers patrolling the shtetl tempered their movements, and Havah and the boys stepped gingerly along the cobblestones, three figures propelling forward holding as still as possible.

Yehudith spun around the bakery, cleaning and serving, chatting and rolling. She was a force of nature. Her husband Gedalia Yosef was more deliberate, removing his cap every few minutes to wipe his brow along his sleeve. Even when he took off his hat, his head remained covered with a *yarmulke*. "For the Jew who goes without a cap, I wear two," he says. "So God never loses."

"Both my *yingalehs*!"Yehudith rushed to Szulim and Abraham, offering hugs and a small piece of pumpernickel for each to snack on. "Eat, eat!" she motioned with the back of her hand but they took small bites to make the afternoon surprise last as long as possible.

Yehudith handed Havah a stack of matzahs wrapped in paper, and the maid and two young boys walked across the street. As much as they wanted to nibble on a small piece of the cracker-like bread, they knew God would not allow it. From Purim to Pesach, Jews refrained from eating matzah in order to build up anticipation for when matzah was the only bread allowed. In a few days, after the second seder, Havah would open the paper carefully on the dining room table and the boys would take turns breaking the matzah into pieces, rolling the pin over the crackly bread, breaking it up even smaller. Havah would take over, both to ensure that the crumbs stayed on the paper and to do a proper job. The matzah needed to be extra fine for Mama's sponge cake.

SZULIM WOKE ON Erev Pesach to Havah opening the dining room table and dragging chairs from the front room. There would be no cheder or school today; everyone was busy with preparations. While the children polished the silver, Pop carried the generator from across the street so that they would have enough light after the sun had set to read from the *Hagaddah*, the book that tells the story of the ancient Israelite's enslavement in Egypt and their eventual exodus to the Promised Land.

Pesach was Szulim's favorite holiday. He couldn't wait to search for the *afikomen*, the middle matzah from the *seder* plate taken when no one was looking and hidden for the children to find. What would he get if he found it? New clothes? A coin? An extra bite of compote? Szulim could already taste the gefilte fish made with ginger especially for the holiday. He could hear the voices of the grown-ups getting louder throughout the long meal as they drank the four cups of wine. Even the children got a sip, though it made Szulim's tongue pucker. Sara and Rivka would include Szulim this year in their lookout for Elijah, taking turns keeping watch over the Kiddush cup of wine at the center of the table poured for the prophet who visited seders all over Poland, all over the world, drinking from the cup and bringing peace. Szulim really hoped Elijah would visit this year in particular.

And as the last prayer would be recited, Pop closing the Haggadah with the declaration, "Next year in Jerusalem!" no one could imagine that this - a modest table in a German-patrolled shtetl, a table seating 13 members of a loving family plus an oirech - would be as close to holiness and peace and togetherness as they would see for a long time.

———

As the weeklong celebration of freedom ended, another family moved into Szulim's home.

"What are you doing, Pop?" Szulim watched as his father and a man he had never seen before moved a bed from his sisters' room into his own.

"This is Mr. Kozorek. He and his family will be staying with us."

"For how long?" Szulim asked.

"As long as they need to. He's got two little girls, almost the same age as you and Abraham. Go on into the kitchen and say hello."

Szulim walked out to the patio. What good were girls? He already had two sisters. He looked back into the house and saw his father move Abraham's crib from his parents' room into Sara and Rivka's. What next? Would the armoire get moved into the kitchen? Between all the kids using his front room for school, and now this new family, his house felt very crowded. At least the weather was warmer and he could play outside.

The Kozorek girls were too young to play with Rivka and Sara; one was even younger than Abraham. They mostly clung to their mother's skirt as she helped clean the house. Szulim noticed that Havah didn't open up the table for dinner like she normally did when they had company. This family, Szulim quickly understood, was not company. His parents were happy to help others in need, but there was not enough food for four additional mouths. Already, their own meals had begun to shrink.

Szulim overheard his father speaking to his mother. "See Perl, this is why we must stay on the good side of the Judenrat. We could have gotten a much different family."

"I know, Chaim. We're lucky. They respect us, this house."

"They're like us, Perl. Jews like us. Thank God we didn't get some intelligentsia who don't observe the Sabbath."

Everyday, the father of the girls left the house. Szulim didn't know what kind of job he had. The man didn't have a store like his parents, that he knew. He didn't have as much money. Szulim could tell by the dinners the family ate. They were even more meager than his own meals had become.

"Why can't Mr. Kozorek just go to the old man at the end of the marketplace?" Szulim asked his father. "He can sign a *wexel* and get money."

"It's not that easy," his father said.

Szulim sighed. Mr. Mesinger, the old man who handed out money at the marketplace, was mean. Szulim always saw people walking away from him with their heads lowered, their hands pulling at their pockets. And when *zlotys* were no longer acceptable currency, villagers went to that old man with the big beard to exchange their useless Polish bills for ghetto notes. Szulim wished he could find the hole in the ground where all the money was kept.

SZULIM QUICKLY CHANGED into his nightshirt, shivering. Despite spring's thaw, nights were still quite chilly. The heat from the kitchen didn't make it to the bedrooms, no matter how much wood or coal Pop fed the stove. Szulim couldn't wait to jump into the bed and snuggle with Abraham under the down cover. Though the movement of furniture bothered Szulim when the Kozorek family moved in, he was happy they needed the crib. Thankfully Abraham was old enough to sleep in a bed like a big boy, even though he still wore a cloth diaper wrapped tight around his bottom at night. Soon he'd do his *notznik* in the ceramic pot next to the bed just like everyone else who didn't want to go to the outhouse so late; he was almost three already. Szulim had always thought it unfair that Pop and Mama got to share a room, Rivka and Sara, too, and he had to sleep all alone. Now all four children slept in one room; the girls in one bed, the boys in another. Though it took several nights for Abraham to learn to settle down, Szulim was happy for the warmth from his little body.

Telling: Summer 2009

I FLIP THROUGH my notebook before calling Sal. It is filled with questions, hundreds of questions I've jotted down while watching the VHS tapes Sal had sent after I agreed to write his story. The tapes were a video testimony he had given for the Shoah Foundation a decade before. They only scratched the surface.

Sal answers the phone, anxious to begin, and Sandy also says hello. She sits in the den, in their house in Tampa, prepared to listen in as I ask Sal about his past. Questions, Sandy later tells me, she herself had wanted to ask for years, but had been afraid. Not out of fear of what she might have learned, but of what fissure she may have torn inside of Sal. She could see the pain lying just below the surface. She'd tried over the years, carefully. But with every question, she had felt like an intruder trying to work her way into a building that was meant to remain locked.

"What were you talking about?" she'd ask Sal as they drove home from family get-togethers.

"We were just talking."

What were they joking about? she wondered. *Why the screaming?* Sometimes he'd explain, and other times he'd clam up. She told Sal how uncomfortable it was to be in this situation. How it hurt to feel as if his devotions were split, as if she was not his number one. But he never apologized. The word 'sorry' was not in his vocabulary. "We were talking about things you don't need to know."

All those years, Sandy knew it had something to do with the Holocaust; she knew he was a Survivor. But he had no tattoo. She had looked, early on in their marriage, running her fingers along the inside of his arms and up his legs while he was sleeping. So she thought he had left right before the war. Or during. She had been unclear on the details and Sal seemed unwilling to share, not because he was hiding something from her, necessarily, but rather from himself. Sandy sensed a grief that lay deep and felt a duty to shield Sal from it. To protect her husband from something inside him.

Now, as Sal sits in the other room speaking of his past, she takes it all in.

"How do you remember it all with such detail?" I ask Sal. "You were so young."

"I suppose it is hard to accept," Sal says. "But there are memories, sensations as clear to me now as they were some 70 odd years ago. They swim through my mind, with traces of understanding I had as a child and reconciliations I've come to in my later years."

I think about my own life, my childhood. I can remember the sounds of my parents' voices outside my bedroom at night, nightmares that roused me from sleep. We all have our traumas and our relative normal, I suppose.

"I simply had the time, as well as the need, to focus on what had been pleasant, once my life was no longer so," Sal says. "When there was no food to eat, I savored the memories. Day in and day out, for weeks and months on end, what else was I to do? If I wanted to live, I had to remember what it was I wanted to live for."

"It's funny how the mind works," I say. "Time heals, but it also opens the floodgates, no?"

"I'm not washed over with this thing ... recovered memory? Not really. But it seems that every time I tell the events of my life, new memories surface."

Sandy listens to Sal lay himself bare and struggles to reconcile the man on the phone now with the man she has been married to for over 45 years. She recalls the time long ago when she went to see *The Godfather*. Was Sal with her? He rarely goes to movies. "What's the point?" he always said. "They're a waste of time." Maybe, but she enjoys the escape.

That movie, however, wasn't an escape. It was eerie. Sandy had to pee, but couldn't move. She was riveted to the character of Kay Corleone. There she was, a nice Jewish girl with two babies and a bowling league, feeling a kinship with the wife of a Mafioso. It wasn't normal, she admitted to me during one of our private calls. But there she sat, transfixed, watching her marriage play out on the big screen, only with Italian accents. And guns. Sandy realized that she, like the wife on screen, was married to a man with a secret, married into a family that from the outside seemed so normal and loving. But underneath the crocheted tablecloth and gefilte fish and kisses lay a confidence that she was not privy to.

Until just recently.

Sal continues. "Of course, there are details that, no matter how much I strain to recall, don't come back. Faces and names of friends long gone. And then, there are those memories that, even now, I wish could have disappeared along with my childhood."

Summer 1940 — Winter 1940

"Where are you going?"

Szulim turned to Havah with his hand still on the doorknob. "To play. The sun's out. I want to look for my friends."

"Why don't you play on the patio?"

Szulim could not understand. Only the chickens were on the patio. He couldn't play *Comme Comme Tir* with the chickens. Besides, he knew to hide inside the house if he heard a tank coming. Tanks were very good at running people over. "I'm going to the store."

His mother stood behind the counter, her lips moving and the pencil scratching the paper, so Szulim waited until she was done adding up numbers before he spoke.

"It's summer. Why can't I play outside?"

His mother sighed, wrapping her arms around him. "There are restrictions. It's a part of life. You need to be careful so you don't get punished."

His parents had never punished him before for playing outside. It must be the Germans. They didn't seem to like children very much. His sisters were lucky. They got to go to school all day. Well, not school. But they went to someone's house where they'd get their lessons and see plenty of other children. Szulim went to cheder for a few hours each morning, but other than reciting the letters, he couldn't talk with the boys, or play. And the basement was so dark.

Szulim walked outside and looked down the street. His eyes rested upon two Gestapo soldiers standing with their legs wide and their arms behind their backs, laughing at someone on the ground. An old woman, older than his Bubbe Wajnberg, bent and shaking. Szulim took a few steps closer, without being seen, and watched her arm move vigorously back and forth along the sidewalk. In her hand was a toothbrush.

"You missed a spot!" Even though the soldiers spoke German, it was close enough to Yiddish that all of the Jews understood the Nazis' taunts. What the villagers didn't know until later was that their Yiddish accents were unfamiliar to the Germans. Not that the Gestapo cared enough to bother with comprehension.

The taller of the two shiny boots spit on the ground, right next to where the woman scrubbed the sidewalk. Without looking up, the woman rubbed her toothbrush over the soldier's spittle. "Dirty Jew!"

Szulim ran back inside the store and hid behind his mother's skirt.

———

For a Tuesday, the marketplace was quiet. Szulim's parents had not opened their store. Jews in Zelechow were refraining from commerce, cutting hair, even wearing leather as they observed the ninth day of the Hebrew month *Av*. Since the destruction of the ancient temple in Jerusalem centuries before, Jews around the world followed the rules for mourning as they commemorated that anniversary, and the tragedies that have befallen their people, coincidentally, on that same summer day. Two years from now, when the residents of Warsaw would be forced from their ghetto and rounded into cattle cars, pious Jews would not be surprised at the date. *Tish'a b'Av*.

Szulim wandered around the patio, kicking at some pebbles. Abraham was napping in his room, the little girls napping in the room that used to be his sisters'. Pop and Mr. Kozorek chanted *kinnot* in the front room, reciting the sad poems from *Eicha*, the Book of Lamentations. His mother and Mrs. Kozorek sat with Rivka and Sara at the table as the girls crocheted tiny blankets for their dolls.

"I'm bored." Szulim came into the house, eager for some company.

"Let's go for a walk," Rivka suggested. Sara, as usual, followed Rivka. They didn't look like sisters; Rivka had long blonde hair and light eyes, Sara's eyes and hair were dark. But, being only 18 months apart, they did everything together. To Szulim, they were a unit. Sweet, calm and gentle. Pop never had to hit them with the gartl.

The three children touched their chests, unaware that it had become instinct to feel for their stars before they stepped outside. The sun shone brightly, but the heat wasn't as bad as it had been lately. A pleasant breeze rippled through the leaves of the birches and oaks lining the streets. A murmur of activity could be heard from the plaza since the farmers had come into town to sell their wares. Lucky for them, the non-religious Jews carried on as usual. The children walked in the opposite direction of the marketplace, past wooden houses and small patches of grass. It wouldn't be a good idea to wander among so many goyim.

They moved to the side of the road when they heard the horse's hooves clomping along the cobblestones. They stood, waiting for the droshky to pass, looking down in order to avoid the eyes of the driver. They had to wait for several minutes as the horse did its business and the driver jumped down from his bench to clean up. Finally, the old wagon continued, veering to the right as it rumbled along.

Szulim noticed first.

"Rivka, why is he sleeping in the street?" Szulim pointed to the man lying on his back a block away in the middle of the road. He didn't look very comfortable with one arm stretched out to the side, the other flung across his chest; his legs bent awkwardly. Szulim liked to sleep on his stomach with his knees bent under his tummy. "He should have just gone home."

"He's not sleeping, Szulim," she said quietly. "He must have fallen down and died."

Died! Like Zayde who was dead. But Zayde didn't lie in the street. He was sick in bed and then no longer.

"When he's done being dead, will he go home?" Szulim asked.

"When you're dead, you're dead forever," Rivka said.

Szulim couldn't yet count to forever. Suddenly, he didn't want to be outside anymore.

———

ROSH HASHANAH MARKED a year since the flying samochods created a different life for the people of Zelechow. Just two months before, the Germans had confiscated all Jewish property. The Jews of Zelechow now had to pay rent on the homes and businesses that had been owned for generations. Days grew shorter, pleasant breezes turned brisk. And any hope for a peaceful new year faded along with the sunshine. Even the bright yellow of the stars sewn to jackets had dulled.

Szulim and Havah walked quickly from cheder, Havah carrying Abraham so they could get home faster. Szulim carried nothing; his siddur left in the rebbe's cellar so that the Germans would not find out a young boy of four had been learning his letters. They heard the dog barking nearby. Only one guard – a guard with even shinier boots than his comrades, as if that was possible – patrolled with a dog. But the dog was even more ferocious than the guard, and both scared Szulim equally.

On Shabbat, Szulim's aunts traded stories of friends who worked for the Gestapo. Women who used to walk freely into homes and borrow sugar from neighbors now needed passes to enter houses where they'd work as servants.

"Oy Frajda, you know her from the mikvah, her legs are black and blue," Mimeh Sara whispered to Szulim's mother and his other aunts. "She had just finished sweeping and mopping …" she stopped to see if Szulim was listening. "The guard's wife held up a sugar canister and dropped it. The thing shattered and sugar spilled everywhere, all over the wet floor. The *shiksa* screamed at Frajda 'you're so stupid you can't even clean properly!' and her Nazi husband came in and began hitting her with the broom."

Mimeh Tertza said, "You heard about Pinchas Damuch. Shot in the marketplace."

"Why?" asked Mimeh Foigel.

"Why? Why any of it!" Szulim's mother said. "Like anything is for a reason. The wind blows, their minds change, boom!"

The women sat quietly as Szulim walked into the room and nestled into his mother. "Mama, who was shot?"

"No one you know."

Now the grown ups were asking 'why,' but Szulim was disappointed that even they got no real answers. His parents had to work, his sisters had to learn, he had to play. They had no choice but to live their lives. So every day, his parents carried on with their hearts walking around outside their bodies, responding to questions they could only answer with "that's why we want you to stay inside."

———

WITH THE STAR secure to his chest, Szulim walked towards the marketplace, the *grosz* coin deep in his pocket. It was too small to be changed into the new money Jews had to use, so his mother had said he could keep it. He hoped the woman who sold ice cream would still accept it. Even though the weather was turning cooler, he could still practically taste the sweet, cold cream on his tongue when he pushed open the door to the little shack.

"Hello Mrs. Szapiro. May I please have some ice cream?" Szulim had been practicing, under his breath, how to ask politely as he walked to the plaza.

"None today. Sorry." Mrs. Szapiro, a large woman in a gray shirt and black skirt, lifted her chin out of her hand and rose from her stool as she explained that the milkman and his cows were outside the ghetto. *Ghetto?* Szulim had been hearing that word more and more.

"The fish, too? Are they outside?" Szulim thought about the river at the end of the road, past where he was allowed to go, and how he hadn't tasted Mama's gefilte fish since Pesach, back in the spring.

"Yes. But the fisherman, he's in here, with us."

Szulim felt for his star as he walked out the door.

Streets may have had names, but no signs marked the roads. Everyone knew where to go, or how to direct someone. *Walk past the shoemaker; turn left by the brown cow.* The 500 or so homes in the town sat close together, some touching. Birch trees and oaks rose above the wooden one-story houses. As Szulim walked back along the perimeter of the marketplace, he looked down each street that led from the center of town. He saw the river with the fish he couldn't eat, farmland reaching farther than his eyes could see, the woods.

SZULIM WANDERED INTO his parents' store. "What is a 'ghetto'?" Szulim asked.

"It's like a neighborhood, where we live now," his father explained. Szulim didn't understand. Where he lived now was where he had always lived.

"Janek left." Pop turned to Mama and Mimeh Foigel to report on the latest movement of people in and out.

"So, who moved in?" Mama turned from where she stood restocking soap.

Szulim leaned against the counter and listened to a conversation that had become all too familiar, especially at the dinner table where he sat quietly and looked from his mother to his father, trying to keep track of all the names. Agata and Jacek Sawicki. Czeslaw Krol. Marek and Dorota Gorski. Not that he had ever met these people. They were goyim. Szulim wondered if they'd still come and buy sugar from the store.

"The Frenkiel's and Zamosc's. Together. Nine kids in that small house."

"Oy gut." Mama looked down at a scrap of paper.

He didn't understand why some Jews had to move closer to the marketplace. Did they need to be closer to shul? Nothing was too far in Zelechow. But from what he could tell from the way his parents spoke about this ghetto, it sounded like Zelechow shrunk. And all the Jews had to live in this new, smaller village, while all the goyim moved out. But where was "out"? As far as he could tell, "out" was still in the town he had known his whole life. The whole thing was too confusing.

———

SZULIM WALKED HOME with Pop after shtiebl, looking up at the sky, searching for the moon. Was something wrong with his eyes? Everything seemed darker somehow. He looked at the windows of the houses they passed, the glow dimmer than usual. He knew Mama would have lit candles just as the sun was setting, before the third star twinkled in the night sky, before the Sabbath set in and she couldn't strike a match.

Szulim took off his coat at the door and walked to the table where his mother, sisters and Abraham waited to make motzi for the Sabbath meal. He saw the flames from the short, thick Shabbos candles in the six silver candlesticks, a candle for each person in the family. But the carbide lamps that Pop usually turned on before the sun set, or the thickset candles in glass lanterns that would provide light through their meal and afterwards, were not illuminated.

"Why is it so dark?"

Szulim's mother turned to his father who sighed. "There's a curfew now, Szulim. We can go to shtiebl in the evening, but that's it. Mietek won't be able to come after dinner."

No Shabbos Goy? Szulim remembered his father reporting one evening that Mietek had moved to the outskirts of Zelechow. But he couldn't understand why that meant the gentile who came to their house every Sabbath to perform the small tasks they couldn't, like blow out the pillar candles or turn down the carbide lamps, was not going to stop by tonight. For as long as Szulim could remember, there'd be a knock on the door when they finished their dinner and one of the girls would open it and let Mietek in. Always clean shaven, but with sloppy dark pants tucked into big black boots and a long-sleeved shirt made from a flour sack, the Shabbos Goy would smile and nod at the family. He'd brush his blond hair from his eyes and quickly go about his business. He had a few dozen other houses to take care of on their street. Mama paid him for his services on Tuesday, when he'd come to the store. Mietek was the only goy Szulim knew who could speak Yiddish.

"What about the heat?" Sara looked nervously from her mother to her father.

"Oh, he can come during the day, bubbeleh," Mama assured her. "You'll see. Tomorrow he'll come and put coal in the stove."

Szulim couldn't figure out why his parents seemed so sad over this curfew. He had never been allowed to play outside in the dark. And in the summer, he had to go to bed before the sun even went down, unless it was a holiday or Shabbat. He actually liked that the curfew made his parents come home earlier from the store, though he kept that a secret, just like his parents were keeping their own secrets now.

"Shh!" He heard his mother through the walls of his bedroom one night. "God forbid the kids hear you talking of bandits and murderers! They repeat that to a friend out on the street one day? You've seen what these Gestapo do. To children, too!"

"You're right," his father had said. "From now on, we'll only speak of all this mess in Polish."

———

THE JEWS OF Zelechow had to be extra careful walking home from shtiebl on Friday nights. Though the Germans had allowed them this dispensation, walking from worship after sundown on Fridays, Gestapo agents wielding their carbines were known to be fickle. Szulim's fingers felt squished inside his father's large hand, and he could tell that Pop was nervous being out after dark.

As they stepped quickly but carefully along the dirt walkway, Szulim followed his father's gaze, past the houses that used to be in Zelechow but were now considered "outside," and up towards the thin rope that stretched round the perimeter of the shtetl. This *eruv*, symbolically extending the boundaries of a home, allowed Jews to carry personal items outdoors on Shabbat like a handkerchief or a prayer book. Pop didn't need an eruv to carry Szulim or Abraham when they grew tired. The laws of God posed no restrictions on carrying a child.

"Would you believe our *mashgiach* needs to get a *pzshepuska* now?" Pop told the oirech walking home with them. Part of the eruv lay outside the ghetto, based on the German's decree of the borders, so Welwel, the man whose job it was to check the rope each week, needed a pass.

"Bet that's still no guarantee he won't get beaten for stepping a foot outside," the oirech said. Pop cleared his throat and looked down at Szulim. The oirech smiled and stopped talking.

Szulim pictured Welwel climbing on his ladder to check the eruv every Friday afternoon before the sun set, the old man holding extra rope in case it had been cut, as it sometimes was by a gentile kid who'd lie in wait. Welwel would fix it, reestablishing the barely visible border around Zelechow. It used to be that another man helped Welwel because he was elderly. Now, having nothing to do with age, a Jewish policeman walked alongside the mashgiach, careful to remain inside the nebulous ghetto boundary, and warned him if a soldier came nearby. The policeman was prepared to serve as a witness, if need be.

Szulim's father shook his head. "And we thought it was bad when some Polish boys used to hide and throw stones."

"If only stones were our worst problem," said the oirech. "How much did he need to pay for a pass?"

"Ach, to get it signed from the president of the Judenrat, and then by a German? Probably more than he makes as a mashgiach!"

Szulim had heard people talking about pzshepuskas and how hard they were to come by. Chane Rofowicz told Szulim's mother how she needed to buy a pass from the Judenrat just to go inside the school building and peel potatoes for the Gestapo, and Rochla Kaplan had to do the same just to shine their boots. *Veyismere* if someone needed to see a doctor in another shtetl; those passes were nearly impossible to obtain unless you had a good amount of money and connections. Pzshepuskas were the talk of the town, the lucky ones who could obtain them merely saying, "I've got my ways."

Pzshepuskas weren't the only critical items in scarcity these days. The influx of Jews from shtetls too small to justify German occupation, or those who felt there was safety in numbers and thus came to Zelechow to be part of a larger Jewish community, put a strain on the food and water supply. Not as bad a strain as would come later, when Jews from other countries marched weakly into town seeking refuge. But enough of a strain that ration cards became necessary. These slips of paper permitted families to buy an allotted amount of food and supplies each week, and dictated how much of an item Szulim's parents could sell. When someone died, or disappeared, the Judenrat took back that person's ration card. Members of the Judenrat and their families rarely went hungry.

Szulim began noticing the change in the dinner conversations between his parents. Mama's questions to Pop weren't "who moved in?" anymore; now they were "should I have?" His mother had no problems ignoring the German dictates and providing neighbors and friends with additional supplies. She could look aside for those she knew. Slip more into canvas sacks. Exchange quiet nods. It was the unknown Jews, the mothers entering the store with pleas for sick babies who needed extra flour. Those people broke her heart. But good people were shot for soft hearts.

"Chaim, should I have?" his mother asked each night.

Pop closed his eyes and shook his head. No. She could not take that chance.

———

Szulim stood in front of his house, hoping one of his friends might be outdoors. It had been a while since he enjoyed the company of his playmates now that the weather had forbidden it. He looked towards the marketplace and saw an old man shuffling along the street. His shoulders were hunched in the way of the elderly, though it seemed as if all Jews, young and old, walked now with a stoop. As if the star pinned to every chest was so heavy that it strained the neck and curved the upper back. All of a sudden several guards approached and the old man froze. Though the guards were very loud, the way he'd seen men get loud after drinking too many glasses of wine, Szulim couldn't hear what they shouted. But he saw.

Szulim stood frozen, like the old man, until his legs began to work again, allowing him to run. He ran across the street, past the pickle barrel and behind the long counter, into his mother's arms.

"They could have cut him!" he said, between gulps of air as he told his mother and Mimeh Tertza what had just happened. How the soldiers took the bayonet ends of their rifles and raised it to the old man's chin. How they grabbed hold of his long, thick beard and with one swift movement, chopped half of it off, laughing as they tossed the clumps of gray and white into his face, spitting on the fallen hair as it drifted towards the snow. Causing as much pain as if they had actually drawn blood.

Spring 1941 – Winter 1941

Szulim shook the *grogger*, holding it with two hands in front of his chest, rocking his whole body. He, Abraham and little Berl tried to outdo the other with the noise, laughing as the pebbles rustled around inside the small cardboard boxes. Pop had helped the kids fashion the noisemakers in preparation for *Purim*. Meanwhile, the girls adjusted the paper crowns they wore in an attempt to be as beautiful and courageous as Queen Esther, the Jewish heroine of ancient Shoshan who had convinced King Ahashueras to foil Haman's evil plot to exterminate the Jews. During the reading of the *Megillah*, the scroll that contained the book of Esther, Jewish children everywhere would hiss and shake their groggers every time the villain's name was uttered.

"Haman … Hitler," Feter Moshe Szyfman pointed out after they returned from shul. "Where's our Queen Esther now?"

"You don't really believe he's trying to kill us all, do you?" Mimeh Gitel said to her husband. "This nonsense, it's just more of the same as it's always been with the goyim."

Szulim's mother sniffed. "Well, this 'pogrom's' been lasting long enough now."

"I don't know what to believe anymore," Pop said. "But I do know today we must make merry."

The two families sat down to eat and Pop poured four large glasses of wine. Szulim dimly remembered when Purim had been really fun. Not last year, but before that, when he was almost three-years-old. Children and adults wore masks, and men danced in the streets, singing loudly long after the sun had set. Now they had to remain inside. And the effects of the wine seemed to put a pallor over the once boisterous atmosphere.

Nevertheless, Szulim was excited about his new grogger. He needed something to play with as it had been months since he could enjoy his bike rim. The weather had been so bitter; he only went outside to walk to cheder, or to visit his parents and aunts at the store. And even if Havah would have allowed him to push the metal ring around the house, there was no space — between the children using the front room for school everyday and the other family living with them. He had tried to make skates for the bottom of his shoes when the pond froze over, whittling down an old piece of wood, but he only ended up cutting his hand.

Sitting around the dining room table, Szulim could barely stay awake despite the din of the conversation amongst the grown ups. Berleh had actually put his head down and fallen asleep. Pop walked around the house blowing out candles and turning off the carbide lamps. He opened the front door slowly and peeked outside. After looking up and down the street carefully, he motioned to Mimeh Gitel and Feter Moshe and they hurried out, carrying their sleeping child to their home behind Gedalia Yosef's bakery. Pop looked out the window to make sure they made it across without being spotted by the Gestapo. Unfortunately, Szulim's other aunts lived too far to celebrate with them this evening. They couldn't risk walking home after curfew.

•

———

A MONTH LATER, extra chairs were dragged to the dining room table, but this time to accommodate the Kozorek's. Normally the two families would eat dinner in shifts. But tonight marked the beginning of Pesach, and there could be no shift of a *seder*, when the meal was an integral part of the celebration itself. The Israelite's journey to freedom would be told and retold over many courses of food and four glasses of wine.

Tonight also marked the end of the week. And since the shabbos goy could not come into the ghetto after dark, Pop devised a system of turning off the electricity without anyone having to flip a switch. After all, they'd need the lights long after the sun had set to read from the Hagaddah. Szulim sat at the table staring as his father worked intently. Pop wrapped a piece of string around the switch that operated the small generator and attached a small weight to the end of the string. He took some more string, a much longer piece, and tied one end to the switch, keeping it in the "on" position, and then threaded it into a candle so that it touched the wick near the bottom. When the candle burned down and the flame caught the string, it would snap, releasing the pull of the long string on the switch and allowing the weight to pull it down into the "off" position.

Szulim should have been amazed at his father's ingenuity, but he was used to it. Pop could do anything.

Szulim had gone to bed late, on account of the seder, and had no idea if it was morning or still night when he woke up and smelled something burning.

"Pop! Pop!" he called.

His father came running out of the bedroom, yanked down the burning drapes, and put out the fire. The string Pop had tied between the candle and the light switch had turned off the electricity, just like he had planned. But it also set the curtains on fire. Once his heart stopped beating so fast, Szulim fell back asleep, feeling very proud. Five years old and already, he was a hero.

––––––

The sun shone brightly on the wide cobblestoned plaza as Zelechowers milled about, cautiously trying to barter personal items for food. The non-Jewish farmers had come into the ghetto hoping for business; it was market day after all. But they had no interest in ghetto money, just clothes or housewares. Ghetto money meant nothing outside the crowded Jewish quarter. Szulim's parents were lucky. They had relationships with non-Jewish businessmen that went back generations, so they were still able to get goods for the store or food for the family, though with greater limitations. For a suit, they could get a sack of potatoes; a chicken for some soap. They didn't know how much longer these restrictions were going to last, or worse, how much longer they could count on the goodwill of some of their business contacts. Anti-Semitism had always been prevalent in Poland, always. But instead of a low and constant rumble, it seemed to be rising to a fevered pitch. In fact, four Jews had been sentenced to death for smuggling sugar into the ghetto. A fifth was shot for trying to exchange a fur coat for something to eat. Szulim's parents knew the danger and dealt only with farmers they could trust. Though trust, like food and water, was in short supply.

Szulim looked around. He didn't understand how everything could look the same yet different somehow. The people he had known all of his life, the people he had come to know, shuffled along slowly, marked by yellow stars. That was nothing new. What he noticed for the first time were the people who didn't have stars. The farmers, the gentiles. And for the first time, Szulim felt different.

His parents had always told him that they were different. They were Jews. But the way his parents spoke of this difference, the way he had seen it all around him, being Jewish was special. He was lucky to be one of the people who dressed a certain way, who ate certain foods, who prayed in the synagogue. Even at a young age, Szulim knew that Jews were smarter. They sent their children to school as soon as they could speak. They were cleaner, going every week to the mikvah. Jews, in Szulim's understanding, were better somehow.

But today, looking around the marketplace at those who were visibly marked by this difference, Szulim began to wonder. He could see how the people who didn't have stars stood a little taller, swung their arms a little higher. They seemed not to have an invisible weight on their backs, a weight he noticed his parents and aunts and uncles carrying. And for the first time, Szulim understood what it meant to be a Jew. What, exactly, the star signified.

He also noticed that there seemed to be even more people than usual with yellow stars. Families he didn't recognize, holding small cardboard suitcases and staring wide-eyed around the crowded square. Mylech Szarfartz, the head of the Jewish police, stood on a crate surrounded by townspeople. He read names off of a list and pointed to the people holding suitcases. One by one, a man or woman that Szulim recognized would walk up to an unknown family, exchange words and take a suitcase, leading the stunned people away in the direction of a house.

Szulim tugged at his mother's skirt. "Who are all those people?"

"Jews from other shtetls. They're going to live in Zelechow now."

"Where?"

THAT AFTERNOON, SZULIM heard a knock on the door. Havah answered it and told Szulim to run across the street and get his father. Pop came out of the store to greet the people standing on the front stoop of their house with a silver menorah. Szulim pushed his wheel back and forth along the dirt path as his father scratched his head and put his finger to his chin. Then Pop and the people he didn't know walked into the house.

Szulim followed and saw his father going through the armoire, pulling out blankets.

"It's so hot out. Why do we need blankets?"

"We don't," his father said. "But this family will use them for beds on the patio."

Sleeping on the patio! With the chickens? "Pop, what about their own homes?"

"They don't have homes anymore."

"But why did they bring their menorah? Hanukah's in winter."

"Go play with your wheel." Szulim's father didn't know how to explain that Jews fled from their homes with whatever valuables they could carry, hoping to pay their way into the good graces of a home in Zelechow. But no matter how many jewels they carried, most people could not find a home. Szulim hoped no one would come and take his bed away. Where would he and Abraham sleep?

———

SZULIM BURST INTO his house and practically knocked Abraham down as he lunged towards Havah. He buried his head in her skirts and sobbed. He could barely catch his breath as he clutched her, Havah hugging him and asking, "What happened?"

He couldn't stop crying. And even if he did, how could he put into words what he had just seen? He had been pushing the rim of his bicycle wheel down a dirt road, tapping it with a wooden ruler, one side and then the other. When his wheel veered to the left, he turned to catch it. That's when he saw. A young woman walked towards him holding an infant wrapped in a thin blanket. She was only a house or two away. Maybe she was visiting a friend, or stopping by her husband's workplace. Perhaps she was trying to find some extra food for her baby. A Gestapo strolled past holding his rifle with the bayonet pointing up. They always patrolled with the pointy ends facing the sky, as if they intended to pierce the heavens. For no reason whatsoever, the guard lifted his rifle, and before Szulim could look away, smacked the young mother in the head with the butt of his gun. Szulim had never seen the Gestapo hit a woman before. Men, yes. For months he'd been witness to kicks and punches, even shots from their guns. But never a woman. He wished he hadn't seen this, wished he had been playing on another block. Yet he could not turn away. As the woman fell to the ground bleeding, the guard grabbed the baby out of her arms and threw it, still bundled, against the wall of a house.

Szulim didn't know what to do. Nothing worked; nothing seemed to move. Even the wind stopped blowing. The only sound came from the bleeding woman, on her hands and knees, pulling at her hair. A sound like a wild animal. "My baby! My baby!"

He turned around and ran. He didn't see the people nearby, others who may have run to help. He just raced the two blocks home, hearing her rabid screams, "Gutenyu! Oy, gutenyu! My baby!"

Szulim saw what happened; he saw it with his own eyes. But who would believe him? And how could he ever get that image — a baby flung like trash — out of his head? He never would. The howls of the mother would echo in his ears forever. He was still sobbing when Mama came home from the store and began rubbing his back. She didn't have to ask what happened. She had already heard.

———

SZULIM STOPPED ASKING "why." Did it matter? What mattered was the fact that there was never enough food or water. That more and more people lived in Zelechow than ever before. That there wasn't even space for the notznik pot with all the children sleeping on his bedroom floor. Every time he thought his house couldn't possibly hold any more people, his parents would answer the door to another family crying. Begging in Yiddish for shelter from the cold.

Summer had turned to fall, and fall to winter. The Jewish New Year had come and gone with obligatory ritual but little fanfare. Still a celebration, but tempered. Everything tempered now.

There were new faces straggling into the ghetto daily. Strangers with yellow stars like him, yet these people weren't like his family at all. The men did not go to shtiebl on Shabbat like his father. The women wore bright colored clothes, dirty now after walking the 20 kilometers from Sobolew where the trains had left them off. They didn't speak Yiddish. They came from far away, his mother had said. Holland, Belgium and France.

"Is that in Poland?" Szulim couldn't understand why they'd come here when there was no place to sleep, nothing to eat and the Gestapo guards were so cruel.

Szulim overheard Mimeh Foigel whispering with his mother in the store. "These people have no ration cards. I'm afraid to sell anything. A Zelechow Jew, I can give extra bread. What if these new Jews are spies?"

"I'm surprised they even come in," his mother said. "Looking at us like we're peasants. Just because they speak another language, that makes them better?"

"Aren't you hungry?" his mother had asked the oirech last Friday. The old man had cut away all the fat and left it on his plate.

Szulim knew it was rude, but he couldn't stop staring. He and Abraham eyed the meat, hoping that Pop would be practical and scrape the uneaten portion onto one of their plates. Who was this man who didn't eat fat? Szulim was lucky his family could still afford to buy such good meat. The poor families had to eat lean cuts of beef on Shabbat. If they ate any meat at all.

Szulim never got used to the dead bodies. Every time he saw someone lying frozen on the ground, he ran to the store to tell his aunts or parents.

"These people are from far away," his mother said. "They're not used to our food and our weather. They didn't take care of themselves."

Szulim wanted to believe it was their fault. That freezing to death was something he and his family had control over. That it was as simple as brushing your teeth, or eating fatty meat or wearing your gloves. That he was somehow immune to becoming one of the families who had no place else to live but the cemetery. Families who washed their few items of clothes in a stream and hung them to dry overnight on trees; these shirts turning into ghosts – white, headless bodies frozen into a strange motionless dance. Arms with no hands hanging limp, or flung out as if trying to grab those who came too close. Yet walking to cheder everyday, seeing arms and legs poking out of the snow like broken branches of a tree, Szulim wondered if his mother was telling him the whole truth.

Spring — Summer 1942

When the ground finally thawed, not all limbs rising from the earth flowered into life. The spring melted the snow and revealed corpses that had lain hidden underneath the blanket of white. The bodies provided employment; the Judenrat paid Jews in ghetto money to serve as undertakers, burying the dead in ground that had just begun to soften. Szulim was six years old.

As the snow turned to streams trickling down hillsides, the fever ran through Zelechow, leaving even more bodies in the street. When Szulim was too tired to go to cheder, too weak to wander around, Mama made him chicken soup, and it wasn't even Shabbat. Pop came home from the store early to do *bankes*; he was an expert at the cupping method of healing. Szulim could barely see straight, but watched from his bed as Pop attached gauze to a long wire, dipped it into pure alcohol, and then set a match to the soaked cotton.

"Can you get your shirt off, Szulimeleh?" Pop pressed the banke, a little glass cup with no bottom, to the middle of Szulim's back and lowered the fiery cotton into the hollow. The burning puff came so close to his skin, but Szulim hadn't been worried. He felt his skin rise into the banke and he held still. Even though he was tired, it was really hard holding still for so long. Szulim listened as Pop talked about the week's Parshah, the Torah portion that told how Moses called upon Aaron and his sons to make an offering unto God. Szulim could smell the fiery cotton as Pop talked about the burnt offerings that the Lord had commanded, and how Aaron's sons Nadab and Abihu did not listen, making instead their own offerings of incense. Just as his father got to the part about God punishing Nadab and Abihu, he pressed down gently on Szulim's back and Szulim heard the "thwap" of the suction releasing as his father removed the glass cup. It was over.

Pop had poured some camphor oil into his hands and rubbed Szulim's shoulders and back. Between the sharp, cold smell opening his nostrils and Pop's heavy, warm hands, Szulim melted — both with fatigue and relief that his parents were there, caring for him. Relief that the doctor didn't come to his house with leeches, like he did for the goyim.

But the bankes didn't work, despite Pop pressing the glass cup to Szulim's back for days on end. Around the clock, his mother and his aunts sponged him down.

"Eat, Szulim," pleaded aunt Yehudith, the baker's wife, holding a spoon to his lips with the soup she had made. "Just a little sip. I'll bring you a special bread. The ends, your favorite part."

He didn't remember tasting the soup — for two weeks time disappeared in a strange, foggy dance of sleep and wake — but Yehudith's' broth must have worked. Because when Szulim could finally sit up, she brought him pumpernickel rubbed with salt and garlic, just the way he liked it. Gedalia Yosef had figured out a way to bake a small loaf made entirely of heels, especially for Szulim.

"Szulim, you're afraid of the droshky!" Rivka teased when he could finally talk to his sisters and brother. "When the doctor came to give you an injection, you kept mumbling, 'In comes the droshky and the droshky driver takes the whip and pushes it into me very, very deep.'"

Szulim didn't care that Rivka laughed. He was just happy he could see straight. His parents and aunts were relieved, too, thanking God every two minutes, it seemed. They had the means to keep Szulim clean and hydrated. And no one else in the family suffered. Not everyone in Zelechow had been so lucky.

———

JUST AS SZULIM came back into health, his father got picked up for work camp. Every few weeks, German trucks sped into town on Tuesday mornings, the commander stepping down from the cab, pointing his baton. Any able-bodied man strolling by would be fair game. In the past, Pop had been able to pay his way out of service, offering money for a substitute. He was the man of the house, needed by his family to run the store and take care of the home. But on this market day, he hadn't been lucky. He joined the 15 or so other men on the 13-kilometer march, escorted by German guards on motorcycles, to the uninhabited town of Wylga.

The Judenrat came to the store to tell his mother. She had already heard from friends who had seen the line up of men leave the ghetto. Sara and Rivka knew as well. Only Szulim and Abraham didn't understand why their father wasn't sitting at the dinner table that night.

"He's at work," Mama said.

But Szulim knew that Pop worked at the store, and the sun had set which meant that he should have been in the house. So his mother explained that he went away on a business trip.

"When will he come home?"

Mama couldn't answer. One week, two weeks? She knew that often times men came back bruised, their faces unrecognizable from the beatings. Some men didn't come home at all.

"Later. Pop will be back soon." She pressed her lips together in a smile, but Szulim thought her eyes looked sad.

For days, weeks, Szulim had other questions, but he couldn't ask. His mother was too busy working double time at the store, doing the jobs Pop usually did. He didn't like it, but what choice did he have other than to accept the situation? Ever since the airplanes came, he'd had to accept the situation.

LATE ONE AFTERNOON, the door opened and his father shuffled in.

"Pop!" The children ran to their father, jumping into his arms and wrapping around his legs and waist.

"Oh, thank God, Chaim. It's you!" Mama brushed the kids away and sat him down. "You must be exhausted." She ran to get him some bread and tea.

"I am, but I feel good. I haven't worked like that in a long time." He told them about the enormous boulders they moved, the land he helped to clear. "The most I do at the store is carry heavy bags of salt."

He took off his shoes and stretched his legs. "I missed you all. I am very happy to be back, believe me. But it felt good being so productive."

———

WHEN HIS FATHER got picked up again, at the beginning of summer, Szulim didn't have to go to bed each night wondering if he'd see him again. He knew Pop would return. So he just waited, passing his time with his bicycle rim and stick, wandering around with Abraham. The warm weather called them outdoors, despite the fact that Havah begged them to stay inside. On market day, when the farmers came in to sell food, exchanging potatoes or onions for candlesticks or shirts, Szulim noticed a new way in which the Jews and the goyim spoke to each other. Instead of pointing to their carts, the farmers motioned with their hands to the fields beyond the boundaries of the ghetto, waving their arms to the sky. The Jews stared out into this distance and shook their heads, refusing to see, all the while hugging themselves and covering their mouths with their hands. Some actually trembled. Szulim had never seen trades like that before.

WHEN POP WALKED in the door two weeks later, Szulim didn't jump on his father. None of the children did. He looked different. His mother ran up and reached out to his face. No bruises showed on his skin, but Pop was clearly suffering. He sat down but didn't smile.

"We didn't do anything." Pop stared straight ahead. "We just moved the rocks back."

He looked at Szulim's mother. "The only reason they take us there is to break us, Perl. Our morale. I'm not going back again."

FOR THE REST of the summer, every time he heard the roar of the truck, Szulim's father ran and hid. It wasn't easy. The Judenrat knew in advance when the Germans were coming and they'd round up their fellow Jews, helping the Nazis pluck men from the street. Mylech Szarfartz took advantage of his position of power, showing off to the Nazis how strict he could be, and he punished those who tried to run away. Afterwards, members of the Judenrat would go to the homes or workplaces of those men and boys, informing the families that their loved ones were taken. Szulim's father did everything he could to avoid being picked for forced labor, and for several months dodged it successfully.

———

THE WARM WEATHER brought peace and quiet to Szulim's slumbering. Children who once slept on the floor of his room now camped on the patio with their parents, or under a tree in a nearby park. The sun had set hours before and the only light came from the moon, which shone brightly through the windows. Szulim lay sound asleep with Abraham, his sisters in the next bed, when his mother's gasp pierced the quiet of the night. Szulim sat up, pulling the covers around him, and heard his father whisper.

"Don't worry, Perl. Germans would bang much louder."

Szulim tiptoed to the bedroom door and listened to the noise coming from the living room as his father slowly opened the front door.

"Yitzhak!" his father cried. "Oy gutenyu!"

Szulim wandered out of his room and saw his father embrace a man he did not know. A short, muscular man with a red beard, like Pop's. The man trembled and couldn't stop looking over his shoulder. He complained of hunger and thirst. His mother turned towards the kitchen and saw Szulim standing in his nightshirt.

"Go back to bed, bubbeleh. It's okay. It's just your daddy's cousin from Ryki."

Szulim slid next to Abraham and pulled the covers up to his chin. He was tired, but couldn't fall back asleep. He heard the grown ups talking; Pop's cousin telling stories about liquidating a train, piles of shoes — was it burning shoes? Shoes that smelled like flesh? He heard this Yitzhak Bialebroda talk of falling down and scooting under, holding onto an axle, waiting all day, riding beneath. He heard talk of barbed wire and skies full of smoke. He could hear his mother crying softly, his father saying, "I can't believe it. The farmer's stories are true. Oh God, no."

"And when the train slowed to turn into some woods," Szulim heard from the living room, "I let go. It rolled away and I ran."

Szulim fell asleep with these words in his head. A story that seemed to greatly upset his parents, though he didn't understand what was so sad about people taking off their shoes to go on a liquid train ride.

––––––

SZULIM NOTICED THAT his parents spoke in Polish more and more often. From the urgency of their whispers, their hushed and frantic tones, Szulim guessed they weren't talking about new clothes for him or Rivka. He heard the words "Treblinka" and "Turek", *wiszedlenia*, relocation. But he didn't know what any of it meant. He asked Rivka what all the talk was about, but she just shrugged. Not the same shrug when she didn't want to tell him what was so funny about the Hershele Ostropeler stories his parents used to laugh about with their friends. But a shrug that made Szulim understand that she, too, was worried.

His parents pointed to various objects in his house. "Pack it," his father would say. Or, "That'll sell on the black market." Szulim thought about the marketplace on Tuesdays. The cobblestones were light gray, not black. And people only came out during the day when the sky was blue.

"Not this?" his mother asked. Pop shook his head. Where were they going? His father rarely smiled any more and his mother stopped pretending that everything was going to be all right.

All this *chichiying*, this talk in lowered voices. His parents didn't even bother hiding it from Szulim and his siblings. But Szulim noticed that his parents got quiet when the other family was around. Szulim could see his mother's mouth begin to open when she and Mrs. Kozorek sat in the living room. And then it would shut and his mother would smile with her lips close together. The way Mama smiled at Mrs. Kozorek, Szulim could sense a sadness, a fear and something else. Like a question that no one could answer.

September 29, 1942

MEN WOVE LEAVES over and across broken tree branches, allowing for a canopy of stars to peek through makeshift roofs. Throughout Zelechow, Jews celebrated *Sukkot* by erecting wooden shelters, open on all sides as prescribed by tradition to welcome the traveler seeking food and refuge. Zelechow certainly had its share of travelers now. In fact, the structure Szulim's family used every year to build the sukkah where they'd eat all of their meals during the harvest festival had not sat empty. Nestled in the corner of the patio, refugees had been sleeping in it all spring and summer. But now, despite the arrival of Sukkot, it remained unadorned. Szulim could not remember a time when his father did not fully observe a holiday or ritual, and wondered why he hadn't built the sukkah this year. It was as if his father knew a secret. A bad secret.

On the fourth day of Sukkot, the morning of market day, a German truck swept through town. Szulim's father was unable to hide.

His mother ran from the store when she heard; she knew her husband would be devastated about going to Wylga. She could sense that he knew something, had some sort of feeling that would make leaving even harder. She grabbed a piece of bread and cheese, his coat, and ran to the plaza where he was lining up with 18 other men and boys, both Feter Moshes and Szulim's older cousins, Berl and Herschel, among them. Szulim had been playing inside with Abraham and Havah, so he didn't know. He didn't hear his father whisper in a hurried voice, "Send the girls tonight. You go with the boys tomorrow."

When she returned from the center of town, Szulim's mother rushed back and forth in the house, pulling things out of cabinets, wrapping them in bundles. "I'm busy. Go play with Abraham," she said when Szulim asked why she wasn't at the store. On Tuesdays, even Mimeh Foigel and Mimeh Sara worked there.

THE DINNER TABLE seemed lopsided. Szulim and Abraham sat on one side and Mama sat at the head. But the other seats remained empty. Szulim already heard that his father went to the work camp, but where were his sisters?

"They're staying at a friend's tonight." Mama waved her hand towards the door and spooned some soup into their bowls. Szulim hoped that meant he could have their portion of dinner.

"Boys, we're going away tomorrow afternoon. On a trip. So I need you to prepare your things." Szulim got excited. They must be going to the woods! For two years now they hadn't gone away in the summer; he missed the vacation house. But then he remembered that it had been getting colder. Too cold to run barefoot and sleep in the cottage meant for summertime. Besides, his mother always loved going to the woods, enjoying long stretches of relaxation and playing with the kids. Now, sitting at the dinner table, she didn't sound happy about leaving.

SZULIM FELT AS if his body had melted into his bed. They had been up late packing, and with only he and Abraham in the room that night, he fell into a deeper sleep than he could ever remember. But he didn't get to enjoy it for long. Szulim couldn't tell if it was the dogs barking or the guards screaming, *"Raus! Raus!"* Loud noises, scary noises, shook him from slumber too early in the morning. He looked towards the windows and wasn't surprised to see darkness still.

"Szulim! Abraham! Wake up!" His mother rushed from room to room, back and forth, her arms flailing. She reminded Szulim of the chickens that sometimes fell out of the shochet's hands when he sliced their necks, the birds running in circles. Szulim rubbed his eyes and tried to get his body to move. He didn't know what was happening.

"Szulim, I need you to listen to me," his mother said. She was out of breath. "I need you to be a big boy, a good big brother. You must listen to me and help me with Abraham." His little brother stirred in the bed, still half asleep despite the shouts and the occasional gunshot.

"Put your shoes on. Get your brother up. We have to leave."

Szulim started to ask where they were going, but something inside him stopped his lips from moving. He knew this was serious. He had never seen his mother in such a panic, so desperate. All the bundles that had been prepared the day before lay on the table, untouched. As he felt for his star, buttoning his coat and helping Abraham into his shoes, he heard screams. Sirens. Guards shouting, "Get out! Get out!" Polacks hollering a word he didn't know. Sharp thuds echoing through the dark as batons and rifles beat on doors and walls.

The sack Szulim had packed the night before with his collection of rocks and pebbles lay on the floor of his room. His mother hoisted Abraham onto her hip and grabbed Szulim's hand and they hurried out the door.

"Havah," said Szulim, turning back towards the house. He didn't know where she went. He hadn't seen her in all the chaos.

"Come!" his mother said, pulling on his hand as he struggled to keep up in the dark outside. The crowds pushed to the right, towards the marketplace. Szulim's mother dragged him and his brother down the street to the left.

"Perl!" A young man appeared in front of them as if from nowhere. Szulim recognized him as Chiel, Mimeh Tertza's fiancée. "Go to my shop," he said. "Quick!"

Szulim had to trot to match his mother's hurried pace. They scurried along their dirt road, passing houses with doors flung open, lamps turned on. Szulim saw Jewish police screaming in Yiddish, forcing people from their beds, expelling them out of their homes. One of these kapos stepped out of the dark, stopping Szulim's mother and pointing in the opposite direction of where they were headed. "You need to go that way! To the marketplace!"

Szulim saw crowds pushing slowly towards the town square, lugging small wooden suitcases and bundles. Even those who clutched nothing but a loved one's hand, their movements, too, seemed to carry a heavy weight. Like they were walking in a dream, a very scary dream. Stumbling and pushing and straining through a haze of bewilderment. Old people, children, men too terrified to move, all shoved along by the butts of rifles. Szulim wondered why his mother left without taking anything.

"I need to find my daughters," his mother said. The policeman knew Szulim's family and let them pass. "Hurry," he warned.

Szulim could barely make out where he was. He held tight to his mother, panicked at the thought of losing her grasp, petrified by the pandemonium. He wished he were still asleep with Abraham, his sisters in the next bed. He closed his eyes and tried to recall that peaceful sensation from not even an hour before, but he just stumbled on the cobblestones.

He didn't ask where they were going, why they weren't following the crowds. He knew he had to trust his mother and just do whatever she said. Abraham whimpered as he bounced crudely on her hip. They turned left, then right. Nothing looked familiar in the predawn darkness. They passed by one building, another, the houses looking all the same. Was his mother lost? Szulim just held tight and did his best to keep up. Every few moments, his mother would stop and look around. Her eyes darting across streets and in windows. Finally they arrived at what looked to Szulim like a small factory. His mother yanked open the door and shoved them inside.

HIDING
The Attic

SEPTEMBER 30 — OCTOBER 15, 1942

THE SKY HAD not yet turned from navy to coral when Szulim, Abraham and his mother arrived at their destination, firmly shutting the door of the storefront, trying to block out the horrible noise of the ghetto round up. Only darkness made its way through the dusty windows of the workshop where they stood catching their breath. Szulim blinked, straining to take in his surroundings.

"Mama, where are ..."

"Shh!" she said. The only sound came from Abraham who had stopped crying, but whose hyperventilating breaths came out in short bursts between sniffles. Szulim could detect traces of grease and metal, a smell of rubber. He looked around to see if he was at the shoemaker's. From the little he could see, nothing looked familiar. His mother craned her neck, too, though her feet stood planted.

"It's me. Perl!" she spoke softly into the dark room.

"Climb up! Quickly!" A man's voice came from above. Szulim did not know who it was, or where he was hiding. But as he looked towards the back of the room, he could make out a ladder reaching up to a hole in the unpainted wood ceiling.

Mama grabbed Szulim's hand and pulled him deeper into the store. "Go Szulim." She gave him a gentle nudge. "Start climbing."

He followed her orders. Though his heart had been pounding ever since he woke up, he still felt sleepy. He was nervous climbing up the steep ladder, not knowing where he was going or who would be waiting for him above the ceiling. As he neared the top, a pair of arms, men's arms, reached out to him.

"It's okay, Szulim," his mother said from below. She was pushing Abraham up the ladder, stepping on each rung after him.

"Come, bubbeleh." Mimeh Sara! Szulim felt a wave of relief hearing her voice and seeing a faint outline of her slender, beautiful face poke through the hole. He stepped with more assurance and clambered onto a rough and dirty floor. "Over here, next to Berleh."

He stumbled over legs as he crawled across the wood planks that had been nailed crudely to some beams and made his way to the area where the tin ceiling sloped down to this makeshift floor now floating above the store. It was even darker in this loft space, though within the hour a few pinpoints of light would begin poking between the rafters of the rusted roof. He reached out his hands and felt his younger cousin.

"Thank God you found us," Mimeh Tertza whispered.

"Did anyone follow you?" a man asked. Szulim later learned that Chiel had two brothers who repaired bicycles and sewing machines. They owned the shop in which Szulim and Chiel's family now took refuge. These brothers had developed an improved sewing machine, and word had gotten out about this new model with a double bobbin, so the men built a crawl space above the workshop to hide their invention from interested Germans and Poles. Little did they know that space would hide 39 people.

"No," said his mother. "I don't think so. I zigzagged. Just to be sure."

Szulim sat pressed against his brother and cousin Berl, everyone cramped together whispering, sharing details in as few words as possible as the man who first spoke pulled the ladder up into the crude attic.

"Who?"

"Gitel, Berl, Sara, Foigel, Tertza, Laicha, Sara, Chiel's family..." Szulim lost track of the whispered names in the list of all the people hiding in the small space.

"The girls?"

"Sent yesterday," his mother answered, reminding Szulim that his sisters were not among them. He wondered where they were. And though he had never given them much mind, being girls and being older, he found that now he missed them immensely. His aunts muttered their "thanks God."

"Mama, where's Pop?"

"Shh, he's all right. We'll see him soon."

How would Pop know where to find them when he came back? He hoped Mama had left a note at the store.

"Please God ... a few days, we wait quietly," Mimeh Foigel said. "It will all be over."

"Oy, I hope so."

No one had to tell Szulim and Abraham to be silent. They knew. Everyone sat completely still, listening to the liquidation of Zelechow. They couldn't see what was happening outside. But they could hear. Gun shots, beatings, cries. The kapos'

Yiddish screams overlapping with German orders shouted through bullhorns. The actual words incomprehensible; the anger, however, piercing the silence in the attic like knives. Ferocious barking from a whole pack of dogs. Where did these dogs come from? Szulim had only ever seen the one that had patrolled the shtetl all these months, marching alongside the man with the shiniest boots.

They didn't know then, and most of that group in the attic would never find out. But history would tell that on the last day of September, known to Zelechowers as the 19th of *Tishrei*, a small group of people fled into the forest. Another group who had difficulty making their way to the center of town – children, elderly and the ill – were murdered on the spot by SS troops, along with those caught trying to escape. Almost 300 people shot dead on the streets they called home. After the round up, after the nearly 15,000 Jews were marched to Sobolew where they'd board a train to Treblinka, Germans hunted down and killed 800 more hiding throughout the village. The only Jews left wandering around Zelechow were the 50 members of the police force and fire brigade, charged with burying the dead and collecting property.

But that came later, during the calm. In the meantime, fear and fury continued to ricochet through the marketplace, down streets and around corners, seeping its way into the hiding space just below the roof, communicating to those huddled in the dark, cramped space the hell that they had somehow managed to escape.

SOMETIME IN THE late morning, the screaming ceased, the sounds outside began to fade. No one in the attic could see what was going on, but they sat completely still and listened. Angry orders became more distinct, footsteps more organized. Aside from the sound of an army truck roaring by on occasion, the tapping of the Judenrat patrolling the streets, or guttural German curses, Zelechow seemed eerily calm, devoid of the clamor of everyday life. The atmosphere inside the attic hung thick with worry. The air, or lack of it, stifling; but not hot. Thankfully, the season's oncoming chill saved the 39 hidden Jews from the fate of Zelechow's deported; those 15,000 souls crated into cattle cars and rolling to Treblinka. Had it been summer, the sun beating down upon the corrugated metal roof would have converted their refuge into an oven.

SIXTEEN DAYS. SIXTEEN mornings, afternoons, nights – one minute indistinguishable from the next, bound only by silence, dread and the feeling that each moment might be the last. The grown ups were afraid to even whisper in case guards or the Jewish police stood outside. If small amounts of air could seep in through the rafters, certainly their voices could float out and give them away. Even their breathing had to be done without a sound.

Szulim, Abraham, and the other children sat on the perimeter of the loft, since the ceiling sloped down and there was less room. At night – no different from the days, just darker – everyone slept where they sat, lying in rows pressed against each other, unable to move. Szulim twisted in his sleep, plagued by a fear once thought unimaginable in a boy so young, a fear he had seen first hand and had suffered during his waking hours, too. He woke up crying.

"Shh, Szulim," Mama said. "You have to be quiet."

Abraham jerked in his sleep, as well, and on the fourth night, his arm flailed out and banged against the metal roof. Everyone sat up in a panic. Once they realized the SS wasn't bursting in on them, that the loud noise reverberating out into the silent night hadn't attracted attention, they went back to sleep – but not before moving the children to the middle of the room so that errant limbs could not imperil the lives of others.

SZULIM'S MOTHER HAD arrived at the attic empty-handed, but many of the people brought what little food they could grab. Chiel's family had been preparing meals ahead of time, though they never expected to feed 39. Two days, three at most, they all thought, and then they could climb back down the ladder and find their way towards safety. But after the sun rose and fell, and then rose and fell twice more, adults crawled to each other to speak amongst themselves in whispers.

"What's going on? Why haven't they left yet?"

"How much more could they possibly find to loot?"

"I'm hungry." A child, Szulim couldn't tell who.

"We know. Shhh. We all are."

They could still hear German and Polish voices, working together to pillage the abandoned homes, stealing valuables and selling off property. Dogs still roamed the streets, their barks echoing off the walls of empty houses.

By the fifth or sixth day, the scarcity of food and water became a problem. Szulim's stomach had stopped growling, cramping instead from the emptiness. When darkness of night blanketed the attic, Chiel and his brothers crept down the ladder to search for provisions. They carried the buckets of waste to empty outside, though by that time, with such a lack of food and water, the buckets hadn't been used as often. Troops didn't patrol at night anymore; the town had been liquidated, so there was no one left to force inside after curfew. Szulim imagined the Judenrat, the police and the Nazi guards dining happily with their families in spacious homes. Candlelight flickering across cloth-covered tables, dishes filled with food no longer rationed. Sleeping in warm, soft beds blissfully unaware of his existence.

The group cloistered in the attic sat quietly, praying that the three men might find something for all of them to eat without getting caught. Chiel and the others stole into homes now abandoned, poking through cupboards that yielded modest portions. They returned with bread and water, but little else. Not even word of what was happening in their village. Not only did they avoid German guards, they took great care not to see anyone at all. They didn't know which member of the Judenrat they could trust, which Jewish policeman might be friendly. What if the three men saw others seeking refuge, additional souls who might try to join them? None of this, however, mattered to Szulim. He cared only about food.

A WEEK INTO their confinement, they heard the door to the workshop creak open. Two men entered, speaking in Polish. Szulim recognized one of the voices as belonging to Mylech Szarfartz. After Pop returned from Wylga the second time, he spoke freely of the Chief of Police, the well-built man now standing right below them. Szulim had heard his father and big Feter Moshe talking about Szarfartz's slaves who cleaned his clothes and polished his shoes. "What, he thinks he can be a Nazi with those shiny boots of his?" Szulim's father was not alone in his hatred of Mylech. Practically every Jew in the ghetto resented the Chief's inherent joy in taking bribes, as if the thrill came long before the necessity. The fact that Szarfartz and this gentile man had entered the workshop was itself the result of a bribe.

"Trust me." Szarfartz's voice was muffled, but the 39 Jews holding their breath above his head listened intently. "The sewing machine is in here somewhere."

"We need to find that prototype before the Germans get their hands on it," the second man said. "At the very least, the plans."

"Must be a big job, you being the head of the Institute."

"Yes. Important work coming out of there," said the Polish man, who turned out to be the Dean of the Warsaw Polytechnic Institute. "When we heard about this Jew in Zelechow ... let's just say there may be a place for you at Polytechnic if we find his invention."

Szulim had heard the Jews called many names by Germans and Poles, but he had never been referred to as a 'bobbin.' He didn't understand why these two men searched for 'bobbins' amongst cabinets and drawers. Not even a baby could fit in a desk drawer.

Szulim knew to remain silent. He slowed his breathing, everyone did. But when they heard a tapping right underneath them, a hushed panic swept amongst the hidden. Szarfartz and the Dean had found brooms and began poking at the false ceiling of the workshop; every thud right under Szulim's tuchas sending a snake of fear up his spine. One of the Jews motioned to the trap door and mouthed, "Should we sit on it?" But he was too late. Light flooded the once concealed garret as the floorboard began lifting.

"I found the storage space!" Mylech Szarfartz said to the Polish man. "Help me push it up."

Before anyone could react, Chiel's uncle Rafel, an old man wise enough and brave enough to take a risk, stuck his hands out through the opening. Everyone froze. Time stopped, breathing halted. Szulim didn't understand what was happening, but he could feel the tension. A hum that couldn't be heard, but resonated through the air in the split second before something very fragile shattered.

Yesch ludzhi! "There are people up there," the Dean said in a loud whisper. "Let's leave. We can come back another time."

Everyone in the attic held on until they heard the door close. Then a collective exhalation of breath swept through the room, punctuated by a nervous hiccupping.

"Oh my God, oh my God."

Rafel, the old man with the long gray beard spoke first. "I knew we couldn't prevent them from coming up."

"You knew Mylech was a crook."

"That I knew. But I hoped the goy had a conscience."

"Thank God he was a mensch."

"Or simply afraid that if they turned us in, the Germans would steal the prototype for themselves."

"Szarfartz would have loved to turn us in."

"For the right price, he still might."

For a week, Szulim had felt himself grow more and more limp from lack of food and movement, malaise and foreboding weakening his muscles, turning his bones to mush. He'd lift his arm, only to have it fall back to his side; *like Sara's doll*, he thought. So that every time he felt this sensation in his arms or legs, he thought about his sisters, wondering if he'd ever see them again. And then he'd think about his father, before squeezing his eyes shut to stop the painful thoughts from burrowing deeper into his head.

But now, the rising of the ceiling panel was like an injection, shooting fear throughout his thin body. He felt hardened and awake again, as if Pop had turned on a generator inside him.

For ten more days, they sat. Silent. Waiting. Wondering how long it would take until Zelechow emptied. Wondering if they would leave the attic alive. Wondering if freedom could possibly outrun starvation or capture.

The generator inside his body had since shut off and what Szulim felt was more than sleepy; it was the woozy fatigue from when he had suffered the sickness. They all felt it. For a couple of days now, the only thing that passed between their lips had been water. The last time the men crept out to scavenge for food, they came back empty handed.

"The abandoned homes now have people," Chiel and his brothers reported. "It looks like farmers, families outside the ghetto, they've moved in."

Their breathing slowed and their energy levels allowed for little more than sitting around or sleeping. Which is all they had been doing anyway. The cramping in their bellies radiated down to their hips and legs, which had barely moved for over two weeks.

Sixteen days into their confinement, as the sun prepared for its descent, they heard Yiddish coming from outside the workshop. A couple of Jewish policemen strolling the sidewalk spoke in much louder voices than necessary for a twosome walking right next to each other down a deserted street.

"The reason it's taken so long is that there was a lot more to loot than in other towns. And the closest train is in Sobolew."

All the adults in the attic perked up.

"I overheard the chief Gestapo. They suspect the Jews hid valuables in walls and attics. Starting tomorrow, they're going house by house to set fires. To uncover the jewels."

It was a warning. They listened as the policemen walked on. Their voices fading, but repeating in Yiddish the same conversation. Szulim would not know until many years later the fate of those police and the members of the Judenrat. When their job had been completed – when the Jews in positions of power finished rounding up and hunting down and burying the people they once prayed with – the Germans had no use for them. Some were killed right then and there, others perished in Treblinka.

But on this fall day, the 4th of *Cheshvan*, the kapos saved others from their own fate. As soon as the sun finished sinking from the sky, those hiding in the attic began their descent, quickly and quietly scrambling down the ladder. Like Noah's animals, they left two by two, letting 15 minutes or so pass between each departure, allowing time for the pairs of escapees to set off into the darkness.

Szulim's mother said goodbye to her sisters, quickly and with little fanfare. No hugs, just a brief "I'll see you soon." So different, he remembered, from when Mimeh Foigel had left for Warsaw way back before the war ever started. Then, all of the sisters were hugging and crying and hugging some more. Now, Mimeh Tertza left with Mimeh Gitel and little Berl; Mimehs Foigel and Sara, a pair to themselves, matter of fact, as if they were walking across the street to the store.

Szulim was anxious to leave the deplorable conditions of the attic and sat near the trapdoor, waiting, wondering when it would be his turn.

"Laicha," Chiel whispered to Szulim's remaining aunt, the wife of big Moshe Boruchowicz and mother to Berl and Herschel, "why don't you and Sara go with Perl? She shouldn't be all alone with two young boys."

"Sara and I will go alone," Mimeh Laicha said. "Five will be too much of a crowd."

So Laicha climbed down the ladder with her daughter, Szulim's cousin Sara, a redhead nearly five years older than his own sister Sara. The mother and daughter stole into the night. Szulim never saw them again.

Telling: Summer 2009

It's been over a week since our last phone call and I feel caught between two worlds. The sheer normalcy of life in New Jersey now sits in high contrast to an increasingly ever-present backdrop of shtetl life during the war. Meanwhile, Sandy and Sal are adjusting to a routine of evening phone calls that leave them hollow. Sandy is prepared for tonight's conversation. She settles into the sofa holding the receiver, and a box of tissues.

"This is like a movie," I say to Sal. "All the plot twists."

Sal laughs. "I don't go to movies much. But even I, who lived through it, have a hard time believing sometimes. The fact that my father told my mother 'Send the girls tonight' as he lined up for Wylga."

"How did he know?"

"My whole life, I've wondered. How did he know? How did he know not to build the sukkah, that we wouldn't be there to celebrate the harvest? How did he know my mother should send my sisters away the night before our town was liquidated? Did he have a gut feeling? Or did he have information?"

Sal sips from a glass of water. He, too, is prepared for a long conversation.

"My younger years are all about secrecy. My parents speaking in Polish when they didn't want us kids to hear them make plans. Sneaking an education when the schools were shut down. Hiding like fugitives in our own village. The distrust, the constant need to be on alert."

"When did you stop looking over your shoulder?" I ask.

"Ach, who knows. But I'll tell you something. My father, may he rest in peace, believed in the power of a confidence. 'The problem with a secret,' he used to say, 'is that you're the only one who has it. If someone else knows it, it's no longer a secret.'"

Sandy thinks about how good Sal has been at keeping secrets.

"I am not interested in idle chitchat or gossip. I don't have a need or a desire to talk with others and share stories," Sal says. "Sandy and I have gotten into many fights about this."

"This is true!" Sandy laughs, her voice faint through the phone. She told me about her book club from years ago, when she and Sal lived in Miami and the kids were in junior high. The group had read a book about the Holocaust and she shared with them a bit of Sal's past, just the few details she knew at the time. Sandy thought it was relevant to their discussion. The women were shocked. In the following weeks, some of them approached Sal and said, "Wow, I had no idea." Sal had felt completely betrayed and he and Sandy had another one of their fights — about her saying too much, him not enough. "I don't want to be the subject of people's conversations," he had said. But she needed to open up.

She listens to him now talk about this long-standing source of friction between the two of them. "Sandy thinks there are no secrets in a marriage." Sal sighs. "That what I know, she should know. But if I am told something in confidence, it remains such. And I expect the same from others. This I learned from my father."

Sandy holds the phone, reflecting on this notion of secrecy, and remembers the vacation she and Sal took long ago. In 1973, the Communist Bloc had just opened to travel, so they booked a tour of Warsaw, Berlin and Moscow. She and Sal had already been to Israel and parts of Western Europe, but no one they knew had ever been to the Soviet Union. It seemed like such an incredible opportunity to see an unknown part of the world. Granted, Sal was from Poland, *but what would he remember?* Sandy had thought. He was a little boy.

They sat on the plane, that late September, waiting for takeoff. Sandy picked up her book, looking forward to some peace and quiet, a break from her life with toddlers. She could see Sal gripping the arm rests. The stewardess stopped at their row to take their drink orders.

"A coke please," Sandy had said. Sal just shook his head.

He needs a drink, Sandy thought as she watched her husband's eyes dart around the cabin. *Something, anything to calm his nerves.* But Sal had never been a drinker. "I was drunk once in my life," he had told her the night of their wedding. "Never again."

Sandy knew the only thing that kept Sal's motion sickness at bay was to talk. So as the plane rose towards the clouds, Sandy asked him what, if anything, he remembered of Poland. And that's when he told her. Flying over the Atlantic, eight years into their marriage, Sandy first learned about life in the ghetto, hiding in an attic, how her husband survived the war.

"When we land in Warsaw," Sal had said, "I need to find some people."

"What people?" she asked.

Sal answered, "The people who hid me."

Sandy shakes her head now thinking back to that vacation. She can't believe she hadn't taken into account how that trip might have meant something else to Sal, that his agenda for going would have been so different from hers. But then again, he had never talked about his past. Ever.

Now, on the phone with me, it's all pouring out.

"How did your mom keep you and your brother entertained in the attic?" I ask. "You were sitting still for so long."

"You must understand that for kids in Poland, in my shtetl, there was no concept of being entertained. We were expected to behave in a certain way. You sat at the table respectfully; you ate, you didn't talk. We were born into a different code of conduct, not like today."

"Definitely not like today," I laugh, but also panic knowing that my boys can't sit at the table for two minutes. "My kids would never have been able to sit quietly like you did."

"Yes, they would have," Sal says. "My brother and I possessed a fear, a fear that had been instilled in us from the start of the war. You see people killed right in front of you, you understand very quickly what 'be quiet' means. We had been living with this fear and precaution for two years already. I suppose it came naturally. We understood enough that we knew, without a doubt, that we must remain silent."

"But still," I say, "you were six years old, your brother five. Young boys have *shpielkes*. Your bodies are wired to move. It's instinct. Sixteen days to sit in silence, not moving. How did you stifle that little kid energy?"

"My brother and I, everyone really, must have possessed some sort of survival instinct. I don't know how else to explain it. Yet from every account I've read, there are no instances of a one- or two-year-old surviving under these kinds of circumstances. The only babies who survived were the ones who were given away to gentiles. You had to have some understanding of consequences."

I think about my three sons and wonder if they would have been able to shut down that innate need to move and make noise, if they would have been able to hold back the sobs. "You and your brother were so lucky to have been the age you were."

"Yes," Sal says. "By age six, I knew the consequences all too well."

I pause for a moment and can't help but think that my middle son, just five, is the same age as Sal's brother when he was pent up with fear and deprivation.

"By the way," Sal says, "the Germans did find the brothers' prototype. In the 1950's, a German sewing machine company called Pfaff announced their 'latest invention' – a new machine with a special double bobbin that could do a variety of stitches. Bastards."

FLEEING
The Woods

October 15 – 17, 1942

"IT'S ABOUT TIME we got out of there," Szulim said. He had begun to wonder if he'd ever see the outdoors again, if he'd grow into an old man, still sitting in the dark attic with knees to his chest, hungry. It felt good to breathe in fresh air and stretch his arms; he hoped his legs still worked.

"Shh!" Mama laid a firm hand on his head. "Not a word."

Szulim was grateful he had on his good shoes, the ones with strong laces and made of thick black leather that came up around his ankles. His short brown pants buttoned just under the knee, but the cuffs were loose and he felt cold air seeping through. He pulled up his socks, the same shade of brown, and tucked the hem of his pants inside them. He drew his navy blue coat tight around his body, grateful that he had thought to put on his gray sweater over his long sleeve shirt when he had been dragged from sleep that awful morning.

As he followed his mother through the streets of Zelechow, tying the earflaps of his *hittel* under his chin, he felt as if he were walking through a dream. As if everyone in the whole world had disappeared, and he, Szulim, was left to swim through the silence.

They passed by houses, all of which were intact, despite the many doors and windows that had been broken into. Szulim saw his home and wanted to stop. He wanted something, anything, he didn't know what. A reminder, perhaps, of the two little boys and two little girls, the family, that had lived there. A reminder of the childhood, his childhood, which had been left behind.

"No time, Szulim. " His mother gently tugged at his hand.

The quiet, the lack of food, the walking by his house as if it were someplace forbidden, as if his bed and his pen knife and rock collection did not belong to him anymore, but to a ghost or a memory of the happiness that used to reside there.

The sadness sank to his feet, heavy like two cooking pots filled with marbles, but he walked on. He had no choice.

Light from the almost half moon glinted off the leaves, and walking through the woods, Szulim held tight to his mother's hand. He had never been out this late before. The stars sparkling in the sky above did not comfort him, but made him feel small. Small and very afraid. He imagined they were eyes, a thousand pairs of German eyes staring down at him through the branches.

The woods did not feel peaceful now like it did in summers before the war. Then, when they travelled the long road out of Zelechow by horse and buggy to the cottages nestled among the thick trees, friends and family surrounded Szulim. Those nights, gazing at the stars before bedtime, brought joy. Here, walking forever in unknown directions towards a place he had never been, Szulim felt very alone.

All he could do was focus on putting one foot in front of the other and wonder how long it would take to get there. But where was "there?"

"Someplace where we'll be safe," his mother had said. From how long they had been walking already, it didn't seem like safe was anywhere near Zelechow. Szulim prayed they'd arrive without getting caught. Please, he prayed, let there be food.

His mother stopped looking over her shoulder early on into their journey. Soon, she let go of Szulim's hand. "Hold onto my skirt." Mama needed to carry Abraham who wrapped his arms and legs around her waist and neck, and laid his head on her shoulder. Szulim wished his mother could carry him, too, but Abraham didn't have on his good shoes; his feet hurt from the cold.

Thankfully the chill wasn't as severe in the forest; the branches and leaves protected against the wind. The only sound came from the leaves rustling, twigs cracking underfoot, his mother's voice mumbling every so often, "Did I go this way already? Left or right?" She'd pause and look around. Szulim could see nothing. But he trusted that his mother knew where to go. *This must be what people do when they walk at night* he thought. *Stop and talk to themselves so they don't get lonely.*

He didn't ask "how much longer?" What was the point? They had to keep silent. His mother didn't even say "keep up." She just tugged at his hand. Szulim could tell that she was concentrating and he didn't want to interrupt.

Szulim peered through the trees and saw a clearing, what must have been a road, or more likely, a dirt path. It would have been much easier to walk on that path. But then someone might see them. Szulim knew they were far from Zelechow; they had been walking for what seemed like hours without passing a single home or store. As he passed each tree, he wondered if a German might be hiding behind it, standing so still, so tall. He squeezed his eyes shut to block the moon shadows that played tricks on him, but this only made his feet drag and his mother pulled on his hand harder. In the distance, he saw a cluster of small buildings belonging to a farm. They had to be extra quiet now; God forbid they woke anyone.

More than anything, Szulim wanted to stop and rest. He wanted to eat. He wanted to leave this cold, dark, never-ending forest and be with the rest of his family.

"Another few minutes," Mama whispered as she put Abraham down and grabbed both of their hands. "We're almost there."

Szulim held on tight, knowing his mother would eventually find their destination. But he also knew his mother could do nothing to ease his exhaustion and despair until they got there.

SZULIM NOTICED THE color of the sky had changed slightly, turning from black to purple. He thought it must have been his eyes getting used to the dark. His mother noticed it, too, stopping and scanning the horizon.

"I don't think we're going to make it tonight." She pointed to a large building becoming more visible in the early morning light. "Let's see what's over there."

Szulim and Abraham held their mother's hand as they snuck across a field towards a barn. Gently, his mother pulled open the door and they slipped inside. Szulim smelled the animals before he saw them. The sun had begun to rise and they looked around, able to see inside the stable. Horses and cows stared back at them and Szulim wondered if animals could distinguish between Jews and gentiles. He hoped they wouldn't cry out to the farmers. On the other side of the barn, sacks of grains piled high. Near the back, Szulim spotted the biggest mound of hay he had ever seen reaching almost all the way up to the ceiling. A ladder stood propped against it.

"Climb up boys, this will be a good place to rest. Nice and warm."

Szulim had never climbed a ladder before in his life, and now twice in less than a month! "Lay keppeleh, my bubbelehs. We'll stay here until it gets dark again."

His mother didn't have to tell him to be quiet. He already knew. Not that he had any energy to make noise; he had been awake since sun up the day before. Szulim was so relieved to lie down, to take a break from the endless walking. How wonderful that his mother found a place for them all to relax. He didn't even care that there was no food, or any place other than the hay to do his notznik. He fell fast asleep.

COLD AND HUNGER interrupted Szulim's slumber; shivers and cramps battling it out with exhaustion. On and off he'd doze, occasionally sitting up in the scratchy hay, looking around. Had it gotten dark yet? The relief he first felt at finding someplace to rest had begun to fade; his mother seemed anxious to resume their journey. Szulim felt that this night they'd actually make it. They followed the sun's descent, noticing the light growing dimmer as it poked through the cracks in the wood. They climbed down the ladder, Szulim and Abraham surer of their footing, and stole out of the barn. His mother took their hands and walked purposefully towards the woods. She seemed to know where she was going.

"Just a few more minutes, boys." Szulim didn't take comfort in his mother's estimation of time or distance, but he followed along, clutching her hand. They walked through the woods, tripping over thin tree branches. How much easier if they could walk in the path meant for horse and buggies. But they weren't animals able to trot freely, fearful of nothing but lightening. They were Jews on the run, sheltered only by fate. Caution and fate.

THEY EMERGED FROM the forest and saw a house in the distance, across another field. A lamp glowed through the window, the only home among the handful of others they had passed with a source of light coming from inside of it. Someone must be awake. Quietly, they walked into the yard, stopping next to a clump of bushes. Szulim could not see an entrance.

"Where are we?"

"Wilcziska." His mother tugged at the boys' sleeves and led them to some bushes a distance from the house. "Sit here until I come get you. Do not move."

Szulim pressed his body as far as he could into the leaves and held his brother's hand, watching his mother walk around the house. He hadn't been this far away from her in over two weeks. They watched as she knocked on what must be the front door.

"Is this where we're sleeping tonight?" Abraham asked.

"Shh!" Szulim only hoped this house had some food and a bed. He thought finally they would be okay. Finally there would be no more hiding. They'd stay here for a few days before going back to the rest of his family in Zelechow, back to cheder and the store and his bicycle wheel.

His mother stood at the front door and motioned for them, waving her arm, but they stayed hidden. She had said not to move until she came to get them and they knew by now how to listen. She rushed back to the bushes and grabbed them. "Hurry!" She choked on her words, barely able to contain the excitement in her voice. There must be several beds and a whole table full of food, Szulim thought.

When he stepped inside the small farmhouse, Szulim saw the stove and clay hood first, beyond that, a table. He glanced around and noticed a burlap bag hanging in a doorway leading to another room, the only other room in the house. A man he had never seen before stood in front of him wearing a nightshirt and a cap like a long stocking that hung down his side. His bedclothes didn't look comfortable, but rough; the fabric the color of rye fields. His feet were bare.

"Let's go, quickly," the man in the nightshirt said. His eyes darted around the empty room, looking from window to window.

Szulim wanted to stand near the stove and take in the warmth, but this man, named Mr. Sokol, seemed anxious to get them out of his kitchen. He must have been asleep already and wanted to go back to bed.

"I shouldn't have the lights on. It looks suspicious."

Szulim followed Mr. Sokol into the small bedroom shared by the entire family. He pushed a huge armoire to the side and Szulim saw a space where a wall should have been. The man in the nightshirt went inside and Szulim watched as he lifted two floorboards. There were no handles, so Mr. Sokol used a long metal tool to pry open the wood that revealed a trap door. A small ladder led down to another door. Where were they going? Szulim felt like he was entering a cave, it was so dark and quiet. Mr. Sokol opened the final door and lowered Abraham down first.

DISAPPEARING
Wilcziska, Poland

FALL 1942 – WINTER 1943

"YOU'RE ALIVE!" SZULIM heard his father's voice and then felt arms grab round his waist. Strong arms, safe arms pulling him down and into a tight embrace along with his brother. "Oy gutenyu! You're here!" His father drew Mama into their circle as she stepped down into the small crawl space at the entrance to the cellar.

"Mama!" His sisters ran to the knot of hugging bodies. Szulim was shocked. He never expected to find Rivka and Sara at this house, in this dank space under the ground. How did they get here? Rivka threw herself at her mother's skirt and held tight. Sara clung to her mother and cried. More people rose from the floor – Szulim could barely make them out in the darkness – all with questions. "Perl, what took you so long?"

"Oh, my *meidelehs*. Thanks God! My precious, precious meidelehs!" His mother's tears flowed with Sara's and she held tight to the girls. "You made it. All this time I didn't know." Szulim had never seen so much weeping, and at such a happy moment. But from the lowered voices, the subdued tone of this celebration, Szulim understood that they weren't free, not really. That still, they must hide from the bad people who were after them.

His mother pulled back and held his sisters' faces, looking deep into their eyes. "Are you okay?" she asked. Sara couldn't speak for her sobs.

Pop let go of the boys and hugged his wife again, whose grasp on her daughters would not loosen. "Every night, we waited." He looked at the four children, all together again, and asked, "What happened to Havah?"

"I asked her to come with us ... that morning when we were rounded up," his mother said. "I begged her. She said she wanted to be with her family."

Szulim felt as if he were walking through a dream, this time a good dream. Though the room remained quiet, it spun with excitement. Hugs, tears, arms and kisses coming at him from all directions. Pop pointed to a space on the floor and Szulim took off his shoes. He wriggled his toes for the first time in what seemed like forever. Szulim and Abraham lay down on the floor and wrapped their arms around each. Though this wasn't their house in Zelechow, and though an empty sack covered his tired body rather than a down comforter, Szulim went to sleep happy. Surrounded by his entire family, he was home.

Szulim opened his eyes and didn't know if it was day or night. He looked around, recalling the events that led him to this place. Endless walking, a haystack, hiding in bushes, a man in a nightshirt. And then his family and all the tears and hugs. He had little room to move; only his eyes could wander the unfamiliar space, long and narrow. So narrow that if his parents stood next to each other with their arms outstretched, they'd each touch a wall. And barely long enough for all of the people lying in a row on the floor. A dark, dank rectangle. Near the top of one of the bare and dingy walls, Szulim saw an opening, like a window with no glass. It reached up to the ceiling, leading outside. Perhaps it was a coal chute, though he didn't see any coal on the floor underneath it. Bushes growing against the wall of the house obscured the light that would have shone through, making it difficult to distinguish day from night. Difficult, but not impossible. Soon the snow would block the air and light completely.

Szulim knew that morning had come as he saw others stirring and sitting up. The movement of one disturbed everyone's sleep, so the group maintained the same daily schedule. He sat up, too, and wondered how long they'd stay in this small, cold, dark cellar. A couple of days? A few weeks? Where would they go after that? The more faces he recognized, the more questions popped into his head. How did his whole family — cousins, aunts and uncles — end up in the same tiny house so far from home? He wondered about his friends from cheder, his neighbors, the people who used to shop at his parents' store. Were there enough underground caves for everyone? Szulim knew not to ask. He knew there were no answers.

Low wooden benches lined the sides of the cellar. As everyone rose from what clearly weren't beds but a bunch of empty sacks filled loosely with straw, they picked up the makeshift mattresses and blankets and stacked them along the side of the narrow room. Pop and both Feter Moshes lifted a table made of milking stools and a board, and moved it from the end of the room into the center. They did the same with the benches. The furniture filled the space and made the room even more confining. There was nowhere to go but where they all were. Just a single, tiny cavern filled with too many people. Szulim sat on a bench, out of the way of the grown ups, along with his sisters, his cousin Berleh, and his two big cousins Herschel and Berl. His older cousins had an empty look in their eyes and didn't seem to share in the joy. Their sister, Sara with red hair, had not arrived. Nor had their mother. Szulim had last seen his cousin and Mimeh Laicha when they left the attic.

The adults gathered round the table and Szulim counted everyone who took refuge in the cellar. His Mimehs Gitel, Tertza, Sara and Foigel. Big Feter Moshe Boruchowicz, thin Feter Moshe Szyfman, and another uncle as well; his father's brother Symcha, who he had last seen when he traveled with Pop to Maciejowice. Three cousins – little Berl, big Berl, and Herschel. An older woman sat among them who Szulim did not recognize, and with her, a grown son and three daughters, two of whom were the ages of his aunts. A large man, who Szulim guessed was the older woman's husband, coughed so heavily his whole body shook. Two other men, also without long beards, stood smoking near the window. Twenty-four people in a storage space not meant for living in, big enough only for a handful of individuals. Who were these people so eager to hear his mother's story, asking questions and making comments?

The grown ups spoke in hurried whispers, low voices that didn't match the levels of excitement, relief and anxiety reflected on their faces; each recounting his or her journey. They had heard about the attic already from Szulim's aunts who had arrived in pairs late, very late, the night before Szulim arrived. The children, as was expected, sat quietly with nothing to do but listen.

"What happened, Perl? We all left the attic at the same time."

"Normally I could walk 11 kilometers in one night. But with the boys ... I had to carry Abraham."

"You knew where you were going, right?"

"Of course. I must have gotten turned around. I couldn't take the road, you know."

"Where's Laicha?" Feter Moshe looked at Szulim's mother, his eyes, like his sons, dimmed with worry about the wife and daughter who had yet to arrive. "You were in the attic together, you knew she didn't know the way here as well as you did."

"I asked her to come with me. They all did." Szulim's mother paused as if unsure how to speak of her sister-in-law's hesitancy at traveling together.

Pop squeezed Moshe's shoulder. "Keep hope. Maybe tonight."

ALL OF THE conversations Szulim had not been privy to in Zelechow, all of the chichiying in Polish, now flowed freely around him in Yiddish. There was no more hiding of information, no more fear that the children may overhear something and share it with the wrong person. In two days, Szulim understood more about their situation than he had in the two years he spent living it. Things a child would not be expected to comprehend, he learned from the adults as they talked openly. Like the fact that when the war broke out, the population of his shtetl was roughly 5,000. Two years later, before angry dogs roused them from sleep, 15,000 people crammed into the tiny ghetto, calling Zelechow their home. Now, the vast majority of those 15,000 waited to be gassed and burned in Treblinka.

"We were only in Wylga a day," Szulim's father said, recounting to Mama how he, along with Szulim's three uncles and his cousins Herschel and Berl, escaped and found their way to the cellar. "You know, normally we'd be there a few weeks. I got suspicious when the Germans changed plans and began marching us back home."

Szulim's father had heard rumors that Zelechow was liquidated the day after they departed for the labor camp. "We came to a fork in the road. Left, I knew, was Zelechow. We turned right. I figured the rumors were true." If they were marching to Sobolew, which had a train station, then they too would be put on cattle cars for Treblinka.

"Somehow Chaim communicated the plan," Feter Moshe Szyfman said. Szulim had trouble picturing Berleh's father being strong enough to lift heavy boulders, let alone walk all that way. But he just stared in awe at his uncles, his older cousins and his father.

"When it grew dark, when the forest was close to the road," Pop said, "I signaled, quietly of course, and we dropped to the ground. We waited until the Nazis passed then we rolled into the woods." This was not the first time he heard his family speak of miracles – the fact that the men were not seen and shot by German guards – and it would certainly not be the last.

"But Symcha!" Szulim's mother asked. "How did you get here?"

"God works in mysterious ways, I suppose," Symcha said. Men from Maciejowice had been sent to Wylga at the same time as Szulim's father. The two brothers, Chaim and Symcha, found each other. As it turned out, Maciejowice had been liquidated the same day as Zelechow. Symcha had no home or family to return to and so he joined Pop and the others on their journey to Sokol's farm.

"You poor boys. Too young to be sent to a work camp." Szulim's mother reached out to his cousins, but Herschel pushed her hand away. "I'm eleven." Szulim thought that if it had been Herschel's own mother stroking his cheek, Herschel would have eagerly accepted that tenderness.

"When we got here and I saw Rivka and Sara, I couldn't believe it!" Pop paused and closed his eyes, shaking his head slowly as if trying to dislodge a sharp rock stuck in his mind. "I didn't know anyone was alive."

Szulim learned that his sisters hadn't, in fact, been at a friend's house the night before his village was rounded up, but had set out for the farmhouse in Wilcziska where they all sat now underground. When Mr. Sokol's son Zsdiszek came to the store that market day, the day Pop had been picked for Wylga, Mama had arranged for him to meet the girls at the edge of the ghetto later that evening, after the sun set. Szulim, Abraham and his mother would have left the next evening. But by then, they had gone into hiding, holding their breath in the crowded, quiet attic.

"I thought you were in Treblinka, Perl," Pop whispered. "You and the boys. Those were the longest two weeks of my life. I tried not to lose hope. When your sisters arrived and told me you were in the attic with them … oy gut."

"Your husband is the eternal optimist, you know." Mimeh Foigel turned to Szulim's mother and told her how worried they had all been. "When you didn't arrive by morning, and then that whole day. We kept thinking 'what if?' But Chaim, he kept us calm."

"I just knew that if you had avoided Treblinka, you'd make it here. Maybe it was something with the weather that delayed you, who knew. But you'd arrive."

Szulim stopped listening to his parents and aunts, and focused on the strangers among them. They were Jewish, he knew that. He understood now the difference between Jews and goyim. Gentiles could walk during the day, wherever they wanted. Jews must hide. If these people slept on floors and spoke in whispers, surely they were Jews, too. But he had never seen Jews puff on small sticks and breathe smoke. Like dragons, he thought, those fire-breathing creatures he had learned about from one of little Berl's books. Always with the smoke, these people. Smoke and Polish coming out of their mouths, not Yiddish and prayers, like his parents. Szulim wondered if they'd stay with him forever. Mr. and Mrs. Popowska, their son Leibl and daughters Hinda, Devorah and Malka. Hinda's fiancée, Hershel Winograd and Hershel's father Noah. Were all of these people part of Szulim's family now?

TWENTY-FOUR PEOPLE crammed into one tiny, dirty, airless room. There were to be no private conversations. Any discussions were to be had by the entire group, and quietly. Szulim learned of the horrors that his parents had begun hearing from farmers over the summer, when they brought information along with their crops to the marketplace on Tuesdays. Newspapers had been limited and radios were forbidden, but farmers who lived near Treblinka told stories of crowded trains rolling towards the town that was too small to hold all the new arrivals. They spoke of trains leaving from the station empty, and then a smoke thickening the sky. They told of a sour smell and their horrible suspicions. But Szulim's parents could not believe it.

"Who, what human being, could devise of such a thing?" Pop said as he described the exchanges he shared with the farmers. "But when my cousin Yitzhak Bialebroda snuck to our house late one night, I knew. Stories from goyim are one thing, but my own flesh and blood? A Jew reporting first hand what he saw? That's when I knew we had to start planning."

In whispers, Pop told the Popowska's about the family store, how it went back many generations on Szulim's mother's side. "I went through my head, 'Which goy do I know? Who do I trust?' I know many goys, but trusting is a whole other story."

Edward Turek, Sokol's brother-in-law, came to the store every week and bought mostly sugar. "I suspected he might be producing liquor illegally," Pop said, looking around the small dark room. "And if he were making all this liquor, he'd need a place to hide it."

Szulim's father took his chances and asked Turek if he could hide a family. At first, Mr. Turek said no. He was sorry, but he was a widower and had a son who was very pro-Nazi and would tell authorities. Szulim sat rapt, remembering back to a Tuesday when his father came home from the store looking very down. Pop and Mama had started right in on their chichying, not even waiting until the kids were asleep, Mama asking, "Who else? This one? Oy, I don't know! Who else?"

A week later, Szulim learned, Mr. Turek came back to the store and said, "I'm sorry I disappointed you. I can't take you in, but my sister and brother-in-law have space and agreed to hide you."

Mr. Popowska interrupted. "I wonder if this is before or after Sokol agreed to hide our family, too."

"It's lucrative, no?" Hershel Winograd spoke up. "I mean, we all had to hand over everything we had as payment – money, jewelry."

"Every week Mr. Sokol came to the store," Mama said. "I gave whatever non-perishables I could. Flour, wheat, clothes. My jewelry went to Turek. I figure he'll sell it on the black market if it comes to that."

"No, Mr. Turek is a good man. I don't think he knew that Sokol had made other arrangements," Pop said. "Anyway, let's not forget the incredible risk the Sokol's are taking in hiding us. They could be killed, you know."

Szulim sat with his siblings and cousins feeling very grown up, hearing it all. Finally, his parents were talking about important matters in Yiddish again. There was nothing left to hide anymore. Except for themselves.

———

THE ROOM GREW silent as they heard above them the squeaking of metal against wooden boards, followed by the trap door creaking open. Szulim's father walked towards the sound coming from beyond the only door in the cellar. He opened the thin wooden board on hinges and ducked into the crawl space only tall enough for a young child to stand upright, a small anteroom with a short ladder reaching up to a trap door. This door was hidden in the opened wall behind

Sokol's bedroom closet. Pop stood at the base of the ladder and reached above his head to get hold of the buckets that Mr. Sokol handed down.

"Szulim, Abraham," Rivka said, "Here are cups for you. See over there?" She pointed to a pair of cups sitting on a bench apart from the rest of the chipped dinnerware and explained that those had been declared kosher for Pop and big Feter Moshe. Szulim looked at his small metal cup with thin cracks drawing paths in the white paint. He was so happy to finally have something to eat and drink.

"Sip slowly," Rivka said. "This is all we get."

As the provisions worked their way through his small body, Szulim felt a sensation he hadn't in several days. He stood next to his father and tugged at his sleeve. "Pop, I need to go." His father pointed towards the door where the food had come from moments earlier. Szulim opened it slowly and before he even climbed the two steps up into this small chamber where a ladder led up to the main house, he smelled the two buckets shared by 24 people. He must have been too tired to notice it when he entered the cellar the night before. It was worse than the toilets in the marketplace.

Buildings in Zelechow were one story, with the exception of a large building in the center of town. Stores occupied the first floor, and above those stores lived families in apartments. Alleyways led shoppers to a large indoor patio behind these stores and apartments – a square inside a square, Szulim called it – where a small rectangular structure with three stalls sat in the center. Inside the stalls were holes dug into the ground and space enough on each side to stand.

The smell inside those stalls was awful, even though the pits were cleaned regularly and buckets of water stood outside each door in case of accidents. Three wooden doors with hook locks gave visitors privacy among the crowds, and inhibitions were lost squatting in the cramped spaces. The toilets provided more than convenience for those who happened to be visiting the square, market day or not. They were a source for the latest gossip. And for many, even the odor could not deter them from lingering in the patio. He and Herschel used to wander around town and avail themselves of the marketplace stalls. He'd listen to his older cousin whistling, wishing he too knew how to make music with his lips.

"Herschel, I don't have paper. You got any?" Szulim had called once over the thin wall to his cousin.

"It'll cost you a slingshot."

Szulim was desperate. Normally Havah made sure he carried old pieces of newspaper in his pocket, just in case. But he had run out of the house too fast.

"Fine. Just give it to me."

A hand reached under the wall that separated the two boys. "Szulim, I'm in the middle of the world!"

"How do you know?"

"Well," Herschel explained, "it's simple. Everybody knows Poland is the center of the world. Zelechow is in the center of Poland, and the marketplace is in the center of Zelechow. These toilets are in the center of the marketplace, there are three stalls, and I'm in the middle one."

Herschel had always seemed to know everything. But now, the one thing Herschel wanted to know more than anything else, no one had the answer to. Nor would they for several weeks. So every night, they continued to wait for Mimeh Laicha and cousin Sara. And an end to this terrible war that forced them underground.

———

THOUGH THEY'D NEVER be able to tell how many stars shone in the sky, from the waning light that came through the solitary window they could tell night was soon approaching. Pop and Feter Moshe began to daven softly in the corner as they mumbled the *Shema* and *V'Ahavta*, the most important of all the Jewish prayers. *V'ahavta eit Adonai elohecha.* And you shall love the Lord your God, with all your heart, with all your soul, with all your might.

Earlier that morning, as commanded by the Torah, they had spoken the same words, sharing Feter Moshe's prayer shawl, taking turns wrapping themselves in his *tfillen*, the black leather straps that dangled from two little boxes which they pressed against their upper arm and forehead. Inside the boxes were scrolls inscribed with these sacred words. *V'hayu hadivarim ha'eileh.* You shall teach these words diligently to your children, and you shall speak of them when you are sitting at home. When you lie down and when you rise up. You shall bind them as a sign upon your hand, and they should be for frontlets between your eyes.

Szulim looked around the barren room with no way out, except for past the buckets of pee, and knew there was no way to inscribe these words of the *Shema*, as God had commanded, on the doorposts of the house or on the gates. Would God be mad?

As the men rocked back and forth in prayer, Mr. Popowska continued to cough while his son Liebl and Hinda's fiancée Herschel sat on a bench exchanging stories. Shabbat marked almost a week since Szulim had been hidden in the cellar. But they couldn't welcome the Sabbath bride in the proper way. Stars provided the only light in the tiny village of less than a dozen farmhouses. Candles flickering from a basement window would have posed a great risk to those hiding, as well as to the Sokol's who had to carry on as if nothing was out of the ordinary. As if two dozen Jews weren't taking refuge underneath the floor of their tiny farmhouse. They could have blocked the small opening in order to light two Shabbos candles, but then they'd have no air. Everyone agreed that breathing took priority. Besides, the silver candlesticks had been left behind in Zelechow.

It was the rare occasion that Sokol brought bread with their dinner, so making motzi over a challah was completely out of the question. Not that there was any way to wash their hands. And certainly no one had kosher wine. Szulim thought about the oirechs his Pop used to bring home. He realized that he and his entire family, the Popowska's too, they were oirechs now. Sokol's oirechs who didn't get a seat at the table.

Szulim looked around at his family wearing the same drab, dirty clothes. This was not like the Shabbats he remembered. He thought about the shtiebl in the living room of his neighbor's house. Would they notice that Pop was missing? Then he remembered the dogs barking, the gunshots and the quiet. How he felt like the last person left on Earth that night he walked out of Zelechow. Everyone was missing; there was no one left to pray.

Szulim looked at his father and Feter Moshe Boruchowicz and felt guilty for being bored. He still had Abraham and Berleh to play with, Herschel and Berl, too, though they kept to themselves. Pop didn't have the group of men to study with on the Sabbath, discussing the parshah, chanting the ancient melodies. He would have no *seudah shlishit*, or third meal of herring, wine, chickpeas and challah at shtiebl before coming home for *Havdalah*, the service that marked the end of Shabbat. Szulim closed his eyes and pictured himself holding the braided blue and white candle with four separate wicks, stretching his arms high above his head to ensure that he'd get a tall bride someday. Custom had it that the youngest child held the Havdalah candle, and Abraham had just become old enough to be trusted with the flame. His father would present the back of his hand to the candle, the reflection of the large flame flickering across his fingernails. Szulim could practically smell the cloves and myrtle leaves in the little silver spice box as it passed from Pop to Mama, and then to all the kids during the brief service. Pop would sing *Eliyahu Hanavi*, and just as Shabbat began with the lighting of two candles, it ended with the snuffing out of the braided candle into some spilled wine on a plate.

There was no more Havdalah, just as there was no more waiting until after dark to sit down to *Malava Malkah*, a dairy meal. There was no dairy. Instead they sipped at their only meal of the day – broth made of cabbage, potato or beets – before the sun set completely and the room became pitch black.

———

"WHEN CAN WE go back to our house?" Szulim asked to no one in particular. Abraham looked around, also wondering. None of the grown ups heard him. Or if they did, no one had an answer. Rivka simply sighed and shrugged her shoulders. He had nothing to do but sit and listen to the adults.

"Hey Chaim, what do you think happened to Szarfartz and the rest of the police? All the Judenrat?" Thin Feter Moshe Szyfman always turned to Szulim's father for opinions, as if Chaim had any greater knowledge than anyone else stuck underground.

"I have no idea. But my guess is nothing good," his father said. "You know, there's something I never told you."

Szulim's father recounted the day that Mr. Engel, the head of the Judenrat, had come to their house right after the war started. Szulim remembered him, the tall man with the big smile. "He asked me to be Chief of Police," Chaim said. "The Jewish police."

"And?" Everyone, even the Popowska's, turned to Szulim's father, with eyebrows raised and jaws dropped open.

"I said no."

"You what?" said Mimeh Gitel. "You could have had special privileges. Your whole family."

"Exactly." Szulim's father scratched at his beard and looked toward the window, thinking about Mylech Szarfartz. "If I ever get the chance, I'd kill that *treger* with my own bare hands."

Szulim, Abraham and Berl stopped playing footsie games and listened. By now, they knew when they were about to learn something important. Szulim's father wasn't the only one with disparaging things to say about Mylech Szarfartz. All the men in the cellar spoke of the crude man who was once a treger, a lower class member of the community with no status or respect, who'd unload whatever truck happened to roll into their shtetl. For a small fee, he'd hoist the crates on and off. The war changed his status. He became the Chief of Police when Szulim's father turned down the position, taking on a job that gave him power over everyone.

"For the very reasons I said no, he said yes," Szulim's father said. "You must know enough about human nature. I don't need to tell you what power does to a person."

Szulim didn't know what that meant, but Moshe Szyfman explained with his recollection of Szarfartz, talking about how Mylech used to beat up Jews for the most minor infraction, just to show the Nazis he was tough. "A Jew himself!" Feter Moshe held up a finger and jabbed at the air.

"Yes, well, I saw that potential for corruption and bribery when Engel offered me the job," Pop said.

"You'd be the natural choice," Mimeh Tertza said. "An upstanding businessman, well-respected." Big Feter Moshe just listened quietly. He didn't have much to say anymore, as if without his wife and daughter, he no longer had a voice.

"I suppose. They came a couple of times. The second time I didn't flat out refuse," said Pop. "I asked if I could select my department. I figured if I could pick those I trusted the most, I'd keep it honest."

Szulim learned, at the age of six, that no one can ever peer into a man's soul. The police, the Judenrat, they may have started out with good intentions. But things got bad, food was scarce, people wanted to take care of their families. Someone needs something, a favor, and what happens next?

"A bribe is an evil thing," his father said quietly. "It sneaks up on you. Once you take it … ach. I bet most of those police and Judenrat felt bad when they first took a bribe. Not Szarfartz. He lived for it. May he rot in hell."

"Why didn't you tell us, Pop?" Szulim asked. He still couldn't believe his father was asked to be the Chief of Police.

"What if you told a friend, Szulimel? I couldn't take that risk. If the Germans found out I had turned down a position of power, I would have been a watched man." He turned to Feter Symcha. "Remember what our father said on his deathbed? 'Shomer, so you won't be seen.' I had to remain invisible."

Szulim looked around at the unkempt faces of his family and the Popowska's, people whose dirty clothes were beginning to hang loosely on thinning bodies. They were surely invisible now.

———

Szulim THOUGHT ABOUT Ruben, Aaron and Mendl from cheder. All of his friends from the neighborhood. Were they hiding somewhere, too, or did they go to Treblinka? And if they were in Treblinka, were they able to run around outside playing *Comme Comme Tir*? Szulim wanted to play with them. He wanted to be 'it' and find that secret door, any door, that led out. Out of this prison and back to the Zelechow he knew before dogs and guns woke them too early from bed. Before frozen bodies poked up from the ground like trees.

Szulim and Abraham started a game of chase and enticed little Berl to join them. They played finger chase since their legs had no room to run around. But Berleh got a splinter from the wooden bench.

"You boys are too rough," said Mimeh Gitel, folding Berleh into her skirt. Szulim and Abraham sunk their heads into their shoulders and sat down on the bench in the center of the room. Szulim wished he had the space or the energy to play as rough as Mimeh Gitel and Feter Moshe always said he did. Abraham poked him in the side and giggled.

"Quit it!"

Abraham stopped, but sat next to Szulim, pressing against him. He smiled as he fixed his gaze on his older brother.

"He's looking at me!" Szulim stood up and walked to his mother, leaning against her while she talked with her sisters. "What do we do? I'm so bored."

"Go play with your sisters."

Rivka and Sara sat alone with their heads together, whispering. "Remember the half-moon sink with the blue tiles in the kitchen?"

"Remember the fancy rug in the living room? Navy blue, with little gold flowers and fringes on the end?"

Szulim didn't remember the rug Sara spoke of, but he sat with his sisters and lost himself in reverie. In his mind, he wandered through his house in Zelechow, noticing as if for the first time all the things he had passed by without a second glance. The wooden cabinet in the dining room that held both the dairy and the meat dishes; the dining room table and chairs made of the same golden colored mahogany; the intricate carvings on the cabinet doors and table legs, a darker shade of brown. The wardrobes in the bedrooms made of inlaid wood. In the kitchen stood two stoves: one that burned wood and cooked their meals, the other that heated the house. Szulim recalled Pop filling the heating stove with wood or coal, how the stove itself stuck out from the wall but the chimney lay hidden behind white tiles. When Szulim stood close to the tiled wall, but not too close so he wouldn't get burned, he could feel the warmth radiating through.

There was nothing in the cellar to keep them warm now other than each other, 24 bodies pressing close in a space no bigger than the front room of his house. Remembering his house in Zelechow lifted Szulim's spirits and occupied him for a bit of time. Until it became too depressing.

———

EVERYONE IN THE cellar got quiet as they heard the closet in Sokol's bedroom sliding across the floor; it seemed too early for dinner. As the trap door creaked open, Herschel turned to his brother Berl and whispered "Mother?" But it was only Mr. Sokol. Szulim's father walked quickly to the ladder expecting a bucket of food. The farmer had only a request.

"Anyone here able to help my daughters with their school work?"

Daughters? Szulim had no idea there were children living above him. He wondered how old they were, how many girls. Mimeh Sara walked towards the entrance since she had been a schoolteacher back before Jews weren't allowed to teach anymore, before Jewish children were banned from learning. She looked down toward her sisters before following Sokol up the ladder.

When she returned an hour later, she sent Rivka and Sara upstairs; Sokol's daughters, who they all learned were named Mietka and Pela, were about the same age as Szulim's sisters. Their older brother Zsdiszek, who had met Sara and Rivka at the edge of the ghetto weeks before, was nowhere to be found. Right after Szulim arrived at the cellar, Sokol's son got word that he was to be drafted, so he ran away. Years later, Szulim would meet him and learn how he ended up joining the Polish army, was captured by Germans and then liberated by Americans in Germany.

And so it began that every so often, when the sun set early in the afternoon, one or two of the hidden Jews would get to go upstairs for a short time since farmers didn't visit each other after dark. In the summer, Sokol's daughters worked in the fields until evening. And they didn't get homework during harvest time. But in the winter, the Sokol family sat in the small room past the kitchen with gas lamps and candles until it was time for bed. Once in a while, an adult could emerge from the cellar for a brief chat with Mr. and Mrs. Sokol, but mostly it was the kids who got to go upstairs and play.

Szulim cherished the times he and Abraham played with the girls. Once a month he could stretch his legs and arms without bumping into someone. He stared at the lamps giving off a light he never thought he'd come to miss. He breathed in fresh air. He stood by the stove and thawed out from the constant chill of life underground. Sometimes Szulim helped them with their schoolwork. But what he loved best was playing make believe.

The two boys, and everyone who emerged from the cellar, were given Polish names just in case the girls were overheard talking to someone about a new playmate. Szulim was careful to call his brother 'Adam' and reminded Abraham to call him 'Mietek,' just like their Shabbos Goy. The four children played marriage, Szulim taking Mietka as his betrothed, his brother belonging to Pela.

"Okay, it's time!" Mrs. Sokol meant business and Szulim knew better than to argue or ask to play longer. He could see in her hunched shoulders and weathered face that she was terrified. What if a neighbor living among the cluster of farmhouses that made up their small village showed up unannounced? He gave a small wave to Mietka, the older daughter, and hurried back through the trap door down into the cellar.

Years later, when Szulim returned as a man named Sal, Sokol's daughters would still call him Mietek.

———

"AFTER GOD MADE the world, he filled it with people. He sent off an angel with two sacks, one full of wisdom and one full of foolishness. The second sack was of course much heavier. So after a time it started to drag. Soon it got caught on a mountaintop and all the foolishness spilled out and fell into Chelm."

And so began the stories Szulim's father told to kill the boredom, to provide escape, to bind them all to a tradition that believed if you could laugh at yourself, no one could truly hurt you.

"The townspeople in Chelm decided to build a new synagogue, so they sent strong, able-bodied men to a mountaintop to gather heavy stones for the foundation. The men hoisted the stones onto their shoulders and trudged down the mountain to the town below. When they arrived, the mayor yelled, 'Foolish men! You should have rolled the stones down the mountain!' The men agreed this was an excellent idea. So they turned around, and with the stones still on their shoulders, trudged back up the mountain, and rolled the stones back down again."

Everyone laughed, but Szulim wondered if the Nazis let his father roll stones down the mountain when he went to work in Wylga. Probably not. Szulim remembered how the Gestapo forced people in his shtetl to stand up to their necks in cold water for hours, or clean toilets with their hands. The image of the mother and baby flashed through his head. No, he thought, surely they made Pop carry heavy boulders on his back up and down mountains over and over again.

In this town of Chelm lived Herscheleh Ostropoler. When Szulim and Abraham had grown too old for lullabies like *Oyfen Pripichik* or *Inter Shulem's Viegele*, Mama told them stories about this Herscheleh. Szulim had never seen a Yiddish storybook, and Mama couldn't read Polish, but she had all of Herscheleh's silly adventures in her head. Szulim used to close his eyes and listen. He could hear bubbles in her voice, and when she chuckled, Szulim giggled, too. But Szulim hadn't heard his mother's happy voice for a long time now.

His father continued the stories as everyone sat listening, even Liebl Popowska and Hinda's ugly fiancée, Herschel Winograd. "Herscheleh Ostropoler was hungry," Pop said, "so he went to shul on Friday night. He sat next to a heavy man in fine clothes, hoping the rich man would invite him home for dinner."

Szulim thought about the oirechs Pop used to bring home from shtiebl. He couldn't remember if any of them were named Mr. Ostropoler. The Herscheleh in Pop's story sat at the rich man's table, his mouth watering as the flames from the candles flickered across the piles of food and shone in all the silver goblets. The lady of the house ladled soup into his bowl. "Chicken soup with noodles for you." Herscheleh thanked her and began to undress.

The rich man stared. "Why are you taking off your pants at the dinner table?"

Herscheleh replied, "So I can go swimming to catch a noodle."

Szulim's older cousins laughed and laughed. It was as if all the good that had been bottled up in them for so long finally got a chance to come out. Maybe Mimeh Laicha would hear her sons' laughter, and it would sound like a shofar, calling her and Sara to the cellar. If they would only arrive at last, his cousins might smile more often. Maybe Herschel would play with him again like he used to in Zelechow.

Feter Symcha cut in. "Did you hear about the *wassr treger*? This water carrier couldn't make a living. What with fixing the barrel, the buggy, paying for the water and feeding the horse, there just wasn't enough to go around. So he decided to train the horse not to eat so much. This went on for quite a while, each day he gave the horse less food, and it looked like he was going to make it." Symcha paused and looked around the room. "Until one day, the horse died. This treger went around crying, 'And I had him trained to eat almost nothing!'"

The stories of Chelm always began with the two sacks. But Szulim knew there must have been a third. And that sack, filled with evil, got dumped on Zelechow.

———

IT WOULD BE a long while before any more laughter could be heard underneath the tiny farmhouse. One evening, Mr. Sokol brought news along with their meal of the day. As Szulim's father traded the bucket of waste for the bucket of soup, Mr. Sokol bent down to speak into his ear.

"Oy gut!" Pop turned to the group and uttered a single word, "Moshe." Szulim's favorite uncle understood immediately and began beating his chest. Laicha and Sara had been found on the road, robbed and murdered.

Herschel's face froze and Berl shouted, "No! It can't be them!" Berl couldn't accept then, and never did, that his mother would have walked on the road during the day, making herself and her daughter an easy target for Polish bandits. Szulim's mother reached out to her nephews, boys who now had no mother of their own, but Herschel turned away, turning instead into his pain.

Szulim thought about the woods, how it used to be a happy place before the war. In the summers, his mother had hired a driver to bring herself and the children by horse and buggy to the cottages at the end of the long road leading out of Zelechow. He'd wave goodbye to his village, noticing how it grew bumpier towards the end of the half-hour ride as the horses brought them closer to the grove of trees. When he saw the row of straw-thatched roofs at the entrance of the forest, his heart quickened. He always wanted to be first to run inside the house and help his mother open the wooden shutters, allowing the light and the summer breezes to stream through the windows that were nothing more than holes in the wood and clay walls.

His mother would pull long, tapered candles out of a box and set them in sticks around the two-bedroom cottage. These would be their source of light come dark, along with kerosene and oil lamps. She'd unpack the two sets of dishes they brought from Zelechow — one for meat, one for dairy. While Mama hung strips from the ceiling to trap houseflies, Szulim would run outside to find the other children whose families could afford to rent a cottage for the week. They'd wander through the woods picking mushrooms and berries. When the sun drenched their bodies in golden warmth, they'd take off their shoes and socks and dip their feet in the same creek where they got water to cook or clean. Afterwards, they'd run barefoot in the soft grass and catch butterflies.

Szulim rubbed his head now as he recalled the time he lay on the *leszak*, the cot his mother left outside the cottage for the kids' afternoon naps. A boy from across the road had run up and Szulim fell over, smacking his head on a tree stump. It bled and bled, even with his mother holding a cloth to the wound. Two months later, when Szulim got his hair cut, the barber commented on the size of his scar.

Even with the memory of that mishap, Szulim had been upset the past two summers when they couldn't leave the ghetto to go on their vacation. Now, he wasn't sure he ever wanted to walk on a quiet, tree-lined road again.

FROM THE DAY that they heard the news, Szulim's two cousins turned inward. They didn't speak to anyone, except for the occasional denial that their mother and sister had been killed. Feter Moshe's large body that used to bounce with laughter now sagged. And he ran out of kisses for the children.

Though they hadn't heard from Pop's mother and sister, no one would assume that they had died. "They must have run into some difficulty," Pop would say. There was an understanding that in these circumstances, people did what they could to stay alive without making it riskier for someone else. And without telephones or telegraphs, how could one person in hiding communicate to another? Nobody sat *shiva* for those who simply went missing. Only after the war, when people came out of hiding and witnesses came forth, did Pop and Feter Symcha establish the *yarzheit*, or anniversary of their mother and sister's death, as the liquidation of Maciejowice on the 18th of Tishrei.

But there had been a witness for Laicha and Sara; bodies had been found. Szulim didn't understand why everyone pretended otherwise. So after weeks of stony silence, Pop gently touched his brother-in-law on the shoulder. "Moshe, it's time." Feter Moshe, Berl and Herschel tore at their clothes, which were already ragged from Wylga, the journey to the cellar, and almost two months of wear. All of the family members were gathered together already, sitting on low benches, unable to cook meals even if they wanted to. There was no mirror to cover, or a Torah to read from, or baths from which to refrain. But because it had been more than thirty days since Laicha and Sara had been killed, they could not formally sit shiva. There wasn't a *minyan* of 10 observant Jewish men (the Popowska's weren't religious and thus didn't count), so they couldn't even recite the Mourner's *Kaddish*.

Szulim looked around their meager accommodations — at this pit with no food, no space or air, nothing to offer by way of play or life — and thought how easy it was here to follow the Jewish customs of bereavement. He didn't like being in a place that was only good for mourning.

———

SZULIM FELT BAD about Mimeh Laicha and Sara, so he sat quietly as Feter Moshe Boruchowicz took on the role of the *melamed*, pulling Szulim aside to teach him the prayers and how to daven. Moshe had a small black notebook in which he marked all of the holidays. Szulim didn't know where he got the notebook and figured it must have been in his pocket the day he was picked up for Wylga. It was like the one in his parents' store that kept ledgers. Every day, Feter Moshe sat and scribed, creating his own siddur complete with the daily and Sabbath prayers. Somehow, Feter Moshe seemed to know when Szulim was about to play with his brother or little cousin; that's when the lesson would begin. Abraham was too young and squirmy, and Feter Moshe's own sons had already learned the prayers. Not that they were interested.

"I'm not the world's policeman," Szulim's father said when big Feter Moshe insisted that the Popowska's refrain from smoking on Shabbat. Though Pop was a chossid, which meant he followed a particular rabbi who he'd visit once a year before the high holidays, he was a businessman first. Feter Moshe Boruchowicz, on the other hand, was a chossid first. He did everything he could to follow his rabbi's teachings despite the change in circumstances, and he pushed those teachings on everyone around him. It never used to bother Szulim back when Feter Moshe had sweets in his pocket.

Szulim thought about all the men in the room. Big Feter Moshe's job was to pray, write in his book and ensure that they followed the rituals. When Szulim looked at Pop, his father seemed to be looking past him, through the walls, calculating the next step. That, the analyzing and figuring and worrying, was Pop's job. Feter Symcha took it upon himself to tease the children. Szulim hated how Symcha rubbed his beard against his chin. Feter Symcha smiled but Szulim ran to his mother's skirt. "He's just trying to make you laugh." Mama kissed

Szulim where it itched and, with a pat on the tuchas, sent him back to play. Feter Moshe Szyfman's job was to sit with Berleh and Mimeh Gitel, complaining about a cold that no one else seemed to have.

Then there was Mr. Popowska. Day and night he coughed into his hands, wiping maroon stains on the legs of his clothes. And when the Popowska's ran out of cigarettes, Hinda's fiancée Herschel, and her brother Liebl made it their job to steal out into the night. Szulim stared at Herschel. *What a schlub!* he thought. He could never understand why Hinda, so intelligent and so pretty, would be engaged to this heavy, balding man who spoke with such poor grammar. Herschel and Liebl would be gone for days, sometimes weeks, finally returning with packs of smokes and stories. Szulim sat rapt as they spoke of blowing up trains and raids, or described battles waged alongside partisan groups they joined. It didn't matter whether the freedom fighters were Russian or Polish, Herschel and Liebl stood victorious. Except for the time Liebl came back with his right arm in a sling.

"Every time you leave here, you take a chance that someone will follow you back," Szulim's father said. Szulim could see Pop's neck stiffen as he faced the two young men. Here they all were with barely enough food to eat and these men squandered their resources for cigarettes. Or worse, beat people up for them. "These 'freedom fighters' actually gave you their cigarettes? Ach!"

The night they came back with guns, Pop wasn't the only one to get angry. The yelling amongst all the adults filled the quiet cellar. Even the women stood their ground, screaming until Devorah Popowska yelled, "Enough! All this noise may attract the attention of a neighbor. If we are to survive, we have to get along."

It wouldn't be until Szulim was a man himself that he understood what Herschel and Liebl were really seeking in the dark. Still, it wasn't right. Mr. Winograd, Herschel's father, made no impression on him at all.

Feter Moshe clutched his homemade siddur and shook it in everyone's faces. "If Hitler destroys everything Jewish in this world, there will be one book left." Szulim didn't know then that this book he learned to daven from, this book that truly taught him how to read – a former accounts ledger now scrawled with sacred words – would someday come to rest in Yad Vashem, the museum in Israel established to remember what the world should never forget.

———

SZULIM SMELLED IT. Unfamiliar and cloying, like sweet gone bad, the odor was metallic and warm. His nose pinched. "What is it?" he asked. "Why do the women stink so bad?" The smell was so different from the men. His mother pulled her skirt from his grip. "You shouldn't ask about such things. *Poo poo poo*."

And so he knew. The women must all have a terrible disease. What Szulim didn't know, what he hadn't learned about at the age of six, is that bodies imprisoned and hidden from the sun can still prepare for new generations. Not that it would come to anything. A whole future would be left buried in that soil.

Spring — Summer 1943

Feter Moshe wasn't the only one interested in Szulim's education. His aunts and sisters taught him how to knit. "That's a girl's job!" Szulim said when he first eyed the wool and knitting needles Mr. Sokol had sent down with their food. Just because he was stuck underground and played with girls upstairs every now and then didn't mean he would do what his sisters did. But boredom came before pride, and within no time, Szulim produced sweaters and socks alongside the women in his family. He started out with just one color and a simple stitch, a basic knit and purl, but soon created sweaters with stripes and interesting combinations of colors.

"Wow, Szulim. You're better than us." Sara cupped her hand under the socks Szulim was working on. "Look, Rivka. He's making it with four needles."

Only after the war would Szulim get to wear his creations. While they hid in Sokol's pit, the *greeb*, they knitted an entire wardrobe for the farmer and his family. It didn't matter. Szulim was thrilled to have something to do.

As they knit, Mimeh Sara taught them Polish. If they were ever kicked out of the cellar, it would be important to speak Polish since Nazis used specific criteria, such as language, to determine the religious and ethnic background of people throughout Europe. For Szulim and his family, the way they dressed made their Judaism obvious. But for the non-religious who wore modern clothes, whose hair and eyes fit into the Aryan prototype, an accurate pronunciation of Polish might be the difference between walking the streets freely or perishing in a camp. Hinda Popowska could speak Polish beautifully. Years later, when Szulim recalled those months in the cellar, he thought it a shame that Hinda, with her blonde hair and fair complexion, never had the chance to pass as a gentile.

Szulim already knew the Polish word for Jew, *Zsyd*. And when the dean of the

Polish Technical Institute discovered them hiding in the attic, Szulim heard him repeat the word *ludzie*, meaning people. On the rare occasions he played with Mr. Sokol's daughters, he called Mietka his *panna mloda*, or bride. But soon, Polish became Szulim's second language. As he lived underground, working the strange but familiar sounds around his tongue, Szulim never anticipated that there would be four more languages he would someday speak with greater fluency.

———

THE SOUND OF the closet scraping along the floor above made Szulim's mouth start to water. As Mr. Sokol quickly and quietly pried open the floorboards, all of the Jews hiding in the cellar rushed to the door. Along with the broth and occasional piece of bread, the little bit of fresh air that came through the opening to the upstairs sustained them. Pop stood at the base of the ladder and handed the buckets of waste up to Mr. Sokol. The farmer, in turn, handed down a bucket of soup that had been heating on the stove.

Everyone froze when they heard Szulim's father cry out in pain. "*Veyismere!*" The bucket had slipped out of Mr. Sokol's grasp and hit Pop on the nose. He stumbled, but managed to do so without dropping their dinner.

"Chaim, let me see." Szulim's mother took her husband's face in her hands and peered closely. "Oy gut, it's black."

Pop rubbed his nose. Even wincing in pain, he laughed. "That's just soot from the bottom of the bucket. It'll go away."

"What's this?" Pop looked at the soup and noticed bubbles of oil floating on the surface. "When has Mrs. Sokol ever put meat in the soup?" With the ladle, he stirred around and scooped up a rat that must have fallen into the bucket while it cooked on the stove. Holding the rodent by its tail, Pop walked to the other side of the room, reached up to the small window and threw the rat outside onto the ground, wet now from the melted snow.

Pop and big Feter Moshe would not eat; the meat, if one could call it that, wasn't kosher. But the children and women got dispensation. God would not want them to starve. Szulim's stomach growled, so he pushed the floating rat out of his mind and pulled out his little cup, the same cup he used for every meal and drink. Once a day it held soup, once a day, water. He'd swish the water around the cup to give it a rinse, and then he'd drink.

Pop poured the tepid broth to the rim and Szulim took a sip. In the beginning, he used to gulp. But soon he learned that slurping it quickly only made the hunger worse, only teased his belly, which stretched in anticipation of a feast. Drinking slowly was much better. If he drank slowly enough and made his one meal of the day last long enough, he could fool his stomach into thinking it was full. Besides, there was no reason to rush. They weren't going anywhere.

This trick, like so many others that got him through the long days and nights, he taught himself. All of them — his aunts, his siblings and cousins, the men, the Popowska girls — they all, cramped together in the cellar, discovered silently and on their own similar methods of survival. And all of the grown ups, the Popowska's included, came to an unspoken understanding that the children needed more food than the adults. As Szulim sipped the flavorless soup with the occasional shred of beet or cabbage, he closed his eyes and pictured himself standing next to the stove in his house back in Zelechow.

"Szulim, bring me the potatoes." His mother wiped her hands on her apron. Szulim handed her the vegetables and wrapped himself in the folds of her skirt as she prepared the *cholent* for Shabbat. Chunks of meat, vegetables and beans went into the huge black cast iron pot. He couldn't yet see over the top into the white interior that had seasoned into a light brown over the years. He watched her fingers expertly fill the skin of a chicken or goose's neck with potatoes, flour, herbs and *grebenes*, those crispy bits of skin left over from rendering *schmaltz*, the chicken fat. Oh, how he loved the grebenes. She sewed up the pouch, the *magelech*, and tossed it in the pot. Everyone looked forward to biting into a piece of the magelech. If Szulim or Abraham got the end, Mom would reach across the table and take out the thread.

Every Friday afternoon, housewives throughout Zelechow improvised, filling their largest pots with various cuts of meat, whatever beans were on hand, some potatoes and water. The richer families, of course, had more meat. Szulim's mother put the lid on the pot, covered it with a piece of newspaper and secured it with a string. She hoisted the heavy pot off the table and placed it into Szulim's outstretched arms. He staggered a bit, but tried not to let his mother see. He was big enough now to carry the cholent across the street to Gedalia Yosef's bakery where it would cook overnight in an oven large enough to fit many pots like this one.

"Come right home, Szulim." His mother's hand would linger for a moment on his wrist.

Mr. Popowska's coughing broke Szulim's reverie and the weight of the cholent pot in his arms disappeared. Despite months of violent hacking, Szulim still couldn't ignore the awful sound. Malka, the youngest Popowska daughter, smacked her father's back to help clear his lungs. The heavy man quieted and Szulim closed his eyes, concentrating on the past and willing himself back to his great uncle's bakery.

Great Aunt Yehudith bustled from the enormous oven to the sideboard, using a large wooden paddle to slide the braided loaves onto the countertop. She looked up from wrapping the bread. "Szulimeleh, you carried that heavy pot?" She helped him lift the cholent onto the countertop. Szulim was proud to be old enough to do what only Sara and Rivka had done. He closed his eyes and inhaled deeply. Szulim thought he was the luckiest boy in Zelechow for living right across the street from the bakery. From his doorstep, he could smell the challahs rising in the oven. When he stepped into Gedalia Yosef's store, draping his arms on the counter and resting his head in the crook of his elbow, that sweet, doughy smell wrapped around his entire body. The scent was as soft as the challah itself, and as long as he could swim in that aromatic sea of yeast and honey and flour and eggs, he knew nothing could hurt him.

Gedalia Yosef, with his yarmulke and hat both, accepted the *groshes* that were thrust in his hand, offering challah in exchange with a nod. "Good Shabbos," he called to the villagers as they walked out of his bakery. Gedalia Yosef knew exactly how many challahs to bake, just enough for the neighboring townsfolk without any left over. With all of the day's challahs prepared and sold, Gedalia Yosef stoked the fire, raising the temperature inside the wood-burning oven so that it would remain hot overnight, even after the fire burned out.

Neighbors walked into the bakery carrying their own heavy pots as the afternoon sun continued on its arc across the sky. When the sun fell below the horizon, Gedalia Yosef would no longer accept payment or even handle the coins. Long after darkness settled over the town and Shabbat prevented anyone from using a stove or stoking a fire, his oven would hold thirty or forty pots of cholent, the lingering heat slowly cooking the stews throughout the night. The name of this stew was derived from the *Mishnah*, the rabbinic text passed down through centuries that prescribed how Jews were to carry out their religious obligations in every day life. To cook food for the Sabbath without lighting a fire, Jews were commanded to "bury the hot."

By midday on the Sabbath, when the men returned from reading the week's parshah at their shtiebls, the cholent would be cooked and still warm. Families throughout Zelechow made kiddish by raising cups of sweet wine and reciting the blessing. On Friday nights, they drank the kosher wine bought from the villager, but on Saturdays, Pop poured his own homemade liquor. The men and boys washed their hands, always clean hands that reached across the table to rest on the challah. Together, they chanted the motzi, signifying the start of the meal.

Szulim and his family would begin Shabbat lunch with gefilte fish leftover from the night before, chopped liver or Mama's egg salad made with onions, schmaltz and grebenes. While everyone ate, one person would go across the street to get the cholent from Gedalia Yosef's enormous oven. Neighbors greeted each other at the bakery as they looked for familiar marks on the cast iron or the pieces of burned newspaper. Though many of the pots were identical, no one ever brought home the wrong cholent.

The eruv winding its way around Zelechow allowed the villagers to carry the heavy pots on the Sabbath. Szulim remembered going out in the winter months to retrieve the cholent, how his hands kept warm holding the cast iron vessel, the half-burned paper disintegrating in the cold wind. Sitting now in the cellar where air never stirred, Szulim recalled how the paper his mother had wrapped around the cholent pot would turn to ash and blow into his eyes. Just thinking about it brought forth fresh tears. Blinking them away, Szulim marveled at the ability of something he could see and touch suddenly dancing upwards into the air and disappearing.

As he'd approach his house with the heavy pot, Sara or Rivka would open the door and Mama would take the pot out of his arms and place it gently on the stove. Carefully, very carefully, she'd unwrap the paper that remained; ripping was not allowed on Shabbat. She'd slowly lift the lid so no bits of paper or ash would fall into the stew. It was a matter of luck whether there was enough water or enough heat, whether the cholent would turn out just right. And that would determine whether or not they had been righteous Jews that week.

"Oh!" Mama would pronounce. "The cholent is good!"

Sometimes it was overcooked, sometimes not cooked enough. But always, the cholent was delicious. Szulim could not recall a Shabbat when the cholent was pronounced anything but good. This, the flavorless liquid he ate day in and day out with a few potatoes or an occasional root, and now a rat, this was not good. Definitely not good. But it kept them alive. Szulim sat in the cellar and thought about the cholent pot left behind in his house. Empty, like Gedalia Yosef's oven.

———

"What are they doing?" Szulim tugged at Mimeh Tertza's sleeve. All morning, his older cousins worked with the other young men, taking turns scraping at the wall across from the small area where the waste bucket sat, where the ladder stood that led out of the cellar.

"I think they're trying to create more space." Mimeh Tertza kissed the top of Szulim's head and went back to her sewing. No doubt the conditions in the cellar were awful; too many people for the small room. If they could expand the area in which 24 people lived, everyone would be happier. Just to be able to stretch out while they slept, rather than lie with their hands glued to their sides, pressing against the person next to them.

The men spent all day digging at the hard, compacted earth, creating a tunnel over a meter in diameter, the excavated dirt forming a large pile in the corner of the cellar. At night, when Mr. Sokol handed down the meal buckets, he gave them empty buckets for the soil, which appeared much bigger than the space it had come from. Szulim's father and uncles filled the buckets, over and over, and handed them back up to Mr. Sokol, who every time he opened the front door, looked around his property before stepping outside into the moonlight. He didn't want to arouse suspicion by disposing buckets of dirt that came from inside his house. By the next evening, after another day of hard labor for the men underground, Mr. Sokol realized there was no place on his property he could hide all that earth. This wasn't a small hole they were trying to create but another living space. Both Mr. Sokol and the men in the cellar realized something else, perhaps even more important. There was no way to insulate between the top of the new dug out space and the room above them. If anyone were to walk on the floor over this hole, the sound would be different than the rest of the house, hollow, which would give them all away.

The men put down their spoons, resigning themselves to their cramped quarters. But at least the kids had a new place to play.

———

ON THE 17TH of Nisan, the coughing ceased. Mrs. Popowska moaned and her daughters wept softly. Szulim thought they should be happy now that Mr. Popowska's sickness seemed to have gone away. Herschel Winograd and Liebl laid him on the floor near the wall. Szulim stared at the man sleeping in daytime who, with arms and legs stiff at his sides, looked like a rickety piece of furniture. Mr. Popowska, who had seemed so large when Szulim first arrived at the Sokol's, now rested on the ground like sticks inside a sack. In that way, he was no different from anyone else in the cellar.

"What timing." It wasn't until Feter Symcha and Pop whispered to each other that they could not bury the body for another three days, until after the Easter celebrations, that Szulim understood. Mr. Popowska was dead.

Just last night, when Mr. Sokol brought them their soup, he handed down a few loaves of bread and said to make it last. The Sokol's family and neighbors would be visiting the farmhouse on and off for several days, as was custom during the Holy Week leading up to Easter when schools closed and no one worked in the fields.

"On Pesach, he brings us extra bread," Feter Moshe had said. "Go figure." Szulim had looked at the bread and looked at his father. He knew he wasn't allowed to eat bread on Pesach, but it seemed like weeks since he last had a piece. Pop cut some for everyone in the cellar except for himself and big Feter Moshe.

The two of them would not eat anything leavened, but Szulim and his siblings were allowed. No one knew it would be Mr. Popowska's last meal.

Szulim looked back at the man who coughed no more. Though he had seen many dead bodies in Zelechow, they were never inside his house. And he never went close to them lying on the street or in parks. Now he'd have to sleep in the same room with the corpse. He hoped Mama would let him and Abraham sleep at the end of the long row of people and not in between his parents like he normally did. He wanted to be as far away from Mr. Popowska as possible.

For the next three days they sat quietly, both out of respect to the grieving family and out of fear of the footsteps parading gently on the floor above them. When the trap door opened once again, Szulim didn't know which made him happier - finally getting food and water, or getting rid of the dead body.

———

"Everyone, shhh!" Szulim's father stood with his fingers extended, as if they were guns ready to shoot. Bodies froze and hearts pounded as they listened to the closet above them moving along the floor. The only sound came from the creaking wood as the trap door was pried open. Szulim didn't need anyone to tell him that it was too early for dinner. Though they had been cut off from the seasons for eight months, they knew it was early summer, which meant Mr. Sokol and his family were working in the fields, taking advantage of long hours of daylight. Szulim heard boots coming down the ladder and looked at his father to see what they should do.

Mr. Sokol's voice could be heard from the opening above them. "These people will take care of you." First the boots, then legs, then a whole body stepped slowly down into the cellar. A Russian soldier stood in front of them all, his eyes adjusting to the dim light as he took in the surroundings. He leaned heavily on one leg and hopped towards a bench. Szulim stared at his filthy uniform, his short dark hair in stark contrast to the bushy beard unkempt from days on the battlefield.

The grown-ups whispered amongst themselves. "Even with Chiel gone, we have room? Oy gut. Another mouth to feed."

He was not family, he was not a Jew, but Szulim's aunts tended to the soldier and nursed him back to health. And Sokol treated him like royalty, assuming that he would be the golden ticket when the Russian troops came to liberate Poland. A farmer who helped a wounded soldier would surely be given privileges. So Sokol gave the man pieces of wood and cardboard, sharp metal and a grinding stone. And this soldier, who they came to know as Tomaitey Tapielkin Voroshilow, changed everything for Szulim.

WHEN TOMAITEY SHAVED off his unruly beard, Szulim saw the face of a much younger man. He sat on the floor and watched as the Russian whittled away at a piece of wood.

"*Tuy hoschesh delyat?*" Szulim had no idea what the man said, but nodded as the soldier placed the knife and wood into his small hands. "*Smotry. Eta tak.*" The Russian wrapped his hands around Szulim's and showed him how to run the sharp edge of the blade against the wood at an angle, working in short, quick strokes. He even helped Szulim fix the hole in his cup. For months, Szulim and his aunts had tried using bits of paper or bread to stop his soup from leaking out of a widening crack. Each fix lasted only a day. The Russian helped Szulim carve a tiny piece of wood that fit perfectly into the gap. Over the next several weeks, Szulim cut every single one of his fingers and turned to the soldier to bandage them. Abraham was too young to whittle, but he sat and watched. Tomaitey taught Russian songs. He made a deck of cards and Mimeh Foigel taught them to play *Bilotka*. Even Sara and Rivka sat at this stranger's side, absorbing everything.

Gradually, Szulim's parents came to appreciate what this soldier did for their children—providing the entertainment that they themselves were too preoccupied to provide, giving Szulim a purpose to an otherwise tedious existence. The Popowska's never got over their resentment of this seeming replacement of their father and husband, but of course nothing short of freedom could diminish the pain of Mr. Popowska's death. And in a year's time, when the Russian's songs and language proved to be more than amusement, Szulim's parents would look up towards the sky and thank God for the miracle of this non-Jewish stranger.

Almost from the moment the soldier came into the cellar, Szulim felt he had a job. So when half of the group left to hide somewhere else soon after the Russian arrived, Szulim barely noticed their absence. He didn't need to play with Berleh when Tomaitey pulled out the cards or the whittling. And it's not like his older cousins talked to him, anyway.

But one day, when Szulim looked up from the chess set and noticed that the cellar didn't seem as crowded, he asked, "Where is everybody?" His father explained that they had run out of money to give Mr. Sokol, plus with the rations, the farmer had a hard time getting enough food for all of them. Neighbors were watching and he couldn't load up his wagon with more food than he would need for his family. So Mr. Turek convinced his brother Wladislaw to hide some of their group in his house. Mimeh Gitel, thin Feter Moshe and Berleh; big Feter Moshe, Hershel and Berl; all of his aunts. They lived in a different house now, in Wladislaw Turek's cellar, only a couple of kilometers away.

Once in a while, after dark, Mr. Sokol would open the door and one of Szulim's aunts would step down into the pit. Szulim loved the extra hugs. "I told him I needed to leave as soon as it got dark so I could make it to you before sunrise. He thinks you all are hiding somewhere far from here," Mimeh Sara said. "Stupid Polack believes me."

"Good," said Szulim's father. "The less he knows, the better. Wladislaw's not the same man as his brother. Edward Turek is a saint. His brother, I don't fully trust." After a few days together, when it was time for Mimeh Sara to go back, she left in the middle of the night, arriving to Wladislaw's right before sun up so he would think she had been travelling for hours.

TOMAITEY LINED UP the collection of figurines he and Szulim had spent the past couple of months creating out of small pieces of wood. He found a piece of cardboard and drew rows of boxes, coloring in every other one. "You ready to learn a little chess?" Szulim had never heard of chess, but he picked up the pieces he and the soldier had carved and learned that the tallest was called the king, the next tallest, the queen. He could tell a bishop from a knight, and now that he looked close, realized that all the little pieces, the pawns, did in fact look alike. Every day, Szulim played chess with Tomaitey and learned to speak Russian, chanting the Communist national anthem and singing songs about machine guns.

Fall 1943 – Spring 1944

THE CRISP, COOL air that rushed into the cellar came as a welcome relief from the stifling heat of the past summer months. But with it came the news that Mr. Sokol's mother had died.

"Condolences," Pop said as Mr. Sokol explained there'd be a wake, that he wouldn't be able to open the trap door for several days. When he left, Szulim's mother turned to his father. "Chaim, all these people coming into their home. The smell from down here! Won't that give us away?"

Szulim remembered how awful it had been in the beginning. Like a medley of the worst odors he had ever experienced – chicken blood and bits of flesh baking in the sun behind the shochet's house on a very hot day, the toilets in the marketplace when someone had an accident, the droshky driver who bathed only in the rain that still couldn't wash away the smell of horse manure – as if someone had gathered all the bad smells in the world and put them into one of Mama's perfume bottles. He knew that's what he smelled like now, worse even than the women and their disease, and thought it was incredible what one's nostrils could get used to.

"Like they smell any better, Perl? How often you think Sokol bathes? Once a year if he's lucky. Remember, goyim don't go to mikvah."

Szulim had never liked taking his bath each Thursday. He felt like an animal on Noah's ark, he and his siblings going two by two. One week he and Abraham would be first, the next week, Sara and Rivka. Mama kept track so there'd be no arguments. When Rivka and Sara went first, the boys waited in the other room until their sisters were squeezed dry and dressed in their nightshirts. Abraham was too little to care, but Szulim never took his clothes off until the girls were out of the room. His body was private.

Here in the cellar nothing was private, though Szulim wasn't allowed to take off his clothes, even on the hottest days. Despite their living conditions, they had to maintain their modesty. Szulim wondered how Mr. Sokol took a bath. Did the man with the horse and buggy come all the way to his farm with big barrels of water? What about the old man with the beard and *peyes*, his gray curls extending down from his sideburns like all the other religious men and boys, who carried two wooden buckets on a yoke across his shoulders? That would have been a long way to walk from Zelechow with water on his back.

Every day, when the man would come to Zelechow selling water, Pop would line the pails up against the kitchen wall. When Mama needed water, she'd fill the kettle from the pails. Pop had rigged up a tank in the kitchen, a painted blue cistern with a spigot and a small sink underneath, but this was only for washing their hands after they visited the outhouse, a custom of all religious Jews. The goyim and Jews like the Popowska's did not wash afterwards. Szulim would know winter was coming when he'd go outside to play and find a frozen puddle next to the steps where the tube from the sink poked out of the wall.

For their bath, Mama would boil water from the old man's pails in her kettle while Havah dragged the large, round tub from the patio into the kitchen, placing it between the two stoves. Metal bands encircled the barrel, which had two planks opposite each other extending farther up the sides with holes cut out for handles. Years of use had smoothed the wood, making it feel slippery to Szulim's hands as he rubbed along the inside. Havah poured hot water filling the tub almost halfway, then added cold water, testing with her fingers until it reached a comfortable temperature. When it was the boys' turn to go first, they'd wait for Havah, standing naked next to the coal-burning stove that warmed the room. They'd get as close to the white tiles covering the chimney as they could without touching the cracks spidering along the wall. Szulim learned the hard way what happens if you touch a crack.

Havah would lift the boys into the drum, wet the peach-colored bar of soap and begin lathering their skin. Szulim liked when his sisters went first because the foam that had rinsed off their bodies and floated on the surface made the water smell like perfume.

"Raise your arms, yingaleh."

Szulim always did as he was told, presenting his limbs and tuchas to Havah for washing. He'd sit back down and quickly rub off the soap while Abraham got scrubbed. Szulim would cup water into his hands and pour it down Abraham's back, rinsing his brother so Mama could lift them out of the tub, squeeze them dry in the towel and dress them in their rough cotton nightshirts. That was the best part, when it was over. Even though Mama boiled kettles of hot water on the stove, and added more after the first group of children finished cleaning, it was never warm enough. Szulim always wished there was a way to feel clean and swaddled without having to get naked and wet.

"Szulim!" Abraham poked him in the side, shaking Szulim from his memory of the bath. He whispered and pointed towards the entrance of the cellar. Malka Popowska, the youngest daughter, ducked into the little room where everyone went for privacy. "She brought the bottle again." The boys craned their necks towards the door, wondering how they could sneak a peak without anyone noticing. This business with Malka and the bottle fascinated them the last time they had to go for days without Mr. Sokol cleaning out the waste buckets. When the buckets began to fill up too high, the men found empty bottles to do their thing in. Szulim and Abraham had giggled, thinking it was great fun to poke their little *schmeckles* into the hole and see how much they could fill. But a woman? How was this possible? The boys weren't the only ones speculating, much to the embarrassment of Malka.

Szulim sat without speaking or moving, as he had been for two days already, not noticing the cramping of his belly anymore. Mr. Sokol's mother was dead, so why were all these people coming to visit her? She couldn't talk. These Polacks were so stupid; Jews never stuck their dead on a table for visitors. Szulim wondered about Mietka and Pela, if they were sad about their grandmother. Or if they, deep down, wanted her dead body out of their house the way he had wanted Mr. Popowska out of the cellar. He studied his fingers, picking at the *schmutz* under his nails. There was no use. He felt the weight of his hair on his neck, his skin shades darker than he ever remembered. He longed for that round, wooden tub. He would rip off his clothes and jump into freezing water just for a chance to wash the layers of filth off of his body.

———

Rosh Hashanah marked nearly a year since they had gone underground. As Pop alone davened, Szulim thought about everything that was missing – not just the people, but the traditions. It used to be that Szulim couldn't wait to hear the *shofar* ushering in the New Year, that ancient call to prayer. *Tekiah!* The wail of the horn sounding throughout the synagogue. *Shevarim!* Short pah pah pahs. *Teruah!* Waves of one note overlapping each other. *Tekiah Godolah ...!* He loved the really, really long one; the way the men's cheeks puffed out then sank, their ears and foreheads growing red, eyes popping. The hurried, fervent murmurs of prayer, quieted for once. He'd feel the call to worship all the way to his toes and imagine a ram in the deserts of *Eretz Yisrael*, the ram whose horn was pressed against the lips of the shofar blower. Eretz Yisrael was a magical place, he just knew. A place even older than his zayde who had died.

On high holidays, the whole *mispochah* – cousins, aunts and uncles – would walk to the large synagogue in the center of town where most residents of Zelechow gathered to celebrate the head of the year, the beginning of the Days of Awe. Szulim thought the shul was magnificent. Towards the front were rows and rows of special seats for each family. Or each family that could afford them. Szulim and his father sat in the Boruchowicz seats with both Feter Moshes and his three cousins – little Berl, big Berl and Herschel. Big Moshe would tickle Szulim under the chin and pull out a piece of candy for which Szulim would be grateful since it was usually a while before dinner.

Szulim didn't understand why there weren't any Wajnberg seats; that was his last name, after all. But these seats were from his mother's family, the Boruchowicz's, who had been in Zelechow for generations. They were lucky to even have special seats. The poorer families had to arrive early since it was first come, first served for most everyone else. Szulim wouldn't actually get a seat other than his father's lap, but it was still better than his mother and sisters who would form a horseshoe in the balcony along with his aunts and cousin Sara, not to mention all the other women in town. Even though Abraham was a boy, he had gone up to the balcony with Mama. He was too squirmy to sit up close.

Szulim would grip Pop's hand, and as he'd make his way through the crowd, he'd find the *bima*, the raised platform in the middle where *Rufe* Goldberg stood in his *kittel*, the long white gown worn by all the grown men on the New Year. Rufe Goldberg wasn't a rebbe like the men who taught cheder, or led services at each shtiebl, men who listened patiently as villagers presented problems or sought interpretations, nodding quietly before making a decision and providing sage advice. Rufe Goldberg acted as an administrator, a liaison between the religious Jews and the non-religious or gentile community, and would give a sermon after the Jews of Zelechow joined together in prayer.

Szulim loved to stare at the ark and the ornate carvings of the wooden cabinet that held the Torah. The ark was the centerpiece of the synagogue; visible from the moment one walked through the doors. Szulim knew to hold himself still as the men in white gowns hushed in the presence of such a holy fixture. Not a single resident of Zelechow could have imagined, as men touched the parading scroll with their *tallit* and then kissed the knots of their prayer shawls, that the ancient text, like the village of Jews who revered it, would be displaced. Or that the Zelechow Torah would travel across continents and come to a final resting place in the Holy Land, in a different ark altogether. Szulim had never imagined that he might one day celebrate the Jewish New Year without his uncles or cousins, stuck in a dark pit underground.

———

"STOP IT! I don't want to live anymore!"

Szulim stood against the wall with his brother and sisters and stared at his mother. She sat on the floor sobbing, his father massaging the sides of her head. "Perl, you have children." His father turned to look at the kids and looked back at his wife. "They need a mother."

Ever since his uncles and older cousins came back to the cellar, without the women or Berleh, Mama could not stop crying. She wouldn't eat the little bit of food Mr. Sokol sent down each night. Szulim had gotten used to her complaints by now; how sore she was from Pop always pressing on her temples. That was the only thing that would wake her up when she fainted. Szulim didn't understand why she crumpled to the floor all the time now, falling suddenly asleep. Mimeh Tertza, his only remaining aunt, was alive because she had been visiting with Szulim and his family in Sokol's cellar when the group at Wladislaw's was discovered. Tertza simply stared into space and whimpered.

"Perl, we have to survive. You have to survive." Pop's pleadings were always the same. "If we give up, then Hitler will have won."

Szulim tried to be extra kind to his mother, stroking her arm, offering her his water. He needed her to get better. If she didn't want them, he and his siblings, his father wouldn't either. He had said so in a loud voice that made Szulim's insides sting.

"I can't take care of the children by myself, Perl. If you kill yourself, I'll kill myself, too."

Szulim wanted to cry as well, he felt like he should. Yet the tears wouldn't come. A heavy gray air, heavier and grayer than the normal atmosphere of the cellar, sat upon them all; another *tsurris*, a worse pain even, to add to everything else. But living like animals, worrying about survival, they didn't even have the luxury to experience the full range of human emotion.

Szulim couldn't grasp what had happened. He heard words, but he couldn't sort it out in his head and have it make sense. His uncles and older cousins came back to the cellar completely traumatized. They spoke of hiding amongst the trees for a week. They talked of Polish bandits, the women and little Berl being taken to the woods, separately. Feter Moshe Boruchowicz speculated that Wladislaw turned them in because their money had run out. Wladislaw knew he would have been killed if the Germans found out he was harboring Jews, so he got rid of his problem by telling the Polacks. Feter Moshe Szyfman couldn't say anything at all. He no longer had a wife or a child. Szulim had so many questions;

why were the women killed, but not the men? Why a little boy? But he knew he couldn't ask. It wasn't the right time. Szulim looked at his mother moaning on the floor and didn't think there would ever be a right time.

———

SZULIM PEERED UP at the little hole in the wall that led outside. He tried remembering what seasons felt like. He imagined the damp of a gray spring day breezing through his skin and kissing his bones. Or a warm sun seeping into his heart and pumping bright yellow throughout his entire body. Now he lived from one extreme to another, only guessing at the actual weather. The color of the air in the cellar was either black or gray. The air itself, either really cold or really hot.

What kept them rooted in time was Feter Moshe's siddur; and according to his little black notebook, it was the 14th of Nisan, which meant it was time to gather round and recount the Israelite's escape from slavery in Egypt. They had managed to save a few scraps of potato peels and Feter Moshe led the Seder. Without Haggadahs to read from or the customary foods, without the rest of their family, it felt fake to Szulim, like letters cobbled together and dribbling from the mouth rather than real words filled with meaning, words to chew over. But as Szulim listened to Feter Moshe recite the ten plagues, he found himself drawn to the story of Exodus. Blood, like what Mr. Popowska coughed up when he was still alive. Lice and boils that covered their own hair and bodies now after more than a year without a bath. The darkness in Sokol's pit, especially when snow covered their one little window to the world outside. And the last plague, the death of the first born. Szulim thought about Berleh. How if they ever did get to Jerusalem someday, as they prayed for every Pesach, his younger cousin would not be there, explaining to Szulim all the things he had read about in his books.

"*Ziest er hot nisht fargesen!*" Szulim's father held up the loaves of bread Sokol sent down with their soup and said, "See, he didn't forget."

It had been months since they had seen a loaf of bread. The days when Mr. Sokol was lucky enough to find some cottage cheese or buttermilk on the black market were long gone. They lived on soup made of potatoes, cabbage or beets, the only vegetables that grew on Sokol's farm. Szulim's mother, once round and full, withered, her body skin and bones. They all diminished in size and health. In two decades, Szulim's dentist in the United States would spend a lot of time fixing problems caused by childhood malnutrition, amazed at his patient's ability and desire to undergo major dental work without Novocain. But now in the spring of 1944, just like the year before, Mr. Sokol managed to find several loaves of the exact thing Jews were forbidden to eat. Feter Moshe just sighed as Pop took the bread and parceled out the bounty to everyone else.

———

"It could be over in two weeks!" Szulim's father and uncles seemed almost giddy. Mr. Sokol passed down word, along with dinner, that Hitler's army was losing on the Russian front. Szulim wondered about the back, and if he was losing there, too. While he sipped at his soup, he listened to the grown ups talk about Stalin as if they knew him from shtiebl and could predict what he would do next. Szulim wondered how Mr. Sokol got his information. Perhaps from someone else who was breaking the law. Mr. Sokol hid Jews; maybe he had a friend who hid a radio. Szulim had never seen a radio, but his father had described this metal box that plucks words from the air and speaks them out loud. Little Berl would have been able to explain how it works. Even if there had been a newspaper, Mr. Sokol couldn't read it. Szulim's father never questioned the source of the information or the timing of events. Everyone was just thrilled to have any word from outside the cavern in which they hid.

But the excitement at whatever news they managed to get didn't last long. It had become apparent that no matter who was winning or losing the war, Mr. Sokol was losing heart at hiding Jews underneath his home. "He's going to kick us out. I know it." Feter Moshe Szyfman was crying again. Szulim thought Feter Moshe actually had a reason to cry ever since his wife and son were killed. But everyone had stopped paying attention to his tears because thin Feter Moshe had always whimpered, as if he suffered more than anyone else who had been cut off from the outside world and starved for movement and light and normalcy. Now as Feter Moshe cried, however, even Szulim's parents looked worried.

"I told him," said Szulim's father. "I said, 'Sokol, you can kick us out, and my wife and I won't breathe a word of what you've done to help us. But my kids? They're children. I can't promise that they won't say anything.'"

"I can keep a secret, Pop!"

"Szulimeleh, I know that. But I wanted to scare him into keeping us here."

Mr. Sokol was sorry he had ever agreed to help, and everyday now, he threatened to evict them. The money had long run out and there wasn't anything else the Jews could offer to sell on the black market. Even their shoes had been handed up through the trap door, not that Szulim's fit him anymore. As much as he wanted to get out of the greeb, to walk outside and feel the sun, to find other children to play with, to be someplace on his own, Szulim knew that Sokol's pit was the only place where he'd be safe. He, and everyone else crowded in the cellar, prayed that Sokol's goodwill, if he had any left, could outlast Hitler.

June 15, 1944

The closet in the Sokol's bedroom moved even though light still streamed through the little window. It was too early for Mr. Sokol to bring food. The days were long and he and his family worked all the way until the sun went down. Besides, he never opened the door in daylight. Ever. As furniture scraped against the floor above them, Szulim heard boots. More than one pair. Mr. Sokol didn't wear boots. He couldn't afford them.

Everyone in the pit jerked and flapped around, bumping into each other. It reminded Szulim of chickens at the shochet running from the knife. Mrs. Popowska grabbed Malka's arm and pressed it against her heart while Szulim's mother jumped up with her hands in balls at her side. Feter Symcha twisted his head back and forth, not knowing which way to look. Sara and Rivka clutched at each other while Feter Moshe davened. His eyes were closed and his face trembled as he raised the siddur to his lips to kiss it. Szulim thought the world must be falling apart.

Soon he heard the trap door being lifted and the scraping of wood was no longer above them. It came from the little room at the end of the cellar, the small space two steps up where they did their notznik in the bucket. Everyone stopped moving, freezing like statues, and Szulim listened as 20 people held their breath. Liebl Popowska and Herschel Winograd crept to the little room, towards the ladder that led up and out. Some of the other grown ups gathered behind them. Liebl and Herschel lifted the guns, the ones they stole from partisans, and pointed them above the buckets towards the trap door. Szulim didn't think they were getting soup.

He turned away from the guns and saw his father at the other end of the cellar. He was holding Abraham up to the little window, trying to push him up and out onto the earth. *Where was he going?* Szulim knew it wasn't safe outside. He heard his brother scream at the very same time he heard a gun shot. His father yanked Abraham back inside; that was when the shooting started. Bullets began flying; people were running in every direction. And then Szulim saw and heard nothing.

THE NEXT THING he knew, it was dark, past when they should have gotten dinner. They were upstairs, sitting against the wall in the Sokol's bedroom. Szulim wanted to hold Abraham's hand. He wanted his mother's arms around him. But they were lined up and no one was touching. There were men, lots of men. He tried to count them but his brain tripped on itself and he couldn't keep the numbers straight. 12? 18? A hundred? They all talked at once, asking questions. Szulim understood their Polish and heard that they wanted gold. "Where'd you hide the jewels?" they asked. "Give us your gold!" The once hidden Jews didn't have gold, but the bandits kept asking. They spit their words and their voices reminded Szulim of the dogs that marched with the Gestapo, barking angry barks. They all looked the same, one face in matching filthy shirts and pants, asking where the jewels were hidden. Two men who had gone into the cellar came back upstairs. They shook their heads. Szulim heard a shout, a Polish word he didn't understand, and they lifted their guns at the same time. He had never seen a gun pointed right at him. It had eyes, staring right into his own. He wanted to bury his head into his knees, but he saw that no one else moved, so he held still.

His father spoke. "If you kill us, then all the money and jewels I hid in Zelechow will never be found." Szulim knew Pop was lying. They had given their valuables to Mr. Turek. Nothing was left because Mr. Sokol sold it all for food and there was hardly enough food anymore. But those men believed Szulim's father. *They are so stupid,* Szulim thought. He was only eight years old and even he knew it was a lie.

"Will you take us there?" The man who shouted orders looked at Szulim's father. He wouldn't put down his gun.

"If you leave my family here, yes. I will take you there."

"Good," they said. "Let's go."

His father spoke again. "I can't leave until we clean up the dead."

Szulim looked around and noticed Liebl lying still, so still, right where the ladder came up from the cellar. His body was open in many places and Szulim could see red. Hinda's fiancée lay in front of them. He looked uncomfortable with his arms bent in weird ways and his legs going in opposite directions. But he didn't move. He slept in a big puddle that kept getting bigger. Szulim knew it wasn't water because he couldn't see through it to the wood floor. It was dark, almost black.

He wanted to cry but he was too afraid. He heard some sniffling from the women and shuffling of feet as Pop and his Feters carried the two bodies outside to bury them. Szulim wondered how long it would take before the *armiekrayowe*, those men from the People's Army, killed them, too.

Pop came back inside. His shoulders were moving up and down, jerking so fast. He was making sounds, as if small animals were trying to escape from inside him but he wouldn't let them out. Mama looked at him. Szulim could see she had a question but she didn't ask. Her eyes were big, stretching as if her words might come out through her tears instead of her mouth. Pop pointed to Szulim and crooked his finger. "Come." He tried to say Szulim's name, but covered his mouth, as if he might throw up. Szulim followed him outside into the darkness. He looked back at his mother, but she just wept.

The first thing Szulim noticed was the breeze. He didn't remember the last time he felt air actually move across his skin or blow through his hair. The sky was pitch black with millions of twinkling stars; the moon glowed bluish-gray. Szulim heard his name and turned to his father's voice. Pop handed him a shovel. "Dig over there." Szulim looked down and that's when he saw.

Rivka. She was lying on the ground right by the front door.

He stared at his sister, looking for ways that this wasn't real. That this 12-year-old girl with blonde hair who looked like his Rivka might actually be someone else; that a dog hadn't been chewing on her arm like a scrap bone, just something for an animal to work its teeth around. *I must be mistaken,* Szulim thought. He stared at her, and though he didn't want to admit it, he knew she was Rivka. He waited for her to move. He looked at her face and his brain couldn't believe what his eyes were seeing. Szulim thought about everyone he know who had died – his Mimehs and little cousin, how he loved them very much. He missed them, but he never saw them dead. He saw Mr. Popowska dead, and just inside the house lay Popowska's son and the man who would have been his son-in-law. But Szulim never loved them.

"Has she really been killed?" He couldn't say the word 'dead' out loud. His father started to cry, giant sobs that shook his whole body. Szulim had never seen Pop cry and it scared him. The only man he had ever seen cry was Feter Moshe Szyfman and Szulim knew Feter Moshe couldn't take care of anyone. He needed Pop to stop crying. He needed to know that his father could still take care of him.

It was at that moment that everything became real. All of it. The precautions and the restrictions and the fear. Everything he had lived and seen for the past five years, they weren't stories anymore. They were real. And he understood in a way that he'd never understood before what his parents meant when they said "you'll be punished." This was what could happen if he didn't listen, even for a second. But Rivka always listened. Always.

Szulim was a small boy. His shoulders were narrow and his rib bones stuck out through his chest. His father had hair on his chest, and under his arms, but Szulim was too young to even look for signs of this growth on his own body. He was a small boy who dug four graves. Two for young men who wanted to be heroes, one for his last remaining Mimeh, murdered and lying in the road a short distance from the farmhouse. And then, a final resting place for his sister.

He looked around at who was left; Tomaitey was nowhere to be seen. Devorah, too, had disappeared. There were no other bodies, so maybe they escaped. Mr. Sokol sat at the kitchen table with his head in his hands. He was lucky it was only Polish bandits who discovered the Jews. If it were the Nazis, he and his family would have been killed – along with Szulim's sister.

Szulim woke up yesterday morning, the 24th of Sivan, expecting nothing more than boredom and hunger. Now it was morning again. He had been digging graves through the night. He had no roof over his head, no promise of food, not a single aunt, and only one sister.

Telling: Summer 2009

I'VE REACHED THE questions in my notebook I'm afraid to ask. I admit this to Sal who reassures me over the phone.

"Ask anything; I have nothing to hide. And this is so healing, you have no idea."

I exhale loudly. "Tell me about that day."

"Over the years, I've tried to reconstruct it. And my memories mingle with what I've learned since. In the chaos of it all, Devorah Popowska disappeared. Whether it was during the shooting, when my sister Rivka and Aunt Tertza tried to escape, or sometime later, I do not know. She is the only one of the Popowska's who survived. Last I heard she was living in Israel."

"What about the Russian soldier?"

"When Tomaitey identified himself, the bandits ordered him to leave. He just walked towards the east and I never saw him again. He was the first Russian I had met, but not the last."

"And the Sokol's? Where were they in all of this?"

"Mr. Sokol was there, perhaps ordered to sit in the kitchen while the bandits questioned us. Apparently, he helped us clean and bury our dead."

"I'm surprised they let you do that."

"These murderers, they weren't a sanctioned army. They were hooligans who ran through the night looting and killing. They didn't want to get caught by the Germans, either. Or be seen with a Jew. My father — I have no idea how he could maintain his composure and negotiate with these bastards — said that since it was getting light and they shouldn't travel by day, we would go down and hide in the cellar. He said they should come back after dark and he'd take them to the gold."

"And they believed him?" I am incredulous. But I just listen.

"They say Polacks are stupid, and from this alone, you should know it's true."

I bristle a bit, but say nothing. I understand that Sal comes by his intolerance honestly.

"No sooner did those murderers leave than we left, too." Sal is silent for a moment. "You've heard the Polack joke, I'm sure. Not for nothing they make fun of them. I'm not saying it's right, please understand me, just that it's based on historical fact. At the time of the war, 85-95% of the Polish population was illiterate. Jews, however, were educated."

"Why was this?" I ask.

"Going back to the 19th century there were laws forbidding Jews from owning property," Sal says. "We couldn't farm, so the only way to earn a living was by going into a trade that required an education. Even the Poles admitted that Jews were more educated."

"Perhaps that's part of the reason you were a target."

"Perhaps. Why do you think Sokol let us play with his daughters? We helped them with their studies. Here I was, two to three years younger, yet I helped them with their homework. See what I mean?"

Sandy listens as Sal explains how the Poles couldn't read newspapers and instead got their news from church every week. "Let me tell you," Sal says, "it wasn't love and goodwill to all mankind that they preached in those churches."

"Aren't things different now, Sal?" Sandy's voice comes gently through the phone. "Don't you think they're more educated and aware now? Maybe even tolerant?"

"Oy, I hear that. I'd like to believe that's true. I do think the Germans are genuinely sorry. But I'm not so sure about the Polish." Sal reflects for a moment. "Please know, when I say these things about the Polish, it's not that I look down on them for being uneducated. No. But when I think about everyone I loved who was killed in the Holocaust, everyone who mattered to me – with the exception of my grandmother – they were all killed by the Polish."

Sandy thinks back on their trip to Poland over 35 years before. When they landed in Warsaw, she had barely noticed that the plane had touched ground. As Sal stood to collect their carryons from the bins above their heads, Sandy plucked the crumpled tissues from her lap, around her legs, the seat pocket in front of her. She held the wads in both hands and realized they went through three entire packets. Actually, the tissues were mostly Sandy's, the tears mostly hers.

In a previous conversation, Sandy described to me how composed Sal had been the entire plane ride, how calmly he had recalled his past. Like he was offering a lesson in history, teaching her about something she should have known. At times she'd say to him, "If you can't talk about it, that's okay." But then he'd collect himself and reveal more. She was in shock, hearing it all, thinking about Andy and Robyn on the other side of the Atlantic, wondering how Sal could even relate to how they were raising the kids. It was as if that plane ride was the single moment in time dividing before from after. She still had so many questions, yet as she stepped down from the plane onto the tarmac, she felt the weight of Sal's secret lifting off of her shoulders.

Sandy had breathed in the Eastern European surrounds, a refreshing change from the recirculated air on the plane, and when she looked at Sal, she panicked. Her husband, a man who had always been so self-assured, so decisive and confident, was transforming before her eyes. His shoulders sagged; his breathing grew heavy and labored. He couldn't stop turning his head. *Is he having a heart attack?* Sandy had wondered. Not a heart attack, no. It was as if his whole body had become inhabited by someone new. Was he coming undone after opening up, sharing too much too quickly, the way he gets lightheaded after blowing up the kids' toys at the beach? Sal's voice had lowered to a whisper. His footsteps got lighter, like he was walking on something fragile or hot. Sweat formed on his brow.

Sandy didn't ask, "Are you okay?" She could see clearly that he was not. The voices around her sounded different, more guttural. Soft J's and V's and *tz tz tz*. Foreign sounding, for sure. And then she understood. Sal was frightened. This language, Polish, was not foreign to him. To Sal, it reverberated with meaning, with loathing. She saw in his posture that he felt unwelcome, still, in the land of his birth. His history was coming to life before her eyes, manifesting itself in a physical transformation of the man she loved.

Sandy shakes her head at the painful memory and focuses on what Sal is saying now. The bread. Sal has mentioned this before. For months of their captivity, Sokol gave them soup only, no bread. Yet on Passover, he managed to find several loaves of the stuff they were not allowed to eat.

"Here was a man harboring Jews who was deep down an anti-Semite," Sal says.

"He might not have known it was Passover," Sandy interjects. "Maybe he didn't do it out of spite."

"Oh, he knew," Sal says. "I spoke of the blood libel, no? This was preached every year in every church for weeks leading up to Pesach. I'm telling you, anti-Semitism was in the fabric of their culture."

"And yet he hid you," I say. "He risked his life and that of his family's to hide you. Maybe that whole bit with the bread was less about spite, and more his curiosity. Like he really wanted to understand true conviction, witness first hand the depths of faith."

Sal was silent. "I never thought about it that way. I accept that this could be a possibility. Who knows?"

"People are complex," I say.

"That's for sure. For years, I've been ruminating on this. What started out as righteous became an impossible situation. I don't know. I think when he first agreed to hide us, he did it as a favor to his wife's brother, Mr. Turek. A favor sweetened by some cash. No one thought the war would last as long as it did. He simply had the space; he needed the money."

"But that can't be all, can it?" I ask. "This was such an incredible risk. He had a son in the army, a son who ran away, two young daughters in school. If a neighbor found out he was hiding you and turned him in ... could he have been that desperate for money?"

Sal sighed. "To this day, I still don't quite understand Mr. Sokol, what moved him. For months, when the money ran out, he threatened to evict us. He told us over and over how he regretted ever taking us in."

Sandy thinks back to their Poland trip. They only had two days in Warsaw before they had to rejoin their tour group, so despite jet lag, they threw their bags in the hotel room and went to the front desk to inquire about a driver. Sal wanted to go to Wilcziska to see the Sokol's. Sandy stood by Sal's side in the hotel lobby, waiting for him to speak to the concierge. But nothing came out of Sal's mouth. She squeezed his hand and whispered, "What's wrong?"

"How do I know they won't take us someplace else?" he whispered back. "They might know we're Jewish."

"Honey, this isn't the 1940's anymore." Sandy rubbed his arm. "We're okay. Just ask."

Sandy could tell, after bumping along dirt roads and rolling through fields for an hour, that they had arrived at the farm. It was just as Sal had described it to her on the airplane, a tiny house with a broken roof and dingy clay walls. Her knees shook as they stepped out of the car and she couldn't imagine what Sal must be feeling, revisiting the past like that.

Chickens and pigs roamed the overgrown yard and there stood a lone, large tree providing some shade. Behind the farmhouse was a smaller structure, like a shack, and Sandy realized it was their toilet. She saw a woman tending to the chickens and recognized her at once as Mrs. Sokol, even though she had never seen a picture of her. She wore a long, shapeless red and blue striped skirt with a shirt of an entirely different color and pattern. A scarf, different still from both shirt and skirt, covered most of her head, with a few scraggly gray hairs poking out the sides. Her face reflected years of fieldwork and harsh sun. She just stared at them, unsmiling, while several other women in similar dress, younger than Mrs. Sokol, came out of the house.

Sal spoke. He said hello in Polish, and then "Mietek" as he tapped his chest. One of the younger women grabbed Sal's arm and they made a gesture for Sandy and Sal to follow them inside the house.

A wood-burning stove filled the small kitchen, and on its mantle sat a battery-operated transistor radio. The house had no electricity and the radio was the only item in the home dating from the 20th century. A burlap sack hung in the doorway between the kitchen and what Sandy assumed was a bedroom. It was the only door she could see.

Mrs. Sokol grabbed a couple of plates and a bowl filled with some food Sandy didn't recognize and walked back outside. She made a motion for the American couple to sit at a picnic table as one of the young women, her daughter, brought a cloth to cover the planks of wood. Sandy tried to smile politely. Little children ran around the yard, touching her clothes and hair. Sandy could see Mongoloid features in their wide grins. She was curious about the cellar, wondering if they'd be able to go down and see it. Wondering if she even wanted to.

Sandy hadn't known what to expect of the visit. Perhaps she had some fairy tale idea of a joyful reunion with tears and hugs and exclamations of, "I can't believe it's you! How wonderful to see you looking so healthy and strong!" Not that she thought they would speak English. But the Polish words Sal exchanged with these women did not reflect any joy. If anything, the tenor of the conversation seemed businesslike. As if there had been an expectation of payment.

As it turned out, Sal had been sending money to the Sokol's for years, though he had never discussed it with Sandy. Mrs. Sokol spoke, holding out her hand, pointing to the roof of their house. Sandy could see that Sal was shocked by the way he raised his eyebrows until the driver leaned over from the end of the table where he had been sitting quietly and said, "Don't worry. A million zlotys is only about 500 U.S. dollars if you don't exchange it at the bank." Sal opened his wallet and placed several travelers cheques on the table.

My voice brings Sandy back to the present. "What about the Popowska's? Their son is killed, a fiancée, a daughter is missing?"

"Mrs. Popowska and her two remaining daughters joined us at first," Sal says. "But Mrs. Popowska wasn't strong enough for the journey. So, as I later found out, she returned to the Sokol's farm, begging Mr. Sokol to take them back in. After several weeks, Germans discovered them hiding in the Sokol's hayloft. Mr. Sokol swore he had no idea they were on his property and the Popowska women corroborated. So rather than burn down the barn and kill Sokol's whole family, they murdered the three Popowska's and Mr. Sokol."

Sandy listens to this, even though she had heard it already, and reflects on the visit to the farm long ago. Those women suffered their own losses as a result of hiding Sal's family. And on a gorgeous fall day, out of nowhere, a man showed up from their deep dark past who had been, in a large way, responsible for the killing of their husband and father, responsible for the shame that must have fallen upon their household once it became known amongst the townsfolk that they hid Jews.

Sandy had described to me the relief she felt when Sal stood up and shook hands, saying his goodbyes. In the car back to Warsaw, Sal told her that the cellar didn't exist anymore. She just touched his arm. She knew not to ask any questions.

I wonder what went through Sokol's mind at those final moments. "Was he filled only with regret and fear?" I ask Sal. "Or might he have felt any pride for taking a stand and doing the right thing?"

"People are complex. And yet, look at Turek. I've said it before and I'll say it again, Edward Turek was a saint." Sal's voice rises in conviction. "Everything he did, he did out of the goodness of his heart. A real mensch. Sokol, I don't know."

"He lost his life for you." I don't mean to argue; I just want to understand.

"I know. I think a lot about this." Sal has been talking without stop and needs a sip of water. I listen to him drink and wait for him to continue. "He put his entire family's life on the line. That's a very tough thing to do. Everyone today talks as if they, in that situation, would have hid someone; it's the right thing to do. But I deep down ask myself, would I have risked the lives of those most important to me for someone I did not know? When I'm really honest with myself, I have to answer … maybe not."

WANDERING

The Rye, The Wheat

June 16 – July 28, 1944

No one had shoes. With bare feet unaccustomed to pebbles and twigs and grasses, the hidden Jews, no longer hidden, rushed from what had been safe haven as the sun warned of its approach in tiny splashes of pink across a still darkened sky. The group turned to Szulim's father as if he had answers. But answers did not exist.

"I know a farmer in Maciejowice," he said. "Maybe he'll take us in."

"How far?" asked Feter Moshe Szyfman.

"About 30 kilometers."

"Oy gut."

Based on a bit of information they had gotten from Mr. Sokol in the preceding days, they felt liberation was imminent. The Russians had broken through Stalingrad. Even the United States was in the war. That morsel of hope, along with the bucket of water and some bread from the Sokol's, might sustain them.

They couldn't travel during the day when Poles or Germans could see them, so they stopped to hide in a field of rye as the morning sun inched upwards. Szulim's father seemed to know exactly where to enter the expanse of skinny shoots rising to the sky and everyone followed. Szulim's eyes traveled up the brownish gray stalks that grew nearly as tall as the grown ups.

"Walk in a straight line," his father said. They had to be careful not to mess up the rows so that from the outskirts of the field, it looked undisturbed. The stalks grew very close together, and there was no way to lie on the ground without tamping it all down. Once they got in deep enough, they could rest.

Szulim lay on his back, turning his face towards the sun. He listened to the breeze whistling through the fields and unpinched his nose for the first time in almost two years, inhaling the fresh smell that reminded him of Gedalia Yosef's bakery. He nestled close to the earth and felt like a baby, cocooned in warmth;

as if God had taken a soft brush, dipped it in liquid gold and painted all over his body. But when he shifted, he felt tiny needles poking him. He stared at the little hairs growing out of the grain. If he ran his fingers up towards the end of the stalk, it felt smooth. But when he rubbed back down, it prickled. He had slept on stalks of rye in the cellar, only they had been wrapped in a burlap sack like a pillowcase.

"Be careful," his father said. "It's easy to fall asleep and not wake up."

After the war, Szulim would learn that only hay has the power to intoxicate and relax a body to such a point that is fatal. But hunger kept them all from too deep a sleep anyway.

When night fell, they rose and began their journey. Feter Moshe, Berl and Herschel, Feter Moshe Szyfman, Feter Symcha, Pop and Mama, Szulim and his siblings, Mrs. Popowska and only two of her daughters – they wandered single file through the rye fields, thirteen people in complete silence, searching for food as they walked in the direction of Maciejowice. Abraham was only 7 years old and his legs grew tired, so he rode on Feter Symcha's shoulders. Symcha didn't mind because the *kurepatwa* from which he suffered made him blind at night. Szulim couldn't understand how the strongest man among them could have a disease, but Szulim's uncle became Abraham's legs, and in turn, Abraham provided sight. Szulim walked behind Sara, turning every few minutes to make sure Rivka could keep up.

He kept forgetting. Even though he had just dug a hole in the ground for his sister's body, he couldn't believe they were now a family of five. The events from the night before, the chaos and the bloodshed, kept disappearing from his mind. So he looked for Rivka, as if she might suddenly appear, walking towards them in the fields of rye. As if the hours preceding their exodus were just a bad dream. For six weeks he walked, turning around every few minutes to look back at his missing sister.

SZULIM WOKE UP and looked around. The sun had not set yet and everyone either sat up or lay prone in the tall grain. "Where's Malka? And Hinda? Their mother?"

"They left," his mother said. "Mrs. Popowska couldn't walk anymore."

"Where'd they go?"

Szulim's father shook his head. "She said something about going back to Sokol's. May God watch them, too."

Szulim hoped God could watch both groups of travelers at the same time. He wasn't so sure, however, that God had ever been watching them at all.

Szulim's father knew that in order to keep food from spoiling in the summer or freezing in the winter, farmers dug pantries deep into the earth. Each night they'd sneak onto farms, hoping there'd be no dogs, looking for such a cave. They didn't stop until they found something to eat, which sometimes took until nearly dawn. Other nights, when they were lucky enough, they could stop and rest with a few hours remaining before daybreak. They filled the bucket with water from a well and only took from the food cellars what they needed to get by. Then they'd find a new field of rye, taking care never to rest on the same property more than once. If a farmer had gone out and seen his field ruined, he'd enlist the help of others to search for the hiding Jews.

For almost two years, they had hungered for a glimpse of the moon, the warmth of the sun. But here they were, like wild animals left to fend for themselves against the elements, without predatory instinct or natural defenses. Three days into their journey, their faces became unrecognizable. *Ven fried zich ein hoiker?* Szulim's mother stared at her remaining children and husband and asked, when is a hunchback happy? *Ven er zet ananderin hoiker.* When he sees another hunchback. Reflected in their swollen faces was her own, blistered and burned. She chuckled. But Szulim could tell that she didn't really think it was funny. She had simply run out of tears.

AFTER FOUR DAYS of sleeping in rye, they made it to Maciejowice. They gathered in a wooded area at the edge of someone's property as Szulim's father, Feter Moshe, and his sons Herschel and Berl collected tree branches.

"Like this." Szulim's father stood with a branch to his shoulder, pointing out towards the house. "You all stay here and hold them like guns."

Three years ago, Szulim would have played pretend with his friends; imitating the soldiers they saw patrolling the streets of their shtetl. But he knew this wasn't a game. He watched his father walk to the farmhouse, head up and shoulders back, and knock on the door. Szulim remembered that chilly night he and Abraham hid in the bushes, holding hands while their mother approached Sokol's house seeking shelter. He prayed with all his might, they all did, that this new farmer might take them in. He wondered who else might surprise them hiding in this stranger's cellar.

"No!" Szulim's mother didn't have to wait for her husband to make it all the way back to the trees to hear the news. She could tell by the way he walked.

"Chaim, what'd he say?" Symcha couldn't see in the dark.

"He didn't recognize me at first. But then he said his neighbors were nosy and would tell the Germans."

"*Oy veismere!* What do we do now?" thin Feter Moshe began to cry.

Berl spoke up. "I say we head towards Warsaw. Sneak into the ghetto. At least there will be other Jews."

Szulim's father looked down, as if there might be an answer among the twigs and leaves. "I had enough trouble escaping from one ghetto. I'm not going to put myself, my family, back into another."

"All this wandering around aimlessly, stealing food. That's no good." Even in the dark, Szulim could tell Berl's teeth were clenched. "We need a plan."

"I have a plan." Szulim's father looked at the nine others in their group. "We keep heading east and meet up with the Russian front. It's our only hope." Szulim looked back and forth between his father and his oldest cousin, who at the age of 18 had somehow become a man without anyone noticing. He could tell his father wanted to scream, but they had to whisper. If anyone walked by and heard them, that would be it.

"Well," said Berl, "it's not a good plan. Warsaw's the only place we'll be taken in."

Szulim's father stared at his nephew. "If that's how you truly feel, then go. But we're heading east towards Zelechow. I know the area. I know where there's food. I know that's where the Russians will be coming in from."

Berl could never have known that what remained of the Jews in Warsaw were upturned gravestones, ransacked businesses, empty homes and ashes. So he, Feter Moshe and Herschel walked west towards the capitol. Everyone else headed east. Everyone except Rivka.

"LIE DOWN!" POP's voice snapped in the forest like a broken twig, a sharp whisper swallowed by the wind. Szulim hugged the ground, his heart pounding as he heard footsteps coming from behind. *Please don't let them see us! Please don't let them see us!* Szulim prayed silently.

"Where are they?" A voice called out into the dark. "Chaim? Symcha?"

"*Veyismere*, Moshe!" Szulim's father stood up, panting. "You scared the hell out of us."

"So, let's go." Feter Moshe, Berl and Herschel rejoined the group. They trudged along, a silent concession to Szulim's father, ignoring the dispute of only twenty minutes before.

THEY SETTLED IN a new field of rye as dawn approached, after being chased off a farm by a dog. They hadn't gotten food that night and had to turn to the rye kernels for sustenance. Fortunately, they had been able to fill their bucket with water from a pond before the animal with sharp teeth and a salivating bark rushed at them.

"This tastes terrible!" Abraham spit the pond water from the bucket onto the ground before lying down to sleep.

"Drink it, yingaleh." Feter Symcha reached into the bucket, making a cup with his hands, and held it to his nephew's lips. "With this heat and the sun, you need the water."

When the morning's light arced across the sky, they peered into the bucket and saw weeds and worms. Szulim's throat had constricted as he imagined the slimy strings swimming their way down to his stomach. He lay down in the rye and dreamed of finding a farm later that night without dogs. He hadn't slept long before the shower coming from above woke him. Szulim welcomed the pouring rain, rubbing the rivulets up and down his arms, through his hair. He opened his mouth like he saw his parents doing, drinking the clean water and feeling it course through his body. The rain tasted crisp and felt smooth on his tongue, unlike the pond water in the bucket.

At first, they all reveled in this drink and bath from the heavens, this respite from the beating sun. But the realization that they had no shelter from the downpour washed away any relief and they despaired again at their lack of accommodations, at being so exposed to the elements. For weeks, Szulim's skin felt like clothes that didn't fit anymore. If he smiled, he thought his face would crack apart. Not that there was anything to smile about. When he touched his hand to his cheek, even at night while he walked, it felt like the kitchen wall in Zelechow, radiating heat from the cracks between the tiles.

He wished they didn't have to walk every night. At first, only his feet hurt from walking without shoes through the countryside, his toes and soles gathering information about what lay underfoot instead of his eyes. The goal of reaching Maciejowice kept them going, thinking that in just a few days, any moment, they will have a place to rest. Perhaps some food. But after the farmer's rejection, Szulim's feet felt heavier. The bubble inside his chest pushing him forward had burst, releasing exhaustion that spread throughout his arms and legs. As if his head was like a droshky driver, cracking the whip across the back of a horse, or in this case, his body. If only that farmer had taken them in. Szulim couldn't understand how an old friend of Pop's could shut his door on them, turning them away into the night.

HAD SZULIM KNOWN before he started out what this next phase of their journey would be like, he would have wanted to just lay down in the road and die. It was the not knowing, the small kernels of hope, that had kept them all going for this long. The indignities had come bit by bit. First yellow stars, then no school. A curfew, then rations. Overcrowding and dead bodies and mistreatment – they built upon each other, over time. Szulim and his family took on each struggle as best they could; hoping the nightmare would be over soon, never imagining what new atrocity lay around the corner. They pushed forth because they had to, because human beings are wired for survival.

And so they marched, believing each day that the next would bring freedom.

A MONTH HAD passed. Four weeks of the sun growing stronger, their bodies growing weaker. Szulim no longer noticed the prickly hairs growing out of the rye. As soon as he lay down on the stalks, he fell asleep. In those precious hours when he escaped his surroundings, he didn't have to miss Rivka, or wonder why Sara hadn't uttered a word since they left Sokol's farm. He didn't have to worry about the fact that Pop limped and wore a smile that only went sideways across his face. Big Feter Moshe still carried the siddur and davened, sitting up and rocking in the rye. But Szulim had long before lost his pen knife and chess set. He didn't remember dropping it; he just noticed one night as they walked that he didn't have it any longer. Had he placed it down in the woods, too tired to carry anything? Or left it in a field of rye? It didn't matter. He couldn't eat a chess set.

The sharp "shh!" from Pop woke him and he saw his father sitting up, trying to peer through the stalks that stood up around him. The sky was pink, the sun barely showing over the horizon. Szulim's father held a finger to his lips and motioned with his other hand for everyone to stay back. Not that anyone wanted to move towards the sound. The group lowered themselves into the rye and held their breath. They heard men's voices, a conversation in Polish.

"Looks like a nice crop this year."

"We'll see. Start over there."

Szulim's father poked his head up above the tips of the rye and quickly sat back down. The men gathered their heads close together in a circle while Szulim reached for his mother's skirt.

"He's about 100 meters away. Maybe."

"What do we do?" They could always count on Moshe Szyfman to panic first.

"I say we run for it." Berl looked from his brother to his father for backing.

"You may be able to run, but not me." Szulim's father rubbed his foot. "And neither can Perl or the kids. We're staying."

"But he could cut here and then what?"

"We'll have to take that chance. It's a big field; there are only three of them."

"I don't know," Berl said.

"Even if we outrun the farmer, you want him calling the Germans?"

The discussion was quick and quiet, not like the time in Maciejowice. Everyone stayed put, crouching as low as possible, muttering silent prayers. For the entire day, they did not move or speak. Szulim thought back to his time in the attic; how just a few weeks could seem like an eternity with no wiggling or uttering a word, and with very little hope. At least now he didn't have to worry about Abraham flinching in his sleep. There was no way he could bump into the sky.

WHEN THE SUN finally began its descent and the farmers left the fields, still many rows away from where the group sat vigil, Szulim's parents weren't the only ones to embrace. Everyone hugged, wiping tears from their eyes as their bodies relaxed. Szulim exhaled, relieved to breathe again after twelve hours. He and Abraham let go of each other's hands, stretching out their fingers, as Sara hyperventilated.

"If they're cutting rye here," Szulim's father said, "they're cutting it everywhere. Tomorrow we find wheat."

"But isn't wheat much shorter?" Feter Symcha asked.

"Yes. But it won't be harvested for another six weeks."

Szulim added this latest stroke of luck, the farmer's day ending before he discovered Jews hiding in his field, to the list of incredulities he had started forming in his head. He wondered how many more miracles they could possibly be granted. How much longer they'd survive. His father was so strong and so wise, but even he had no answers now. Every night, as Szulim trudged quietly with the others, he wondered if he'd ever see the inside of a house again, or would he end up an old man sleeping among rye. Maybe he wouldn't ever become a man. Would the hunger and thirst overtake him? Or would a bullet stop his heart, like it did Rivka's.

July 29, 1944

THE SUN POUNDED on their backs since the wheat, shorter than rye by more than a head, provided even less by way of protection. They hadn't moved in several days, only Pop and Berl wandered at night in search of water. They lived on kernels, chewing them slowly. Szulim thought about the Israelites escaping from Egypt. He wondered what was such a big deal about not being able to wait for bread to rise. At least they had bread. Szulim worried that the growls of his stomach would give them away, but for three days now, a louder rumbling shook them all – tanks and artillery that, from the sound of it, were drawing nearer. As they flattened themselves into the earth, they could feel the vibrations. Szulim knew enough by now to understand that everything depended on who was driving those tanks. This was either the end of their wandering, or the end of their lives.

As far as Szulim could tell, no roads ran through the wheat fields. But tanks never much cared whether they drove over roads, crops or people. His father popped his head up every so often to gauge how far away the trucks were from their small group. He didn't seem concerned that they'd be run over. He just wanted to know, they all did, were these Russians or Germans? A battle waged inside Szulim's heart between hope and dread.

By the third day, they could hear voices. Soldiers' voices singing songs. They sat in silence, straining to make out the words. Szulim clenched his teeth and stuck out his chin, squeezing his brain in an effort to open his ears wider. He closed his eyes in order to block out everything but the sound. He wished the wind would stop rustling through the wheat; that the pitter-patter of distant fire would cease. He heard words, melodies. *Vichadilla na beerich katyusha*. Szulim opened his eyes and looked at Sara. She didn't say anything; she just stared into the wheat. *Katyusha*. Tomaitey used to talk about this Russian machine gun.

Szulim looked around to see if anyone else had noticed, but all he saw were furrowed brows, Abraham staring back at him. And Sara's empty gaze. His whole body tensed as he listened harder. He wanted to be sure, absolutely sure, before he said anything to Pop. Could this really be? He heard a different song. *Soyuz nerushimy respublik svobodnykh, Splotila naveki velikaya Rus'!* It was the Russian national anthem. Szulim knew this song; Tomaitey had taught him and the other children this song while he whittled the chess pieces.

He turned to Sara again. "It's Tomaitey's song, right?"

Sara thought for a minute and then nodded.

"Pop! They're Russians! I know it. I know the song!"

"Szulim, are you sure?" Pop stared at him. "Absolutely sure?"

Szulim swallowed hard. He listened again for a moment. "Yes, absolutely."

"Well then, stand up and sing!"

Da zdravstvuyet sozdanny voley narodov! Yediny, moguchy Sovetsky Soyuz! They rose from the wheat, ten people who resembled no ordinary humans, barefoot and burnt, with torn clothes and eyes practically swollen shut. Bodies emaciated from hunger. They put their arms in the air and walked towards the voices. Szulim's father could see now from the markings on the tanks and jeeps that these soldiers were indeed Russian. So with a voice that came from deeper than he knew existed in his body, Szulim marched towards the Russians and sang. He sang and sang until something in his throat blocked the melody.

That's when Szulim cried. They all did. The emotion poured out, first in song and then in tears, and for the first time in years, they felt safe. The irony of the date, Tish'a B'Av, was lost on no one. Szulim knew that even if he lived to be an old man, Tish'a B'Av — which for centuries had been known as the saddest day in Jewish history — would forever mark the happiest day of his life.

"Never again," said his father, "will I fast on this day. Yom Kippur, of course. But not the day of our liberation."

Szulim laughed as his father tried to communicate with the Russian soldiers by waving his arms and slowing his speech. He tried Yiddish, German, Polish … to no avail. Szulim watched the soldiers' expressions; they really were trying to understand his father. So he stepped forward and began speaking the words he had learned from Tomaitey. Words from songs and plays that seemed too formal to come out of the mouth of an 8-year-old boy. But he continued to put words together and surprise the soldiers. Szulim could see the look of astonishment in their eyes at a little Jewish boy from Poland speaking their mother tongue.

"Hush, comrades!" The soldier standing in front of Szulim waved his arm at his fellow soldiers and beckoned for them to come close. As they gathered around, Szulim felt like a hero; the joy at being understood overwhelmed him.

Szulim learned from the soldiers, as he translated between his father and the

Russians, that although the war was not yet over, this part of Poland had been liberated. "The messiah has come!" Feter Moshe Boruchowicz could not stop kissing his siddur. Szulim's parents embraced and his father said, "See, Perl? I told you." He hugged his brother and the children. "Oy gut, we're free!"

"Where do you need to go?" they asked.

Szulim turned to his father and translated. "Zelechow," he answered, turning back to the Russians.

"That's where we're headed, too," the soldier smiled. "Hop on the truck."

The soldiers helped them onto their Chrysler Studebakers made by the Americans especially for the war. Szulim's head was spinning. He had never been on a vehicle powered by anything but horses, and even the droshky rides had been rare occasions. He thought of little Berl who would have been able to explain to him about the engine located under the snub-nosed hood. Szulim saw his father wince as he leaned on his left foot and was surprised that big Feter Moshe climbed on after him. Just the night before, Szulim's uncle davened and whispered the blessings for Shabbat. Surely Moshe knew the laws of Shabbos prohibited riding on a vehicle. But Feter Moshe did not say a word, and for sure Szulim would not mention it. Maybe he believed the Messiah could appear in the form of an army transport.

Szulim had never seen such filthy soldiers. Unshaven and unkempt, even the trucks were covered in dirt. So different from the Nazis with their trimmed hair, polished boots and shiny cars that used to patrol his shtetl. Nevertheless, these Russians were kind. They shared their bread and offered their water. Szulim gulped from their canteens and imagined the inside of his body, like a cracked earth, finally healing and preparing to bloom. He had not known until now just how crisp and delicious freedom could taste.

Szulim grasped Abraham's hand and smiled as the vibration ran from the floor of the vehicle up into his tuchas. His chest felt fuzzy with little flickers of light, as if fireflies were circling around inside his body, flaring on and off. His legs dangled from the bench and he straightened his knees so he could look at his toes. His feet smiled at him, happy to finally not be responsible for moving his body from one place to another.

Szulim saw his mother mouth to his father, "I can't wait to get there." He couldn't hear anything above the noise of the engine. His body jostled as the truck bumped and sped over the dirt roads. He stared at the landscape and couldn't make out individual stalks of wheat, seeing only a field of tan schmeared against a still blue sky. He turned to his uncles and cousins, but they weren't blurry. He never knew air could be so loud, the rush of it against his ears drowning out all other sounds. Szulim had never moved so fast in his life.

They rode with a dozen soldiers whose gestures could be understood in any language – offering bread, patting the seats, holding their hands with their palms up to heaven as they tilted their heads down. No one could speak above the noise of the motor and the wind, but Szulim could tell they were trying to make his family as comfortable as possible. He could see in their faces both happiness and something else. Concern, disbelief, awe. Like the way Pop looked when he did bankes long ago, or the face on the rabbi when he pulled the Torah out of the ark, his mother's eyes that time she held a friend's newborn in the store. These soldiers wore smiles, but their eyes didn't match their mouths. From the way the soldiers looked at him and his family, from their kindness, Szulim couldn't believe they were not Jews like him.

As they bumped and raced through the countryside, Szulim thought how they had survived every step of the way based on miracles. That they hid in the attic during the fall and not summer. That they lived for a year in such close quarters with a tuberculoid, yet no one else had gotten sick. Being discovered by bandits who were stupid enough to leave, thinking they'd wait until night for their return. The fact that they wandered six weeks through the fields when the weather was warm. The farmer not harvesting the rye where they hid. And the fact that, while in hiding, Szulim learned a language that would become their salvation.

The biggest miracle, however, was what they found waiting for them in Zelechow.

Telling: Summer 2009

I'VE BEEN ANXIOUS to speak to Sal again. It's not that I doubt his story, but there's one aspect that has been gnawing at me.

"How do you remember all these dates?" I ask. "It was so long ago. You had nothing on you, it's not like people had BlackBerrys back then. How did you keep track of the number of days you were in the attic? Or when the bandits discovered you?"

Sandy listens in and realizes it's something she, too, has wondered. This happens a lot, apparently, me giving voice to a lifetime of her unknowns.

"This is so hard for people to understand now, this marking of time." Sal shifts in his chair to get comfortable. "You see, the life of a religious Jew revolves around the rising and setting sun, the orbit of the Earth. It is an obsession, this keeping track of the days and seasons, essential to Jewish life. Every Friday night we welcomed the Sabbath; the Torah was our timekeeper as we lived from one observance to the next."

"Interesting." I think for a moment. "This may sound crazy, but I liken it to women keeping track of their monthly cycle. It's innate."

"I had never thought of that, but you're exactly right." Sal looks at the clock on the den wall and thinks about the fact that he had never seen a Gregorian calendar, or even a date written down, until he was a teenager. "Did you know I volunteer at a health clinic? It's part of Tampa General Hospital. I go every Tuesday and Friday morning and sit in the office and wait. They serve a lot of people from Latin America, so if someone comes in who only speaks Spanish, I go with that patient into the exam room and translate."

I wonder how Sal would know Spanish, but then realize he'd lived and worked in Miami almost his whole life.

"In any case, women come in, pregnant women, who may not know which of their suitors fathered their child, yet they know when was their last period. No date books or those little computers with calendars or anything. And I've always been amazed. How do they know? Would I ever remember something like that? But I think you're right. It's something deep inside. Like the religious Jew."

"So that's how you knew."

"Well, I myself was too young to have fully developed that sense of time. Only three things did I focus on – hunger, boredom and fear. But my mother, father, Uncle Moshe Boruchowicz – especially Uncle Moshe – they focused on time. Uncle Moshe must have been the official 'timekeeper.' He marked every holiday or celebration in his little black book. Not that we celebrated. But he made note of it in order to know where we were in time."

"I had wondered if someone had drawn on the walls, like you see in cartoons of prisoners."

Sal laughs. "No, though for sure it felt like prison. You think people in prison keep a calendar to know how much time they've spent locked up, but it's really a question of knowing where you are and what you did during that time. My uncle recorded how long we suffered, how long we survived."

I think about how few of the Jewish holidays my family and I celebrate, how few most American Jews even know about. From some of my research on a website that converts the Gregorian calendar to the Hebrew calendar going back hundreds of years, I see just how many days of ritual there really are.

"So, when I tell you that we hid in that pit for as long as we did, that twice we went for four days without food and water or an emptying of the waste buckets, that everything changed on the 24th of Sivan," Sal says, "I tell you the truth. I know exactly when the war broke out, when it ended. It is how I know still when to say Kaddish and for whom."

I'm amazed. The Jewish calendar, like the moon of those women in the clinic, lies deep.

"Sal, I have another question. I feel a little ridiculous for asking…"

"It's okay. Ask anything."

"There were married couples in the cellar, teenagers." I'm not sure how to pose this question. After all, who wants to imagine their parents having sex? "I know you were little, but were there any intimacies? I think about Anne Frank, and how she had that crush on Peter."

Sal surprises me with his response. "I've thought about this a lot, this question of intimacy. Not at the time, of course. What did I know? But later, as a young man. There was Hinda and her fiancée, Malka and my older cousins. But looking back on it, I have to say physical contact would have been impossible. Whatever was going on in each of their minds or bodies was theirs alone. There was nothing they could do. In Anne Frank's situation, they had some degree of privacy, movement. For us, it was all one small area."

I try to imagine young people with their rush of hormones, stuck with no release. A group of Jews trying to uphold the customs of modesty as they are forced to pee in a bucket practically in full view of everyone else. It is so hard to fathom.

"I'll tell you," Sal continues, "Liebl Popowska and Herschel Winograd weren't just out seeking cigarettes in the night. There are some things even poverty and hunger can't dampen."

RETURNING

Zelechow

Summer 1944

It seemed to Szulim that no time had passed between climbing on the truck and nearing Zelechow, but in actuality, the trip took over two hours. As they rolled into the shtetl, no longer a shtetl now that it housed only gentiles, Szulim noticed the burned-down buildings. The shul, once the grandest building in town, stood like a skeleton.

"Who made these changes?" Szulim asked. He climbed onto his knees and stared at the once familiar streets, wondering what else was missing. The truck pulled up to his house. Across the road where his parents store had been was now an empty lot. They got off the army transport and stood on the front steps of what used to be home; it looked the same. Everyone waited while Szulim's father knocked on the door. That had become his job, knocking on doors. Szulim thought it strange that they couldn't just walk right in, but he had heard the grown ups talking long ago in the cellar about the Germans, how they sold all the Jewish homes to the goyim for practically nothing.

They waited while Pop knocked again. Chances were good that whoever lived there now was out working in the fields. Finally, the door opened. Szulim saw Mietek, the Shabbos Goy standing in their doorway. Had he still been coming to their house every Friday night and Saturday? Mietek scratched his head while Pop talked to him. Finally, Mietek opened the door wider and stood to the side.

"Mr. Wajnberg, Mrs. Wajnberg," Mietek said. "I can't believe it's you."

"I suppose we don't look like you remembered," Szulim's father said. Before they had gone into hiding two years before, Szulim's mother weighed 100 kilograms. She stood now at only 36 kilos. Ten barefoot and emaciated people in torn clothes, skin swollen and burnt, gathered in the front room of a house where for years they had taken so much for granted.

"I don't know how, but I had a feeling you'd be back," Mietek said. "I bought this place, but didn't pay much. This is your home. Give me a few moments to gather my things."

Szulim watched Mietek walk through the house, collecting his personal items. The Shabbos Goy was the only gentile Szulim knew of who could speak Yiddish, having grown up and worked in a Jewish environment. Even though Jews paid decent wages, many gentiles refused to work for them. Or, if they had to, they did so with misgivings and opposition. Mietek was different. He never did his job with remorse or resentment, and instead showed a tolerance that was unusual among the Polish.

"Mr. Wajnberg!" Mietek called from the kitchen. "I have a present for you."

Mietek dragged a chair into the middle of the room, stood on it, and slid open a panel in the ceiling. Szulim remembered his mother and Havah pulling down the boxes of *pesachdike* or Passover dishes from the kitchen ceiling every spring, and storing their everyday plates up there during the week in which bread was forbidden.

"When they burned your synagogue, I saved this." Mietek pulled down the Torah, the holy scroll that Jews around the world read every Saturday, as precious as a human life. Szulim's father's arms shook as he reached out to accept the ancient text. It was as if he were receiving a newborn. For the first time in months, Szulim saw Pop's smile go up the sides of his face.

"All this time, I thought there'd be nothing left," Feter Moshe Boruchowicz said. "I thought Hitler wiped out our entire tradition."

Moshe touched his siddur to the Torah and then pressed it to his lips. He squeezed his handmade prayer book with both hands and raised it above his head. With eyes closed he began whispering *Baruch atah Adonai,* blessed are you oh Lord our God. The rest of the men joined in, raising their voices and singing out loud the final words of the prayer that celebrates special occasions. *She'hecheyanu, v'kiy'manu, v'hig'yanu, lazman hazeh!* Szulim thought they would break out in dance.

NO SOONER HAD Mietek left than a collective sigh echoed through the group. "I'm not feeling well," said Szulim's father. "Let me lie down." He limped into the bedroom while everyone else sat in chairs, marveling at the furniture, though Szulim noticed they weren't the same pieces he had remembered. In fact, he was surprised at how empty his house had become. He knew that the Germans had looted. He had cowered in the attic two years before and heard not just the liquidation of people, but of belongings. Yet he didn't think anyone would take his bed or his toys. The stove remained, and the heater. But the table now sitting in the dining room was not the same mahogany table he had eaten at for the first six years of his life. This one was not nearly as nice. The walls were bare, the rooms empty, save for a few cots to sleep on. Still, it was home. They were home.

———

FROM THE KITCHEN, Szulim could hear the doctor speaking with his father in the bedroom as his mother stood quietly next to her husband. They were lucky that the Polish doctor had come to Zelechow that day, only two days after they arrived home. His father was in bad shape, running a fever and barely able to walk.

"It's gangrenous. I have to amputate."

"When?"

"Now. I won't be back here for another two weeks and that might be too late."

Szulim could barely hear his father's reply over his mother's weeping. "No. I've lost too much already. Not my leg, too."

Szulim waited until his mother saw the doctor out of the house before he began asking questions. "What is gangrenous? What is amputate?"

"Don't worry, Szulimeleh." His mother patted the top of his head without looking at his face. "Pop won't let them cut off his leg."

THE CHILDREN DIDN'T want to wait until Thursday for a bath. Szulim's father could do nothing but grow weaker in bed and his mother was too busy tending to him and trying to get the house back in order, so Sara, Szulim and Abraham dragged the wooden tub from the patio into the kitchen. They filled it with water as they remembered Havah doing, warming a large kettle on the stove and adjusting the temperature.

"Who goes first?" Szulim asked. "The boys or the ... girl." He looked down as his voice trailed off. The room filled with silence. "You go," whispered Sara as she walked out of the kitchen. She would bathe alone.

Szulim stared at the tub and felt like a chair with one of its legs missing. Though he had turned in the rye, silently looking for Rivka, no one had talked about her death while they wandered through the fields. They were too busy searching for food, trying to survive. But now that they were home, the impact came with a force.

AS HE WORKED alongside his mother – washing the few plates that remained, sweeping the floors, stacking wood for the stove – he'd ask, "Why did she have to die?"

"Why did anyone have to die?" his mother said, her eyes pooling. "Rivka, Tertza,

Gitel, Foigel, Sara, Berl..."

His parents and uncles spoke often of how different it would be if his sister, aunts and cousins had not been killed. No death in particular stood out as more tragic; it was a total family loss. Szulim could hear his parents weeping, could see the stains on their cheeks from tears too plentiful to brush away. But still, they were able to talk about Rivka and the rest. Szulim knew, however, that he couldn't talk about his dead sister with the sister that remained. Sara's tears, once they came, could not stop.

Szulim stood on the front stoop of his house and looked up and down the streets of Zelechow. It seemed so empty, save for the thousand or so gentiles who lived here now. As weeks wore on, more people began straggling through the town in torn and filthy clothes, with dirt-streaked and sunken faces. Those who returned to nearby ravaged villages after coming out of hiding would ask, "Where are the Jews?" The answer was always Zelechow; and so they came.

IT WAS THE voices that Szulim noticed first; his own voice. Speaking didn't itch his throat anymore; the sound could come from all the way down in his stomach. He and his family still spoke softly, but their words, once raspy and dry, now carried a melody, like honey rather than matzah. They didn't need to whisper; it was okay to be heard.

Szulim looked through the windows at the sunshine beckoning. The longing to go outside always came before the realization that now he could, in fact, just walk out the door. *Why am I standing here?* he'd think to himself. As his mother lit the Shabbos candles on Friday nights, Szulim would glance at the open curtains in panic until he remembered that the flames flickering against the night sky would pose no danger. He wasn't hiding anymore. They were free.

As he hesitated before opening the front door late one morning, a familiar smell wafted from the kitchen. Ginger and pepper tickled Szulim's nose, and his stomach began to growl in anticipation of his mother's gefilte fish. Szulim wasn't the only one to notice. Russian soldiers who happened to be strolling in front of his house smelled the beets boiling on the stove.

"Your mother making borscht?" one of the Russians asked Szulim as he stood on his front step. Szulim nodded.

"Think she'll sell us some?"

And so it began that the front room, which had served as a kindergarten during the time of the ghetto, became a restaurant. Szulim's mother and sister prepared meals and Szulim served the Russian army, conversing in the language he had learned from Tomaitey.

"Such a little boy working so hard," the officers said. "Where is your father?"

"He's unwell." Szulim found himself telling the soldiers in as brief a manner as possible how they survived. One soldier asked what was wrong with his father so Szulim tried to translate into Russian what he had overheard the Polish doctor saying the week before. "His leg is sick."

"Can you show me to him?" the Russian asked.

Szulim led him through the living room and into his parents' bedroom where his father lay pale and moaning in the bed.

"I'm a doctor," the soldier said.

Szulim translated. "Pop, this man wants to help."

"Does he want to chop off my leg, too?"

"No," said the doctor, who happened to be Jewish and understood Yiddish, though he, like all the other soldiers, spoke only Russian. "I can't let a man who saved his family walk around without a leg." He turned to Szulim. "Tell your dad that if he wants to live, he'll need to come with me to the hospital."

This soldier, Szulim and his family soon learned, was the chief of staff at the hospital that had been taken over by the Russian army. He set up Szulim's father in a bed there and stayed with him for three or four days, watching over the administration of medicine and care.

Another miracle Szulim thought. He knew the Russians doctors would make his father well. Russians had saved Szulim from boredom, saved his family from starvation and death. Surely they could save something as simple as a leg.

———

AT THE AGE of eight, Szulim became the man of the house. There was no childhood for he and his siblings to slip back into. Only chores and responsibilities, a life to rebuild. On market days, he went to the center of town and bought matches and cigarettes in packs of ten. "Look! Real smokes!" Szulim would open up a pack, take out one of the white sticks and light it to show a potential buyer that the tobacco was good. It wasn't hard; he had seen the Popowska's do it often enough. He sold the cigarettes individually for a profit.

The streets of Zelechow looked the same to Szulim; only they were no longer his playground. Not that there were any other children to play with. Out of the 15,000 Jews who had called Zelechow home in the fall of 1942, only 250 remained. Of those, only 53 were originally from Zelechow. And only three of those remaining Jews were children – Szulim, Sara and Abraham. The ice cream store was gone; Mrs. Szapiro had been killed. Though now that his family needed every coin they could get, Szulim wouldn't have spent his hard-earned money on ice cream anyhow. He learned to pass his time walking through the black market and seeing the strange objects people were trying to get rid of – curios dug up from cellars, valuables that had likely been stolen.

"What's that?" Szulim pointed to a large silver barrel the size of a tub. It had a lid with a tube attached to some sort of nozzle.

The seller laughed. "Beer. Don't know it will do you any good."

Szulim knew it would do his family a tremendous amount of good. The Russian soldiers liked to drink but didn't have any more of their vodka. He overheard them talking about *bimber*, some contraband liquor made of raw beets. They spat at the mention of the stuff, but spoke often of it all the same.

Szulim shrugged his shoulders. "How much?"

"Ten zlotys."

Szulim turned away, scanning the other stalls. He began counting in his head.

"Okay," the seller said. "Eight zlotys."

"I've got five." Szulim handed over the coins and scanned the market for a *treger* but there was no one he could pay to help him carry it home. The merchant tipped the barrel onto its side; Szulim crouched low and threw his weight, less than half as much as the barrel itself, into the keg and began rolling it through the streets of Zelechow.

Szulim stood in front of his house with the upended barrel and scratched his head wondering how he would get it up the few steps and into the door. He peeked inside and saw that Russians had already begun gathering in the front room. He signaled to them.

"What you got there?"

"I think it's a barrel of beer."

The soldiers scrambled over each other, fighting to help drag the keg inside the house. His father wasn't there to help him get the beer out. He held the hose and tapped the nozzle, wondering if there was a faucet.

"Here, let me start it for you," said one of the Russians.

Szulim didn't trust him not to take any without paying. "No, you tell me what to do and I'll do it."

The soldier laughed and held his hands up. "Okay! Just put the tube in your mouth and suck on it like a straw. You have to suck hard to get all the air out."

Szulim thought that was easy enough. He bent down, exhaled deeply and put the rubber hose in his mouth. He inhaled as much as he could and almost choked as his mouth filled with liquid. It tasted the way the wheat smelled when he and Abraham peed in the fields. He swallowed it in three gulps and couldn't believe these Russians were going to pay money for the stuff.

A few moments passed before it hit him. He felt dizzy, and ran out to the patio to throw up in the dirt. The air in front of his face filled with gray dots and he stumbled back into the front room to warn the Russians. "Don't drink it! It's poisonous!"

The soldiers laughed as Szulim covered his mouth and darted for the front door. He came back in, wiping his cheek with the back of his hand, reaching for the walls which had begun to spin. He laid down on the sofa in the living room moaning. His mother came out of the kitchen and felt his forehead. "Bubbeleh, what's wrong?"

"I think your boy is drunk," said a soldier who knelt beside Szulim. The soldier saw that Perl didn't understand him but motioned holding a cup to his mouth. He turned to Sara who came out of the kitchen after her mother and said, "Water?" Sara ran to get a glass.

Szulim opened his eyes, hoping it would make the spinning go away. He saw a soldier sitting next to him. It seemed there were many stars on his shirt, but Szulim couldn't keep them in a straight line. "Am I going to die?" he asked the Russian.

"No. You just took in some beer. A small boy like you, no meat on your bones." The soldier wiped Szulim's forehead with a napkin and held the glass of water to his lips. "Just keep drinking water."

He turned to Sara and asked for garlic, salt, bay leaves and some cucumber. Szulim thought he would throw up again as he watched the Russian mash everything up in a glass and pour water over it. "Drink this, my boy. Won't taste so good, but it should help." He looked back at his comrades who stared at Szulim with both sympathy and amusement. "Trust me. I know."

Szulim sat up with the help of the officer and sipped at the concoction. *How could I be so stupid?* he thought. "Just rest. And keep drinking water." The soldier put his hat back on, nodded to Szulim's mother and left with the other Russians.

Szulim's mother put a bucket on the floor next to his head and continued to bring him water. Abraham had been collecting wood for the stove during the commotion, but now knelt at his brother's side, staring at him with an intensity, as if through the sheer power of vision, he could make Szulim well. It was almost dinnertime before Szulim could stand. With Abraham's help, he brought his bucket to the outhouse and dumped the contents into the hole. He was relieved to be back on his feet and felt ashamed at making such a fuss. A real man, his father, would never have been so foolish. Szulim knew then that he would never let himself get drunk ever again, no matter how long he lived.

———

"YITZHAK!" SZULIM'S MOTHER wiped her hands on her apron and ran to greet the cousin who had shown up in the middle of the night two years before with his unbelievble account of the trains and camps. Once again, he appeared in their living room, this time bringing stories of survival. "Oy gutunyu, it's you!"

"I'm here. And you?"

"Rivka, my sisters…" Szulim's mother turned away, lowering her face into her hands. After a few moments, she looked up and said, "Chaim's in the hospital, he's been there for weeks now. He seems to be healing, but he won't eat any meat. 'Not kosher' he tells me. The man hasn't had a single piece of meat in two years and because there's no shochet, he won't eat something to help him get better."

"I'm a shochet."

"Since when are you a shochet?" Szulim's mother asked.

"Since now. I know the prayers. I'll go tell him."

THE MEAT MUST have worked because after spending six weeks in the Russian hospital, Szulim's father walked home – on two legs. Szulim still had to keep up with the household responsibilities until Pop regained his strength. He thought Pop would be proud of him, how he had done such a good job becoming the man of the house. But Szulim could see disappointment in his father's eyes. He gathered the courage one day to ask, "Pop, are you angry at me?"

"No, Szulim. Look at you, a little man! I'm angry at myself. God brought us out of the pit, my family is working to the bone, and what am I doing?" He waved his hand in front of his face. "Ach, this is the worst, just sitting here watching."

———

YEARS BEFORE, WHEN Zelechow became a ghetto, dinner conversation centered around who moved into Zelechow and who moved out; charting the relocation of friends and neighbors, distant villagers. Keeping track of who was living where, and with whom. Now, the talk seemed empty; the silence punctuated by recollections as Szulim's parents spoke of what used to be. Now they only reminisced.

"Remember the Nachman's?" Pop asked shaking his head.

"I wonder where Leah and Joisef are." Mama looked down into her soup and sighed. "We used to meet them often, for a *glezl tay*." There were so many they had met for a glass of tea; too many they'd never meet again.

The language that once flowed freely through streets, between houses and in the center of the town, was rarely spoken. Szulim's family longed to hear Yiddish from people other than themselves. Sometimes, when Szulim wandered around outside, he'd stop. Closing his eyes, he'd stretch out his neck and listen closely, straining to hear what he thought was the laughter of children. It was only the wind blowing through trees. How badly he wanted another child to play with, another person his age to talk to, aside from his brother and sister. He'd stand in the marketplace and imagine the pitter-patter of small feet running across cobblestones, small feet wearing shoes that he would never again take for granted.

The joy of surviving was dampened by the realization that very few others were as lucky.

When the shofar sounded for Rosh Hashanah that fall, he and his family, and the handful that remained, saw in the emptiness what Hitler had done. There was no one to call to prayer. It didn't matter that their dining room table, the one that opened up to seat 20, had been stolen. This year, only half the seats would be filled. Szulim's mother bought three roosters the week before Yom Kippur. Three roosters, but two hens.

Fall 1944

"It's time." Szulim's father looked at his wife. "My leg is healed, I can make the trip. Besides, it'll be easier to dig before the ground freezes."

Szulim's father and the feters hired a horse and driver and set out for Mr. Sokol's farm, along with a handful of other men. They could have walked the 11 or 12 kilometers, but they needed the buggy to bring back the bodies. It might have only required the strength of two or three men to dig up the remains of Szulim's aunts, cousins, his sister and the fallen Popowska's, but it would have been dangerous going to a remote area populated only by goyim. Even several months after liberation, they knew there was only safety in numbers.

"The tiger never changes its stripes," Szulim's father said.

It took several trips to bring back all of the remains, not so much because of the time spent digging, but in trying to locate all of the bodies. Szulim's father had been in charge of burying Rivka and Mimeh Tertza, Liebl and Herschel Winograd. But he hadn't buried the others — Mimehs Sara, Foigel, Gitel and Berleh. Mimeh Laicha and cousin Sara. Chaim tried to remember where Mr. Sokol had pointed only months before when they were discovered, indicating where he, the farmer, had buried Mr. Popowska and perhaps the rest. But Mr. Sokol had been killed soon after they left his farm; only Mrs. Sokol remained to help locate the graves. Though she never said as much, Szulim's father could tell she was happy to get the Jewish bodies off of her property.

Szulim had never been to a funeral before. As they walked towards the cemetery in Zelechow, he grabbed his mother's skirt. Szulim — a child who sold cigarettes in the marketplace, who took over as the man of the house when Pop was sick — became a little boy once again. He had already seen the gravestones upended and desecrated from outside the gates; he wasn't anxious to get any closer. What had once been a peaceful resting place and a haven for refugees now looked like a war zone where a battle ensued between people who hate and the souls who were hated. He held tight to Abraham, squeezing his hand as he tried to squeeze back the tears. But still, they flowed.

V'Yitgadal, V'Yitkadash Sh'mei Rabah The funeral taking place months, even years after the fact was the first time Szulim's father and uncles could say the mourners' kaddish for their children and wives, their sisters and in-laws. Jewish law required a minyan or group of ten religious men to recite the prayer, and now, finally, there were enough Chossid men to make an attempt at closure. All this time they had been a family in mourning who either had no time or no ability to properly mourn. Szulim thought to himself *What if only five or seven Jewish men, in all of Poland, had survived this war? Who would say the prayer for the dead then?*

Szulim, Abraham, Sara and their mother stood quietly and cried. The men spoke of their loved ones with a pain as if they had just departed. "So young. How much more would have lay ahead." Words swallowed by wails. "I loved them so much." Szulim thought about his sister but shook his head against the images. All he could see when he closed his eyes were Rivka's own, staring blankly. Her arm that had been chewed on by a dog. He tried to remember her alive, before the cellar, before the nightmare of ghetto life took hold. But a picture would not form in his mind. Szulim had already seen his father sob, and certainly his mother. But on that day, the tears flowed once again. Tears for his sister and aunts, for friends, cousins and neighbors. Tears for the millions they had not yet accounted for.

———

SZULIM'S FATHER REMEMBERED how Mrs. Sokol insisted no one could get full on noodles. It had come up in conversation during one of the rare occasions when he sat in the small living room of the farm house on a winter afternoon, talking with the farmer and his wife, trying to obtain what little information existed about the war. So when he had traveled to Wilcziska to collect the bodies, Chaim invited Mrs. Sokol to come for dinner the next time she was in Zelechow on market day. He wanted to feed her a mountain of noodles so she could see that indeed, one could be satisfied from a good noodle soup. He and Perl felt it was the least they could do. Szulim sat at the table staring at Mrs. Sokol's hands; they trembled as she brought a spoon to her lips. Was she nervous or afflicted? Her face seemed to belong to a woman much older than her years; a life of labor, and a recent past of worry and loss, having taken its toll. Over dinner, she told them about the Popowska's and the Germans. About Mr. Sokol being murdered, even though he said he had no idea the women were hiding in his hayloft. Szulim looked down into his soup; he felt guilty about it all.

AFTER LIBERATION, GATHERING places appeared in every Jewish community where survivors came to search for their loved ones. Szulim's house became that center in Zelechow. Tacked to the wall were lists of those still missing, those who survived. Individuals seeking someone, anyone, they could claim as family came to the Wajnberg house to register their name and whereabouts. Scraps of newspaper, torn grocery sacks, pieces of paper that had been wrapped around food – all were scribbled on and pinned up in the living room. Some notes were brief, "I'm here. My parents' names were Nosen and Chane." Some detailed epic stories of survival. Everyday, people came to scan the wall, looking for a new name, a tidbit of information, a morsel of hope. Some came every hour.

"Perl, how did you survive? And with kids, yet?" The same questions crossed everyone's lips and Szulim's mother never failed to give their account. And since there was no school, Abraham sat at her side, helping in small ways with all of the chores, taking in his mother's recollections so that he could no longer distinguish between her memories and his own. Mama couldn't get enough, Szulim thought, of telling and retelling their tale. Of hearing about others and how they dug caves in the woods, how Germans and Ukrainians and partisan groups were afraid to go into these woods because of refugees hiding with weapons. Szulim was too busy working to pay much attention. Besides, even though the Germans still fought in distant parts of Poland, as far as Szulim was concerned, the war was over.

"WHAT'S THE MATTER with Sara?" Szulim found the courage to ask his mother. The funeral had passed, they had been home for months, but still, Sara did not speak. She barely looked at her brothers.

"She's still hurting over Rivka," his mother said.

"When will it stop?"

"When the time comes, bubbeleh."

Szulim wondered if the time would ever come.

January 9, 1945

Very often, Szulim's parents had asked the soldiers dining in their restaurant about the Russian who had hid with them in the cellar. "Do you know a Tomaitey Tapielkin Voroshilow? Can you tell us about him? Is he alive?"

One officer had recalled Tomaitey's father, a general. Another mentioned that Tomaitey had joined a different outfit before rejoining his own.

"If you should meet with him," Szulim translated for his mother, "please tell him that the Wajnberg family sends their best regards."

"Platitudes," Szulim's father had said after the officer had left. No one could provide any tidings that would either bring joy or sadness. Later, they'd learn that the Russian army had been trained not to divulge any personal information about a fellow soldier for fear of what the enemy might learn.

One thing was for certain, Szulim's family had been happy to have the Russians around. Not only did they provide an income, their presence in the town kept the anti-Semitic rumblings at bay. But when the winds of Kislev began blowing cold throughout Zelechow, and Szulim's mother fried potato latkes for Chanukah, the Russians began their march west towards the front. Though the Nazis had been defeated in the area surrounding Zelechow, Hitler's army was still waging war closer to the German border. And less than a month after the final candle had been lit, the Russians had gone entirely, leaving the Jews of Zelechow vulnerable to the hatred that had been building around them.

Szulim pulled his coat tight around his thin body and followed his father to the marketplace. Now that the Russians were gone, he didn't have so many responsibilities. The family's restaurant had closed since no one was left to pay for a meal. None of the other Jews had enough money to go out for lunch or dinner, and no gentile would eat in a Jewish home – except for Mrs. Sokol, but she had been a guest.

Now, with no income, Szulim's father was looking to make a *parnose*, earn a living. So on Tuesdays he went to the marketplace to see what he might be able to pick up and then sell for a higher price. Szulim waited until his father wrapped up the tfillen after his morning prayers and together they walked the few blocks into town.

"Funny, seems empty, no?" Szulim's father stood on the perimeter of the square and scanned the plaza. The sun had just finished rising. Szulim stood close to his father as they wandered among the merchants, seeing what was for sale. Szulim was old enough now to notice the looks on the goyim's faces. As if their eyes could say words their mouths wouldn't. *This zsyd is trying to take advantage of me.* There had never been violence, thanks to the Russians, but the feeling was palpable. Icy, the stares and the temperature both.

From a distance, Szulim heard a rumbling, like a samochod. Only he'd never heard a samochod chant. Then all of a sudden, they saw. Farmers, dozens of them clutching guns, axes, sickles and pitchforks, swarmed into the plaza yelling, "What Hitler couldn't do, we will!"

Szulim froze but Pop grabbed him by the arm and screamed, "Run!" Szulim wondered how his father could move so fast with his bad leg. He noticed other Jews running as well, fleeing in all directions. Some ran towards the building in the center of the square, others, like he and Pop, scrambled through the streets of town. He willed his legs to keep up with his father's as the farmers' voices chased him, each word of their song pounding against the cobblestones. *Let's! Finish! Hitler's! Job!*

Their house had always seemed just around the corner from the marketplace, but today it felt like they were running many kilometers away. Szulim was afraid to turn around, concentrating instead on taking as wide a stride as he could without falling over, the way he imagined horses might run through fields if they had men with flames chasing after them. He wanted to shut his ears against the screams of those captured, the rabid threats of the men with pitchforks. But he couldn't. Their murderous mantra pounded in his chest, along with his racing heart.

Finally, they reached home. Without slowing down, they flung open the door and ran inside, slamming it behind them and leaning against it. Szulim could barely catch his breath. He was relieved Abraham had stayed home with Sara and his mother. Szulim doubted that his younger brother, barely seven years old, could have kept up. "Do not," Pop panted, his chin stretching out from his neck in a circular motion, "leave this house. Understood?"

They sat, just looking at each other and wondering if the pitchforks and axes would swing at their door. Luckily, the farmers didn't know which of the homes in Zelechow belonged to the few remaining Jews. The *mezzuzot* had been ripped off the doorposts and melted down over two years before, and those who returned to Zelechow after liberation could not replace the silver containers that held tiny scrolls inscribed with the most holy of prayers. No scribes were left to write the *Shema*, or bless the piece of parchment.

Szulim's parents went into the other room to speak, and before long the screaming and shooting and wicked chanting disappeared as the residents of Zelechow, the gentiles anyway, went back about their business. Szulim could hear horse drawn carts rolling down the street and out of town. Pop pulled the curtains aside and peeked out the window. "I'll be back," Pop said, giving an extra hug to the kids and his wife. His parents exchanged a look and Mama began pulling things out of the cabinet in the kitchen.

"Kids, gather your clothes."

Szulim thought back to the last time Mama packed up their belongings. He held his album, running his fingers gently along the clear pages in which he had carefully placed the stamps from the Russians. Every time the soldiers had gotten an envelope from home, they tore the stamp from the corner and gave it to Szulim. He had amassed quite a collection. It was the only thing he owned – his pen knife and chess set lying in some rye field, his toys from before stolen for non-Jewish children. He put it in his sack with a sweater, some socks and underwear. This time, he wouldn't leave anything behind.

EVERYONE WAS RELIEVED to hear the front door open and see Szulim's father walk into the room. "Oh, thanks God!" his mother said. She grabbed her husband's hands. "How bad?"

"Nine dead." Mama gasped as he continued. "Thirty-six injured. All those people who ran to the building in the center of the plaza."

Szulim's father walked into his bedroom and returned with a small suitcase. "That's it for Poland. These people are Jew-haters and will be for the rest of their lives. We're going to Lodz, and from there, Palestine."

The horse and buggy driver Pop had hired would be along in just a few minutes, which is all it took to gather up the rest of their belongings; barely six months had passed since they had been home. No, not home. Zelechow, the place where Szulim was born, the only place he had ever known what it was to be a child, where his sister now lay buried, was not someplace he could let his breath out and live. He had no home.

AS DUSK BEGAN to settle over the now empty streets of Zelechow, Szulim and his family climbed into a wagon, a large basket really, set atop two axles with wheels. "Hitler didn't defeat us," his father said tossing the last bundle over the side before hoisting himself up onto the cart. "Neither will these stupid Polacks." Szulim glanced at the stupid Polack sitting on the wood plank at the edge of the wagon, raised up near the horses' rears. He must have been happy to make some money in the dead of winter, even if it came from a Jew. Otherwise he'd go back to his barn and sleep with his animals. *Does he care*, Szulim wondered, *if the horses poop on his shoe while he drives?*

Szulim was thankful to be wearing most of the clothes he owned. Once again, the faces of his family grew red on their journey, this time, though, from the wind and cold that bit at them as they chased the last bit of sun creeping down towards the horizon. They hoped to put as much distance as possible between themselves and Zelechow before stopping for the night. It wasn't easy passing the food Mama had packed for their journey. Bumping along the dirt road that snaked west between farms and villages, their arms flopped like noodles as they reached across the wagon to grab hold of potatoes or cheese.

Szulim hunched in his coat, pressing against Abraham and Sara in an effort to keep warm. No one could speak above the sound of the wind rushing past, the clop clop of the horse's hooves, the creaking of wheels laboring along the frozen and cracked earth. Szulim held his pointer and middle fingers to his mouth, inhaling and exhaling, pretending to smoke a cigarette. Abraham giggled as he and Sara smoked, too, flicking their wrists back and forth. They were tired, but it was impossible to sleep sitting on the cold, hard wood floor of the wagon, their backs leaning against the sides. Every once in a while, one of them would move a package and use it as a chair until the horse hit a particularly big bump and they fell off. Szulim's tuchas was sore and he had to pee, but Pop was too scared to stop.

Once again, they were on the run. But this time felt different to Szulim. For one thing, he wasn't hungry. Mama had made borscht and sandwiches, a little cake. And though they were fleeing, they all knew that what they were leaving behind was something painful, not cherished. And traveling now in the cold and dark of night, they were heading towards a better life.

"You'll go to school," Pop told the kids. "You'll have friends." He spoke of the Jewish community that was not only forming in Lodz, but thriving. Szulim was eager to get his boyhood back, and though he would never say it aloud, was thankful that the pogrom had occurred because it forced his family to leave. These past six months in Zelechow, while certainly better than life underground, only served to remind him of everything he had lost. Szulim hunched against the cold, his back and tuchas getting banged up by the minute, but felt happiness at what he could only imagine might await them all. The way his father went on and on, it felt like an adventure.

Until they stopped for the night.

It would take nearly three days to get from Zelechow to Lodz, but Szulim's father wanted to travel through the night when they first set out. It wasn't until they had been on the road for 24 hours and the second night began to fall that the driver pulled up to a farmhouse and Szulim's father got out to knock on the door.

"Whose house is this, Pop?" Szulim asked.

"Long ago, an oirech told me about a farmer in Chodnow. Said he was a real mensch."

Whether the man was a mensch, or eager to accept the money Szulim's father handed him, no one knew, but he agreed to open his door to the Wajnberg family. Now that the Germans were gone, he could offer Jews a place to rest without fearing for his life or property.

"We'll be leaving very early," Pop said as he helped his wife and children down from the wagon. "Just leave everything out here."

The driver unhitched the horses and walked them to the stable where he'd sleep among the animals while Szulim and his family shared a bed inside the house. Grateful for something soft and warm, they fell asleep quickly.

SZULIM WOKE TO the shots of a gun. "'Stay inside!" Szulim's father shouted as he jumped out of bed and ran into the pitch dark.

Psha cref do cholery! Psha cref do cholery! Szulim could hear the buggy driver yelling over and over into the night at the bandits who had ransacked the wagon and run off with everything Szulim's family owned. "Curse the dog to a cholera!"

"It's gone. All of it." Szulim's father came back into the room and sunk onto the bed. "Veyismere. We have nothing."

"Chaim, do you think they were following us?"

"Ach, Perl. I don't know. Who goes through a buggy in the middle of nowhere, in the middle of the night?"

Szulim immediately thought about the stamp collection he had left in the wagon, gone now into the dark. He knew it would mean nothing to those stupid Polacks, but to him it was a treasure, the one relic of anything resembling a childhood. He also knew that he would never be able to collect stamps again. The thought of losing another set was unbearable.

Szulim's father turned to the dresser, on top of which lay the Torah their Shabbos Goy had saved from the burning shul and stored in the crawl space of their home. "Well, we have this." Szulim's father ran his hands along the velvet cover of the scroll. "Thank God I brought this into the house."

Once again, the Torah remained.

SURVIVING

Lodz, Poland

Winter 1945

As THE WAGON carrying Szulim's family — only the family now, and a Torah — rolled into the city of Lodz, Szulim couldn't believe his eyes. The road seemed to miraculously smooth out underneath the wheels of the buggy and the city glowed as night fell around them. Stars twinkled, not just in the sky but right in front of their faces, hovering over streets and dangling from buildings. "Those are streetlamps," his father said. Szulim's mouth hung open, as did Sara's and Abraham's. He closed it to swallow.

Streetlamps. He remembered his little cousin Berl, gone now two years, describing cities that shimmered at night with outdoor electric candles that didn't blow out in the wind or rain. Szulim had been fascinated by Berl's descriptions, gotten from books he had at home, never really believing that they could have been true. Szulim glanced left and right, taking in all of these streetlamps as they passed, too many to count. He had never seen anything more beautiful.

The wagon stopped in front of a building that rose all the way up to the sky. Szulim's gaze travelled up the walls, counting the layers of windows stacked in lines atop each other. Six rows. He nearly fell climbing down from the wagon; there was too much to look at. He followed his siblings and parents inside the building. Mama held Abraham's hand; Pop held the Torah. There was nothing else to carry.

"*Sholem, aleichem!*" Strangers approached, welcoming the Wajnbergs in Yiddish, though they themselves didn't look Jewish. Not the way Szulim's family looked Jewish. "Come, we have food." Szulim looked around the large room in which they now stood and saw people sitting on cots, laying on the floor. People like them with nothing but the clothes on their backs. From the way these other Jews appeared, like filthy skeletons, Szulim guessed that they had just been liberated.

He wondered if that's how he looked when he first arrived in Zelechow after wandering through the rye and wheat.

Two men came through the crowd carrying cots over their heads. They placed them down, three beds in a row. "You kids take them," Pop said. "Mama and I will sleep on the floor on either side of you." The people working at this collection center came back with soup. Szulim's father didn't eat it, not certain that it was kosher. Szulim was happy to lie down on something soft that didn't jostle his bones.

―――――

SZULIM WOKE UP the next morning, forgetting at first that he had arrived in Lodz the night before. Some cots were empty, others still held sleeping bodies. His parents were already awake. "Here, bubbeleh." His mother handed him some bread and margarine. "They gave us breakfast." Pop drank hot tea, while Sara, who had been awake, sipped at a cup of milk. "You kids will stay here for the day," his father said, "while Mama and I look for a place to live. These people will take care of you." He pointed to a group of workers, different than the night before, who were busy handing out food and papers.

A man and a woman played with Szulim, Sara and Abraham, offering pencils and paper to draw on, tying some string together to make cat's cradles. "Have any cards?" Szulim asked. The room began to empty, most of the temporary residents out looking for more permanent housing and work, so all the people who worked in the big building gathered around the children. Szulim thought their jobs must not be so important because they seemed so eager to play, staring at him and his siblings as if they had never seen children before. As he later learned, Jewish children were a rare sight those days.

Right after lunch, Szulim's parents returned. His father glided into the room, practically skipping. "Kids! Wait 'til you see our place!" He turned to the workers and explained how a Russian functionary kicked out some Nazi sympathizers who had been staying in this enormous apartment. And just like that, it would be theirs. He gently gathered up the Torah that had been resting on an empty cot and thanked the workers for their hospitality. Szulim waved goodbye as they walked out into the daylight.

THE ADDRESS WAS Mielczarskego 12. Szulim had never lived in a home with an address. He walked up a flight of steps and into a palace. So many bedrooms, one for everybody in the family if they wanted to sleep alone. The apartment was furnished from the previous residents, the kitchen fully stocked. His parents were too busy organizing and setting up the house to notice him sliding down the stair railing.

"Szulim! Abraham!" He could barely hear his mother calling from inside the enormous rooms. "I need your help!"

He had never seen such a spacious kitchen. He touched the stove that lit up simply by turning knobs and lighting a match. He couldn't imagine not having to collect wood every day. Lights appeared just by pressing a button on the wall. A large basin stood in the kitchen with a faucet. Szulim's father turned the handle and water streamed out. Where was the tank? Or the man carrying two buckets on a yoke? Szulim couldn't figure out where the water came from.

"You boys go out and find some rocks so we can kosherize these pots." If the apartment was any indication of the wonders that awaited them in this new land, Szulim couldn't wait to explore the outside. He taught Abraham how to slide down the railing and they wandered around the street looking for the right stones, like pebbles, only larger. There couldn't be any holes or bumps, the surface of the rocks had to be smooth. They walked back up the stairs, holding the bottoms of their shirts out in front of them with the stones nestled inside. Their mother filled the pots with stones and water from the sink, and then set them on the stove. As the water boiled, the stones would move around inside the pot and knock out any non-kosher residue. The cleansing process took an hour. She placed the glass dishes in the sink and filled them with water. Those would have to sit for three days. Szulim had no idea how Pop could tell which porcelain dishes should soak with the glass and which ones could not be used at all.

Pop found some rags, wet them and began cleaning out all of the cabinets, wiping down the counter tops. He had to get into every corner to make sure there were no traces of traif. Sara sat at the table carefully tearing some old newspaper they found to line the cabinets.

"Szulim!" Abraham came running into the kitchen. "Wait 'til you see the pot where we do our notznik! It doesn't move and there's a string. You pull it and water comes out of nowhere. The pee goes down a hole and disappears!"

Pop laughed. "Yes, I remember that from Warsaw."

Goosebumps dotted Szulim's arms. He couldn't believe they were still in Poland. For the next few days, before school started, Szulim and Abraham wandered Lodz, marveling at the paved paths next to the street made just for walking, trolleys, tiny rooms that moved up and down tall buildings. "You walk in and press a button, and off you go!" they told Sara. "You don't even have to walk up steps!" His body vibrated from the moment he woke up to the moment he fell asleep each night, every day discovering new miracles. He felt like he had entered an entirely different universe, one filled with magic. Was this their reward for everything they had suffered? He wished Rivka were here to see it all.

NEARLY A WEEK had passed since they first arrived in Lodz and Szulim had been eyeing the footed bathtub that stood next to the toilet. Now that Thursday had come, he and Abraham could try out the indoor plumbing. They stood in the bathroom naked, giggling as the water shot out of the faucet and into the enormous basin. What would have normally been a quick soak turned into an hour-long period of play. Szulim leaned into the water, stretching his arm across the surface and creating waves back and forth. "Boys, that's enough," Mama called from the other room, but they couldn't get enough. They didn't care that the water grew cold. Abraham held up his feet so Szulim could inspect the bottom of his toes. Szulim stared at the tips of his fingers. They reminded Szulim of his Zayde's hands, shriveled and wrinkly. He shivered as he rubbed his fingertips together thinking that his skin turned into that of a worm. He had never felt so clean.

ALMOST IMMEDIATELY, POP set up a bulletin board in the living room, and just as their home in Zelechow became the gathering place for Jews reconnecting with friends and loved ones, so did their apartment in Lodz. Szulim looked around the spacious rooms, amazed at how quickly they became filled with people. Feter Moshe Szyfman and Feter Symcha showed up one day soon after they arrived; Feter Moshe Boruchowicz and his sons Berl and Herschel came a few months later.

"Chaim!" Symcha stood at the wall reading the lists. He pointed at a newly tacked scrap of paper. "Mokobodski ... isn't that Mother's maiden name?" He took down the piece of paper and read the address. He turned and ran out the door.

Several hours later, Symcha returned with a woman also named Perl. Fair hair, fluent in Polish, she had survived Auschwitz passing as a gentile. She had first gone to Maciejowice and found no one, but heard that some Jews had gathered in Lodz. Neither Chaim nor Symcha had heard of this distant cousin, nor had they suspected anyone from Maciejowice might still be alive, but they took Perl in. "You're staying with our family," Symcha said. "You are our family."

Months later, Symcha and Perl would marry, and soon after bring a daughter into the world, the second of three babies to be born in the apartment at Mielczarskego 12.

SPRING 1945 – SPRING 1946

SZULIM WAS 9-YEARS-OLD and had never spent a day in school except for cheder, but that was so long ago. There were only three other boys in that dingy basement in Zelechow and they just learned Hebrew letters. This would be a real classroom, with a real teacher, and a slew of boys and girls. He looked forward to entering the third grade and being amongst kids again.

He sat in the classroom surrounded by children, but alone. Abraham was placed in the first grade, Sara a year ahead of him. A woman no taller than the students, but wider by far, limped through the door on legs that hadn't grown in tandem. Her frizzy hair matched the energy she brought to teaching. As she went through her lessons, a janitor walked in carrying a blackboard. He held it up, balancing it against his knees and elbows as he tried to mark the wall where he should hammer in the nail. "Is it straight?"

Es iz azoy glaich vie mayne fis! The room burst out laughing at the teacher's response, and Szulim would repeat that phrase to himself over and over again. "It's as straight as my legs." The self-deprecating humor was not his teacher's alone, but typical amongst Jews who made fun of themselves so that no one else would. Szulim thought about the stories of Chelm his father used to tell in the cellar to pass the time.

LIFE IN LODZ happened so suddenly, as if Szulim had been in the dark for nine years and finally emerged into the light, as if he had been born into a century from long ago and woke up one morning in the modern era. A whole new world opened up to him in school – math, science, geography and history. Soon, Szulim knew all the answers. And on the playground, he learned how to play football with a small bag of stones, kicking it with his heels and his toes so that the sack would not fall to the ground. He and his siblings joined a youth group, *Shomer Ha'Tzair*. Szulim's father hadn't been enamored with the organization, what with its socialist bent and Zionist agenda that promoted politics over religion, but it was the only Jewish youth group in the area, so he acquiesced. Szulim cherished the uniform – the beret and the pins he earned for completing activities like sports, dancing and Hebrew songs. His favorite part was the big handkerchief he wore around his neck, knotted in front and held in place by a metal ring. The metal ring was engraved with a fancy emblem – a fleur-de-lis enclosed within a Star of David, surrounded by wreaths.

Szulim became a child again, surrounded by other children. And one child in particular caught his eye – a little girl in a blue sweater and red skirt with matching suspenders. Even her ponytails were red. Sara saw how Szulim was smitten with this girl who always smiled, who always knew the right answers along with Szulim, and Sara made fun of her younger brother for dancing the hora with this Chane Cytrinowitz at their youth group outings. Szulim didn't even care. He drank in every second of his new life.

He and the children never spoke about the previous years, the horrors that they had endured. What Szulim heard from his parents was that most of these kids had survived by pretending to be Polish and living with Polish families. Not that they hadn't suffered in their own way, but more than likely, they hadn't gone hungry, or dug a grave for a family member.

———

"DID YOU EVER think, hiding in Sokol's greeb, that we'd be living like this?" Szulim's father could not get over their good fortune. Within just a few months of arriving in Lodz, they had a roof over their heads, food on the table. By summer, Pop had a business again and Yiddish flowed freely. The kids sat quietly as they ate their dinner. Even with all of the new experiences and modernities they were itching to share, they knew; kids and fish did not speak. Szulim's mother sat quietly, too. Yes, she was thankful for their newfound circumstances, but something did not feel right. And it wasn't just a matter of missing her sisters and daughter.

SZULIM OVERHEARD THE doctor speaking with his father. "Your wife is with child." He didn't understand. Mama was lying in bed. He and Abraham and Sara sat in a corner of the living room. There were no children in the room with her.

"How can that be?" his father asked. "She went through the change."

"She was probably just malnourished. Most women lost their courses then."

Szulim's father looked up and began uttering a prayer of thanks. The doctor said, "But your wife is very sick." He put a hand on Pop's shoulder. "She might not make it. The baby … it is unlikely either will survive delivery."

There was so much Szulim did not understand. What did it mean to terminate a pregnancy and why did his mother refuse to do so if it would save her? What was water on the lungs and what did that have to do with a baby? He and his siblings were grown kids already. Szulim just stood in awe that they not only lived in a town with its own doctor, but the doctor was Jewish.

Szulim watched his mother grow weaker as her stomach grew larger. From a reclining position, she taught him how to make gefilte fish, peering into the bowl Szulim brought to her bedside, telling him to add pepper or ginger, showing him how to mash it just so. No salt. The doctor was adamant that she had to watch her diet. That was the only treatment he could prescribe. Their apartment became a hive of activity, filled with people helping and reconnecting and praying. A man Szulim had seen a few times before opened his prayer book. "This psalm is appropriate for today. Let's recite it together."

Once again, as Szulim's family went about rebuilding their lives, one parent had to fill the job of two. This time, Pop ran around holding it all together. Late in the summer, he opened a store. When he had to go home to speak with the doctor, Szulim would stay home from school and work behind the counter. Feter Symcha worked in the store as well, but Feter Moshe Szyfman had left for South America, wherever that was. Feter Moshe Boruchowicz and Szulim's cousins, too, had left; sneaking into Germany in order to sail across the ocean to a new life. Szulim's father was trying to save money to get his family to Palestine.

———

DOZENS OF PEOPLE, once strangers but now friends, filled Szulim's apartment on the 10th of Tishrei. They were breaking fast after abstaining from food on the Day of Atonement. Szulim was still too young to fast this Yom Kippur, but he never stopped praying. *Please, dear God, please inscribe Mama into the Book of Life.* His mother's pneumonia had disappeared, the fact of which he added to the list in his head of miracles. The doctor had been coming every day now to check on her. He said if her lungs didn't clear, he would have to take her to the hospital and induce labor. Szulim didn't know what that meant, but was relieved Mama could stay in the apartment. Even if she did just lay on the sofa. No one in the family had talked much about a new baby; they were too concerned with the health of Perl.

All of a sudden, the noshing turned to pandemonium. Women helped his mother rise from the couch and walk to the bedroom. "Get the midwife!" He heard the clang of pots on the stove, the running of water. Soon Yenta the midwife ran into the apartment and yelled for towels. There was a flurry towards the back bedroom, but Szulim, his siblings and his father were sealed off from the women's work.

Szulim couldn't sleep. He stayed up all night whispering *telim* or psalms, any psalms. The prayers that had been fluttering around the apartment for months came back to him and flowed from his lips. He strained to pick up what was going on in the room, but couldn't hear any sounds from his mother, just the woman who attended to her.

Finally, a cry. Szulim walked into the living room where men, still gathered from breaking the fast, clapped Szulim's father on the shoulder and announced, "Mazel Tov!" Pop embraced Szulim and said, "You have a new brother." They named him Berish, after Pop's father Berl. The doctor, who came to see Mama when the sun rose, said, "I never expected they'd be okay."

"The poignancy, Chaim," said Feter Symcha. "So many Jews killed, yet here a Jewish midwife survived to bring forth more Jews. You and Perl did a *mitzvah*."

Szulim's mental list of miracles grew even longer as he thought *Thank God we're a family of six again.*

———

IN THE PAST year, Szulim had eased back into childhood. Though Germany hadn't surrendered until May of 1945, in Szulim's mind, the war ended months before, the moment he walked into third grade. At home and in his youth group, Palestine was the whisper on everyone's lips, the ultimate goal, the final place of happiness and peace. But to Szulim, Lodz was his promised land, the city his playground, available to him for a mere five grosz tram ride. And when he didn't have a few coins in his pocket, Szulim would just reach out and grab hold of the railings as the trolley slowed down. When he saw the conductor coming, he'd jump off and explore a new area of town.

"Lodz is like a ghetto," Szulim's father had once said. "But without the Gestapo and the limitations." They were surrounded by Jews, dependent on no one but fellow survivors. Living amongst such a community, he felt insulated against the long-standing anti-Semitism that the war had only fomented. New life, Jewish life, emerged. First Berish, than Gitl, born to Feter Symcha and Mimeh Perl. A couple named Symcha and Risha Fingezicht married in his parents' apartment and within a year, Yenta the midwife came once again to Mielczarskego 12, delivering to them a baby girl named Sara. Though the seasons changed – summer turned to fall, winter brought falling snow – to Szulim, everyday felt like spring.

Until Feter Symcha went to jail. He had sold a kilogram of sugar for 53 grosz.

August 1946

"THERE'S NO OTHER way." Szulim's father looked to his older children one by one, watching the tears stream down their faces. "If I thought we could get to Palestine any other way, you know I'd do it."

Szulim didn't even care about going to Palestine anymore. For a year now, the leaders of Shomer Ha'Tzair talked non-stop about the land of milk and honey. But Szulim thought of it as a far off enchanted place, a mystical hope for someday declared at the end of every Seder. "Next year in Jerusalem!" But next year had come and gone many times already, and he had friends now. Here in Lodz.

"Why can't we stay?" Szulim pleaded with his father, looking at his mother for help, as Pop laid out the plans. "We're not in danger anymore." True Feter Symcha had been arrested, but they didn't kill him. It was just sugar.

"You know I'd never do anything to put you in jeopardy," Pop had said, rubbing Szulim's hand. "But it's not safe here for us. Never was, never will be."

Szulim knew that the only reason he had survived thus far was because his parents were there to take care of him. Now they were sending him and his siblings on a train alone to France, where he'd board a boat and sail to his Feter Yehuda. He had never met his mother's brother, who moved to Palestine before Szulim was born, and now they were supposed to live with him until Pop and Mama and Berish would arrive?

"You'll make new friends. And maybe some of your friends from school will be on the train with you."

"But who will take care of us?" Szulim looked at Abraham and Sara, who were silent while he alone asked the questions.

"You'll take care of each other." Mama's sobs grew louder as Pop's voice shrunk to a whisper. "There's no other way."

RIDING THE TRAM, Szulim thought about the word *yosem*. He was a yosem now, an orphan. His parents were not his parents anymore. At least that's what his father tried explaining to him on the way to the train station. His mother couldn't talk; she only cried.

Szulim, Sara and Abraham, carrying only one small wooden suitcase between them, walked the four blocks from the tram to the reception hall where the other passengers gathered. Their father spoke as they trudged along silently. "None of the kids on the train have parents and you need to pretend that you don't either. *F'shtai?*"

Szulim nodded, but he didn't understand. Not really.

He could hear the pandemonium from outside the hall. Even with the doors shut, he could see the hugs and hand-offs, the shuffling of papers and dragging of luggage, the hundreds of arms reaching. Feet scurried as grown ups went one way, children the other. Greetings and introductions and weeping filled the large room with high ceilings.

Especially weeping. Before they opened the door, Szulim's mother pulled him close, again, like she had done on the tram, and before that, leaving their apartment. She kissed his nose, his ears, practically sucking the blood out of his face. Her tears mingled with his own, dripping off his cheeks and down his neck. He tried picturing himself and Abraham and Sara under the warm sun of Yisrael, looking up from the banana trees Pop spoke of now, trees that they'd be planting on the kibbutz as his parents and Berish arrived. "Just a couple of weeks," his father said. "You'll see. We'll all be together again with Feter Yehuda."

The last image Szulim had of his father was blurred from the wet in his eyes. But though Pop's voice trembled, Szulim heard his final words with a sharp yet tender clarity. "Remember who you are. Remember who brought you into this world." Pop paused as a strange sound escaped his throat and his voice squeaked, rising like a bird. "Remember that you're Jewish and will always be Jewish."

These words Szulim understood. He couldn't speak, only nod. His father's message would remain with him for the rest of his life, returning often with the memory of that day, clear as if he were living it again.

Then the doors opened. His father handed a large envelope to someone standing at the entrance of the hall and his parents disappeared.

"COME JOIN US! We're playing a game!" Some grown up that Szulim had never seen before reached out to him with a big smile. A man, younger than his parents, with an accent he couldn't place. The man spoke Yiddish, but louder than he had heard someone speak Yiddish in a long time. He gave Szulim a piece of candy.

Pop was right. There were a lot of children, more children than he had ever seen in one place in his life. Szulim wiped his eyes with the back of his sleeve and lost sight of Abraham and Sara. He had no choice but to join in the activities. The grown ups wore smiles that glowed like the sun, and the way they strode across the room reminded Szulim of the Gestapo. But instead of guns, they carried clipboards; their mission – kindness and joy. *Where did they hide during the war?* Szulim wondered if any of them had buried a sister.

The next thing he knew, he was on a truck, riding towards the train with children he had just met. He gripped the handle of his suitcase, thinking about his parents. Were they still on the tram or had they gotten back to the apartment already? Would they be taking a train, too? Would Berish wonder where his big brothers and sister were? *Szu Szu*. At almost one year of age, the baby of the family had already started calling out to his oldest brother.

Szulim wasn't nervous boarding the train; he figured it couldn't go any faster than the truck he had just ridden on. The rows of wooden seats could move to face either forwards or backwards. The *madrich* in charge of Szulim's group, not much older than his cousin Berl who had left Poland already, arranged the seats so that two long benches faced each other. He seemed to know where all the children should sit. Szulim was relieved to find Abraham and Sara; they would all be sitting together, along with a couple of other kids. Sara clutched her handbag and looked terrified. "Remember," she whispered, "we don't have parents. If you say anything about Pop and Mama, I'll tell them they're our Feter and Mimeh."

Szulim looked around for the driver. He couldn't understand how the big wheels would roll along the tracks. He heard the noise of the engine, but didn't see the locomotive. He looked out the window as the train began to move, watching the trees from the nearby woods move faster and faster until they became one big blur of green. The rushing of the forest made him dizzy, so he focused his attention to inside the train. Kids did puzzles, played little games. The dozen or so *madrichim* led the carful of children in song. Szulim recognized the Hebrew words and mouthed along, but without the joy normally associated with singing. Kids got up and moved about the train, some looking for a bathroom, others making new friends. Most of the kids spoke Yiddish like him, but some sat quietly, isolated by the fact that they only knew Polish. Either their families were the intelligentsia, like the Popowska's, or they had been hidden by non-Jewish families, pretending for so many years to be gentile, that they had forgotten how to speak their first language completely. Szulim felt bad for these kids and didn't think it was right that others poked fun.

He looked at his sister. Her mouth formed the words of the songs, like him, but no sound came out. Her lips trembled and on her cheeks he saw a faint stain, the clear trail of a teardrop that had since been wiped away. He knew she meant to hide her pain from her brothers, so he quickly averted his gaze. Sara wasn't the only one crying, but most of the other weeping children were younger and had older siblings or cousins attempting to provide comfort. Sara had to console herself.

As Szulim watched the countryside roll by slowly, and then much faster, he realized that the land of his birth was nothing more than a place of suffering. He tried to focus on where he and his siblings were headed, how there'd be Jews all around him. The novelty of riding on a train, the activities and all of the children, these occupied his thoughts and managed to push aside, for the first few days anyway, worry and concern about his parents. But that would come.

Songs and games helped pass the time as the train rolled along for days, and children moved around and between the cars. The madrichim brought bread and peeled eggs, which they mostly ate in their seats, crumbs and flakes of yolk falling into their laps and around their feet. It seemed the train was always stopping for an hour or two, and it was at these times that the children could enjoy hot soup. Szulim worried that the soup might not be kosher. After all, the madrichim were Zionists, not religious like his parents. But he remembered Pop encouraging him to eat Sokol's soup, even with the rat floating in it. He knew his parents would want him to get nourishment. He knew God would forgive him.

They ate in their seats and slept in their seats, sometimes leaning against each other. When their bodies needed to stretch out fully, they'd sprawl on the floor.

"How much longer?" Szulim asked one of the madrichim. "My Po ... Feter said it would be just a few days."

"Patience, my boy." The madrich smiled at him. "We thought it would go quicker, too. But it's all these inspections. Oy, the train is stopping. Here we go again."

Szulim sighed. Every day, the train stopped at least three or four times to let officials aboard to scan the papers. Sometimes it took these officials several hours to go through all the passports. And before every stop, the madrichim came by with the same questions. "You remember your name? You're an orphan, don't forget."

Szulim never worried that he'd slip up and reveal by accident that he had parents. Maybe Sara thought about that, since Pop had placed her in charge. At ten years of age, all Szulim worried about was that he'd never see his parents again.

TELLING: SUMMER 2009

BOTH SANDY AND Sal look forward to the phone calls. For Sandy, each time she listens to Sal tell his story, the picture of her husband becomes clearer. She holds her breath as he speaks, absorbing every detail, gaining a deeper understanding of the man she has lived with for almost 45 years. And Sal, with every question that he answers, feels that much closer to holding an actual book, the story of his life, in his hands.

"Explain to me," I say, "why your father felt you all had to leave. Didn't the economy affect everyone, not just Jews?"

Sal hopes he can clear up a common misunderstanding. "So many people think that if you survived the camps or somehow hid, then all was good after the war ended in May of 1945. But that is not true. Anti-Semitism didn't sweep in with the Nazis; it was there long before. And it remained even after the Germans left."

Sal knows this is very hard for an American to grasp, especially one my age who never really lived through an era of intolerance. "Things were always right here… for the Jews, anyway. In Europe, nothing was right from the very beginning. I may not remember pogroms before the war, but my parents certainly did. The fear of living as a Jew had always been around."

I think about raising my own sons, trying to instill both a sense of pride in being Jewish and a respect and tolerance for others. I imagine how hard that must have been living in such an anti-Semitic environment. "I'm so curious," I ask, "how you internalized that dichotomy between your parents trying to make you feel proud to be Jewish while the world around you did everything it could to tell you that you were inferior."

"Ach, that's too much philosophy for a young boy. I didn't wonder at the injustice of it all. If anything, I thought that's how God wanted it. It was our lot."

Sal tries to make me understand that they never questioned it; they just lived in their shtetls and kept to themselves as much as possible. "We behaved differently, and we suffered differently. In our eyes, this difference made us better."

Sandy sits in the living room, the phone pressed to her ear, and looks around at all the relics of their Jewish life. Menorahs, several of them, crafted from metal or ceramic, depicting the tree of life, or Jerusalem's stone temple walls; kiddush cups – engraved in both English and Hebrew – that have touched the lips of their family over the years on Shabbat, at a bris or during Passover. Paintings hang on the wall made by Jewish artists. Sandy identifies completely as a Jew, has created a Jewish home; yet she is an American, too, fully assimilated into an even larger community.

As she thinks about this notion of living worlds apart from people right in one's own neighborhood, she recalls going to see the 9-hour movie *Shoah* back in 1986. She remembers the tickets were so expensive, about $20 apiece. Sal surprised her by wanting to go, too. He normally refused to spend money on anything, let alone a movie, but they went together to the Gusman Theater in downtown Miami where it was being shown over the course of two days.

Sandy had sat rapt throughout the film, which consisted mostly of recent interviews with those who survived, those who stood by during the years of suffering and did nothing, and the monsters who perpetrated the hatred and violence. As the movie played, she listened to the audience. The silence of astonishment punctuated by weeping, praying, moaning, sighing, *ts*king and sobbing. Some out loud, some softly. That was to be expected. What Sandy hadn't expected, she told me, was to hear gasps coming from Sal. It was not that Sal possessed no feelings; he simply never revealed them. There in the dark, he let them out.

He was reacting to the hatred that still ran deep among the Polish so many years later. "A tiger never changes its stripes," he always said. His intolerance had bothered her. Sandy wanted to believe that a society could atone, that people could change. She grew up in a Miami with separate water fountains for blacks and whites, yet her kids and I – born less than a decade later – lived in a much more integrated world. She wanted to believe it could be different in Poland, too. But after seeing the film, she knew Sal was right. How could a hatred that strong vanish with the passing of a few generations? Sandy still shudders remembering when the director of the film stopped at a train station and asked an elderly woman if she knew what had happened during the war. Thirty years had passed, and still, the woman replied, "Too bad Hitler couldn't finish his job before they killed him."

Sandy listens now to Sal describing life in Poland after liberation, and she remembers the end of the film when a group of Survivors visited a Polish town, sometime in the late 70's or early 80's. It was supposed to be a scene where the Survivors received well wishes from the residents. The aging villagers tried to put on a good face for the camera, but Sandy could see in their eyes and their gestures a dislike and contempt that was palpable. As if nothing had been learned from that horrible period in history, no remorse. To Sandy, it was a closing scene that had no closure.

The movie had substantiated, in an open way, everything that Sal had felt about the Polish people and was not always hesitant to admit. Sandy had often felt conflicted hearing her husband speak of the Poles. If he held these prejudices, which were understandable based on his personal experience, was he any better than the very people he accused of prejudice and malice? Yet Sandy remembers their trip to Poland, Sal's abject fear and utter transformation. She remembers afterwards, when he told her that he had been terrified the entire time. "I was so scared," he had said once they landed back on American soil, "that if I did anything wrong – chewed gum, bought something on the black market – I'd be detained and conscripted in the army."

On the ride back home after seeing *Shoah*, Sandy had wanted to talk about it. She *needed* to talk. It had been the first time in 13 years that the subject of the Holocaust had come up between them. She took a deep breath, turned to her husband driving and said, "Sal, what a film. I don't even know where to begin…"

He said, "Yes," his eyes fixed on the road ahead. And then he said one thing more. "You have change for the toll?"

Now, twenty some years later, he can't stop talking about it.

"Tell me more about this post-war political climate," I ask.

"I didn't understand it at the time. I'm sure my parents tried to shield us from it." Sal takes a sip of water. "But when the Germans left, and then the Russians, the Polish government took over. My parents called them fascists. The government was actually communist, but my parents didn't want to align the Poles in any way with the Russians."

"I understand that; the Russians were the good guys to you."

"Yes. So the Polish government was in a financial mess and put price controls on everything. The restrictions weren't just limited to the Jews, but don't kid yourself if you think the laws were enforced evenly."

Sal explains to me how sugar may have cost 51 cents a kilogram, and in order to make any sort of living, his father had to sell it for 53 cents. Yet the Polish government set the price at 50 cents. "Everyone snuck around; you had no choice. But one day, an official came into the store. My Uncle Symcha, not knowing this man was a spy for the state, sold him sugar over the controlled price. Symcha was thrown in jail without a trial."

"For how long?" I want to know.

"It took almost two months for my father to make the proper connections and earn enough money for bribes. He visited my uncle in jail a couple times a week, every week. My father thought 'here we go again' and began making plans to leave Poland once and for all."

"Where did he want to go?"

Sal describes how the Polish government had closed its borders by the time of his uncle's arrest in late spring of 1946; no one could leave. "Our dream had been to get to Palestine. After the arrest, my father became obsessed with simply getting out of Poland. Displaced persons bureaus had been set up in Germany, so the thinking was if we could get there, we could get to Palestine. But getting there was a problem. How do you steal into another country? And with children, yet?"

Sal speaks of cousins, distant relatives, who had managed to flee Poland; they hadn't been burdened by young children who made smuggling across borders an even riskier proposition. He tells of his father searching for a guide who, for the right price, could help Jews sneak out of the country. "This smuggling of refugees across borders, it was an incredible gamble, finding someone you could trust, someone who knew the route and who wouldn't desert you – or shoot you – in the woods. And the price was quite steep."

Sal shakes his head. "To get Symcha out of jail, to get us out of Poland, that cost a tremendous amount of money. Remember, we arrived in Lodz with nothing but a Torah. My father had practically just opened his store. We didn't have those kinds of means. This has been a mystery to me my entire life. How did my father come up with that kind of cash? Did he work his connections? It's not like anyone else had riches. Or did he steal it?"

"The things people will do to preserve family, to survive," I say. "We hear about criminals today, but do we know their past?"

"It's true. So my parents prepared to smuggle my baby brother and themselves across the border, but Pop found a convoy for us older kids, organized by a group called Rescue Children. They worked with the Joint. Do you know what is the Joint?"

I had actually written some marketing materials for The Joint Distribution Committee. "It's an amazing organization," I say.

"Well, the Joint used international pressure and legal channels to get children out of Poland. Pop knew it would be much safer for us to leave this way. Of course, I didn't know anything about the risks of leaving, or my father's plans at the time."

"Which I'm sure made your departure even more traumatic," I add.

Sal tells me everything he has learned since that time long ago. That the Rescue Children convoy was a special concession by the Polish government, on behest of the United States and others who were determined to save Jewish children devastated by the war. That they had arranged to take 500 kids out of Poland, but could only find approximately 360. That even though Sal had been terrified that someone might find out he wasn't truly an orphan, the truth was, about 70% of the kids on the train were like him, only pretending. That true orphans simply did not survive the war.

"Here's another thing I later realized. The madrichim were not Survivors. At the time, I assumed they were Polish Jews like me. They spoke Yiddish; there was a certain *haimisheh* feeling, you know what that is?" Sal asks.

"You knew my grandmom," I laugh. "I understand a lot more Yiddish than you give me credit for."

Sal smiles. "I suppose. Well, the manner in which they conducted themselves, the assuredness, their poise, there was no way that someone who suffered like we had could have maintained that sense of self every time we were stopped and inspected. A Survivor would have been absolutely terrified, so soon afterwards, of anyone asking for papers."

"So who were they? Where were they from?" I ask.

"These kids – and they were kids, really, no more than 18 years of age – must have been American and Israeli volunteers. Actually, if I truly think about it, they must have been Israelis. These people had zeal, a fervor. The only ones I can think of with this level of goal orientation are the Israelis."

REAWAKENING

Aix Les Bains, France

OCTOBER 1946 – JULY 1947

SZULIM LAY ON the sacrifice table and sang. Of all the boys at the Hotel Beau Site, he had been the one selected for the role of Isaac in the play. He looked up into the beard of the rabbi, who pretended to be the patriarch of the Israelites, as they acted out the scene from Genesis. As he lay there, he imagined what the real Isaac must have felt, hundreds of years before as he stared into the eyes of his father, watching the man he loved and trusted more than any other raise a knife into the air and speak with God.

Szulim thought about Pop. When he and all the children on the train had first arrived in France, it became apparent that they weren't boarding a boat for Palestine anytime soon. Szulim felt like a bottle of seltzer that had lost all of its bubbles. No parents, no letters telling of their whereabouts. The madrichim did their best to keep the kids informed, explaining how the boats were turned back; how the children were able to take a train, but their parents couldn't. "Just be patient," they urged as they shuttled the kids between prayers and games and classes. Szulim couldn't stop thinking about his parents, though, and when he saw Sara or Abraham in passing between all of the activities, he missed them even more. But he knew they'd reunite in Palestine. His father had never lied to him.

WHEN THEY HAD finally arrived in the French Alps, Szulim, Sara and Abraham were thrilled to get off the train. What was supposed to have only been a three-day trip, a week at most, took six full weeks. A month and a half of sitting in the same seat, sleeping on a hard wood bench, trying to eat while balancing food on their laps.

Szulim could tell that the Hotel Beau Site, their new lodgings, had once been a fancy hotel before transforming into an orphanage; an enormous estate set on a hill with manicured lawns in the front and a huge field in back. Dark wood decorated the white stucco exterior walls, lending an air of extravagance. The walls inside, painted a variety of colors depending on the room, reached up and tucked into molded wood that edged the ceiling. Szulim had never seen a house with so many windows. Heavy drapes hung parted around the glass panes, allowing sunlight to stream through the large rooms and dance across the wooden floors.

What a change from the drab barracks that housed them in Czechoslovakia. When the train had stopped in Prague after nearly a month of travel, they had to disembark. Szulim didn't understand why they left the station, walking along muddy roads to a barren building that held nothing more than cots. But despite having to share the narrow bed with Abraham, the mattress was a welcome relief to the hard wood of the train seats. He had been so nervous that he'd lose their luggage, though it only contained a few articles of clothing. Szulim left the town of Dabilce, a suburb of Prague, two weeks later having learned only a single Czech word, *zmrizlina*. Ice cream.

Here in the French Alps, Szulim had his own bed, sharing a room with five other boys. Abraham had been moved to a room with kids his own age, Sara with the girls. None of them cried when they were separated, they were having too much fun. The madrichim did say that if anyone wanted to remain with a sibling or cousin, they could, but Szulim felt he had grown in the past year. He was a young man already.

There were even more adults at the Hotel Beau Site than there had been on the train. These people were from Agudath Israel and their level of observance reminded Szulim of Feter Moshe. But they didn't police the children, the way his uncle had. They made the daily prayers fun. Almost immediately, the boys who were of age became Bar Mitzvahs, reading from the Torah and receiving tefillen. Szulim had three more years before he would be called for his own *aliyah*. But all of the children celebrated with a big party thrown in the boys' honor.

Every so often, in the middle of the night, Szulim heard a child cry out, an occasional scream from a night terror. The madrichim ran to those children, knowing there were some who needed special attention. Szulim never told anyone about his experiences; they were encouraged to talk only about good things, like how much fun they were having. Szulim did notice some of the younger kids, some of the girls in particular, crying at points during the day. He looked away; allowing them their private moments, knowing the tears could just as easily be his own.

———

"WE DO THIS all the time!" Szulim exhaled loudly and stared at Sara. "We say the same thing. Why do we have to do this over and over?"

"*Shatz!*" The madricha meant business, hushing Szulim and the others who complained about writing letters. "If you don't write to your family, they'll never be able to send anything back." The kids knew when it was time to listen. The madrichim usually exuded such warmth and vitality, filling the old chateau with tenderness and energy. But they had enough problems to deal with – political issues, the children's emotions – bad behavior was not tolerated. Each and every child had already learned during the war, in different and difficult ways, what happened to those who didn't listen.

So Szulim did as he was told, adding a few Yiddish words to the end of the letter that Sara wrote, passing the paper to Abraham so he could do the same. Sara not only had perfect penmanship, but also more schooling, so onto her shoulders fell the responsibility of correspondence. Each week, the letters said the same thing. "We're having fun, we miss you. Kiss Berish." And each week came and went without word from Pop and Mama. The mailman arrived regularly at the hotel with nothing but let downs, and an occasional envelope for a lucky child whose parents managed to smuggle out some communication. Szulim would watch the madricha take a boy to the side and hand him a letter, the child ripping it open eagerly and giving it to the counselor to read out loud. The madrichim tried to be discreet, but that one child's joy permeated the entire manor, intensifying everyone else's disappointment.

"Try not to worry," the madrichim said over and over. They explained world events, providing reasons as to why no one had heard from their parents. Though Szulim could not keep track of the changing governments, he understood that he hadn't been abandoned. Things were simply out of anyone's control.

———

"OKAY, SZULIM. TURN to the left … good!" Szulim looked at the black metal box the madrich pointed at him before facing the wall, then heard a pop and a hiss as a bright light flared in the corner of his eyes. "We're sending your pictures to America for families to pick out who they want to adopt."

Adopt. Again a word he couldn't understand. After spending half a year in Aix Les Bains, Szulim knew he didn't have to pretend to be an orphan anymore. The counselors were not only aware that the children had parents; they made the kids write to them. Yet now these same children, only pretend yosems after all, were being listed worldwide as kids who needed homes and families. Szulim supposed this was just in case his parents could never leave Poland. So once again, he feigned orphanhood to Benjamin and Adele Siegel, a couple in Philadelphia with two children of their own. He thought it was strange that the Siegel's chose him and Abraham, but not Sara. If it ever came time that he and his brother had to actually go and live with these people, he would not go without his sister.

One day, he and Abraham received a care package from the Siegel's; it was the first time they had gotten any mail. The counselors had to translate the letter, which was written in English. *We're excited to meet you*, it read. Szulim thought it was very nice of these strangers to write to him, but he wasn't at all excited about the possibility of meeting them. If he were indeed to go live with the Siegel's in America, it would only be due to the fact that something had happened to his parents. He didn't want to think about that.

Still, he and Abraham enjoyed going through the big box from the Siegel's containing all sorts of presents and treats, despite the fact that something must have happened during the shipping.

"What kind of ball is this?" Szulim held up the mass of brown leather shaped like an eye. "You can't bounce it or roll it."

"Maybe it got squashed in the mail," Abraham offered.

The madrich laughed and explained football. The boys shrugged their shoulders and tossed the misshapen toy to the side. Next they unwrapped some candy and popped it into their mouths as their counselor warned them not to swallow.

"It's chewing gum."

A food you don't swallow? The boys were dumbfounded until the madrich took a piece and showed them how to chew it, explaining through a mouthful of spit that it was sweet. Szulim laughed as a pink bubble emerged from the madrich's mouth and grew larger by the second. Szulim was eager to try it for himself, but found it too painful. His teeth were too weak to chew. The one thing they loved were the cans of hot chocolate. "Looks like army surplus," the madrich said as he showed the boys how to pull off the top and light the wick in order to heat up the contents.

Szulim looked past the sweets that hurt his teeth and the misshapen ball, and thought about these people on the other side of the world who didn't know him at all, yet acted with such kindness and generosity. It made him feel warm all over. Still, he remained cautious in his letters to the Siegel's, taking care not to reveal that he really did have parents, or that he prayed every day to hear from his real Pop and Mama, and dreamed every night of reuniting with them in Palestine.

Not until Szulim was grown and had the means himself to donate money and kindness would he realize the Siegel's never really meant to take him in. The adoption was symbolic. Had he understood this as a child, he wouldn't have been afraid to be grateful.

———

SZULIM LISTENED TO the pretty woman speak in a language that seemed to glue her tongue to the roof of her mouth. She, along with other French teachers, came to the hotel everyday to give lessons. Szulim stared at this tall, slender woman in her gray attire, always gray. He had never seen a woman wear trousers before. He followed the movement of her pencil – first to her mouth where it rested thoughtfully against her bottom lip, then arcing out from her body as she spoke, forming invisible circles near her shoulder. Occasionally this pencil, the eraser with a mind of its own, traveled down to scratch at her crotch. France truly was a foreign land.

IF SZULIM KNEW how to write, and knew that his parents actually received his letters, he would have regaled them with tales of adventure – bike riding along tree-lined roads, new friends, the smell of the fresh air wafting up from the lake. How they all had chores and, in doing so, earned money that they could use to buy ice cream. The enormous room on the first floor where they had morning prayers before dragging the large benches and long wooden tables out into the center for family-style meals. Lots of potatoes and chicken and noodles. Sometimes noodles with cheese. Foods he was used to from before the war. He would have told Pop not to worry about the food being kosher. The people from Agudath Israel were completely observant.

Szulim would have written about the fruits they brought out for dessert – apples and pears. And *ananas*! In Poland, only the truly rich and truly sick would have been able to eat a pineapple. Or an orange. Perhaps once in his life, after Pop had done bankes, did Szulim ever get to bite into that juicy, pulpy treat. And here, they had them every night after dinner. Along with pastries unlike anything he had ever seen in Gedalia Yosef's bakery.

But how would Szulim have put into words the feelings? The same exhilaration that coursed through his body when he skied down the Alps filled his every waking moment. It was a sensation of whizzing back into childhood. Yet right alongside this thrill, a set of reins tugged at him, slowing him down; the sadness of his parents' absence pulled on him like a weight. The joy he had only begun to feel for the first time in his life had a woeful counterbalance.

And so it was with mixed emotions that he received a telegram informing the orphanage that his parents and baby brother had made it to Strasburg and would arrive soon in Paris. The telegram wasn't from his parents, but from Yitzhak Bialebroda, the same cousin who years before had appeared in their living room with stories of extermination camps. He had made it to Paris a year ago, along with another distant cousin, Benyak Rzesnick. Szulim's parents miraculously reached Germany and they found the Displaced Persons Bureau who helped them obtain information as to the whereabouts of their children. His parents managed to get in touch with Yitzhak, who in turn sent the telegram to the French Alps.

The children and madrichim were thrilled for Szulim, Abraham and Sara. They exchanged pictures, and Szulim wrote Yitzhak's address on the back of his. His friends, however, had no address of their own to give back.

Szulim, Sara and Abraham left on a Friday, which had the madrichim from Agudath Israel in a panic. "It's a four or five hour train trip! Please God you'll get there before Shabbos." Szulim, too, was concerned about being on a train after sundown, more so than he was about being on a train without adult supervision. After all, Sara was 13 years old already.

The three children boarded the train alone, excited to see their parents. But it was Berish who had the greatest pull. It had been almost a year and they couldn't imagine how much their baby brother must have changed. The siblings still had only one small suitcase between them, but now they each carried a small burlap tote. Their cherished possessions fit into a small shopping bag.

Two telegrams had come to the orphanage: one for the Wajnberg kids, the other, informing that passage had been obtained for all the children to board a ship leaving for Palestine on July 11th. The madrich had to quickly prepare the rest of the children so they could travel to the South of France in time to board *The Exodus*.

WAITING

Paris, France

July 1947 – April 1948

MR. RZESNICK'S APARTMENT felt tiny compared to the orphanage. But even the tall ceilings of that grand chateau could not have contained Szulim's excitement. He couldn't believe his parents and Berish would be walking into the room at any moment, and he strained, along with Abraham and Sara, to sit quietly and wait. Yitzhak had gone to the station to meet the train while the three kids stayed in the apartment with this new distant cousin. Szulim tried to remain calm, to guard against too much joy, just in case. But his skin tickled and he felt tiny birds fluttering around in his throat, desperate for flight.

Finally, the door opened. Szulim stared. He had been told his parents were coming; but until he saw them standing in front of him, he could not let go of his worry and truly believe. For a moment they just looked at each other. And then they burst.

The flurry of hugs and kisses, the tears. It reminded Szulim of his arrival in Sokol's cellar when the outpouring of love and relief, and the need for skin to touch skin, was so great. But this time, the sun shone through the windows. And Szulim was sure that somewhere, way up high near God, the angels had finally stopped crying and burst into song.

Mama had her arms around Szulim. He fell into her embrace, amazed by her ability to hug three growing children in one fell swoop. But he had his eyes on Berish. They all did. Berish had changed so much and the three older siblings fought over who got to pick up the toddler first.

"He's walking!" Berish was crawling the last time they had seen him, pulling himself up on the leg of the table and falling onto a diapered tuchas. Now he was running around the apartment in big boy pants, bewildered at these strangers but loving the attention.

"He's a mensch already!" Pop said.

"It's so good to see you Chaim, Perl," Mr. Rzesnick said as he hugged them. "It's been how many years?"

"Ach, who even knows any more," Szulim's father answered.

"My apartment is small, but I can always make room."

"Oh, no need. The Joint has set us up in a hotel."

Szulim couldn't wait to see this hotel his father spoke of. He pictured large rooms, even bigger than their apartment in Lodz. He hadn't had a chance to explore Paris and wondered if the women here would be dressed in gray, too, like the teachers in trousers doing funny things with pencils. He hoped he would still get to enjoy ananas for dessert.

THEY WALKED TO the Hotel National on Rue de Faubourg St. Denis. Szulim stared at the buildings that crowded the avenue, looking for the number 216. *Another place with an address*, he thought as he lugged the suitcase he shared with Abraham and Sara. Mama hoisted Berish on her hip while Pop cradled the Torah in his arms. The sacred scroll rescued from the desecration of the shul in Zelechow had snuck out of Poland, traversed mountains into Germany, and rode like a passenger on a train to Paris. Szulim's father never let that Torah out of his sight.

They entered the lobby of the five-story hotel, eager to begin a new life for themselves, but believing their stay in Paris would be temporary. Their ultimate goal, as always, was Palestine.

"Boys, you'll sleep there." Szulim's mother took to organizing and pointed to a chaise lounge next to a large window. She pulled pillows from the closet in the hallway and positioned them on the floor, leaving space in the corner where the walls met, in an effort to fashion a crib for Berish. Sara would share the large bed in the center of the room with his parents. Szulim's mother could see the sadness that hadn't left her only daughter. Szulim looked around the room, too small for a family of six, and gazed out the window at the city that begged for exploring. He had noticed an entrance to the metro right outside the doors of the hotel and was eager to experience a new mode of transportation.

———

POP CAME BACK to the hotel in the evening after strolling through the *pletzel*, a five-block section of Paris that had become an enclave for Jewish refugees. He was looking to make a parnose while they waited, earn a bit of a living until their visas came through. He had a few zlotys in his pocket, but they would do no good in France.

"You wouldn't believe," he said, "you don't even need to speak French. Every restaurant is kosher, even the apple cart had a sign — 'kosher apples.'"

"*Feh*, have you ever seen an apple that's traif?" Szulim's mother asked from the bathroom where she was wringing out Berish's clothes and hanging them on the shower rod to dry. "Anything to buy and sell?"

"You know, a *bissel* this, a *bissel* that. Small things."

"Good. We got *gornisht* here. Nothing."

"Have faith, Perl."

His mother walked into the main room where they ate, slept and did their prayers. "In you, I have faith. Look at us now! Almost to Palestine. Here, I got a little *nosh*." She unwrapped a piece of cheese and broke it into small pieces for everyone in the family.

———

SZULIM AND ABRAHAM held hands as they walked to the park six blocks away. As it turned out, women wore not just gray, or the white and black that he was accustomed to, but all sorts of colors; every color in the rainbow. Strolling through Paris was a feast for the eyes with intricate carvings wrapped around eaves of buildings, wrought iron swirling around signs for the Metro. And the spectrum of reds, yellows, greens and blues called out to him from store windows.

"Abraham! Look at this one!" Szulim plucked another bottle cap from the ground and held it up for his little brother to admire. It went into his pocket, nestling among the other treasures that he and Abraham collected from the glittering city. Normally, an eleven-year-old boy would have gone to school, but they were biding their time, waiting to leave Europe.

While Szulim's parents stayed close to the hotel, or mixed with the other refugees at the pletzel, he and Abraham roamed the streets hand in hand. The greatest discovery was the Bazar de l'Hotel de Ville. Szulim had never been in a store like this. Gone were the dusty floors and pickle barrels by the front door, the crude carbide lamps and old wooden shelves filled with sugar cubes and soap. This, the largest department store in Paris, must have been a wonder of the world. Szulim had already ridden an elevator back in Lodz. But here, magic steps floated upwards, traversing seven stories. He and Abraham couldn't get enough of riding these shiny metal staircases. They clutched each other, holding tight as their bodies lifted, and looked around at all the wares. They'd reach the landing and eye the bumpy brown floor that clanged when they jumped onto it, their collections jingling in their pockets. Laughing, they'd race to the elevator, taking it down to the bottom floor, and begin again their ride up the magic stairs as lights twinkled above, reflecting in all of the mirrored and marble surfaces.

"*Arreter!*" A gruff voice shouted in their ears as they felt heavy hands on their shoulders. Szulim was too scared to turn his head and face his captor. Without knowing who or what was pushing them, they marched past the mannequins and glittering shelves, through a door and into a small, windowless room. "*Videz vos poches!*"

Abraham looked at Szulim, his mouth an "O," eyebrows frozen high up on his forehead. Szulim swallowed hard and tried to smile through fear-clenched teeth. He shrugged his shoulders. The guard barked once more and pointed to their legs. "*Videz!*" He tapped the sides of their pants.

Szulim reached into his pockets and pulled out six bottle caps, two candy wrappers and a handful of smooth pebbles. Abraham copied his brother, revealing a crumpled comic strip torn from an old newspaper, four buttons and a small piece of wood.

"*Que faisiez-vous?*" The man, trim with neatly combed hair and a thin moustache, stood in a guard's uniform with his arms crossed. His tone had warmed ever so slightly as he stared at the two young boys with caps and fringe peeking out from the bottom of their shirts. Abraham looked to Szulim to do the talking, but fear stole from the end of Szulim's tongue what little French he remembered from the orphanage. "*Où habitez-vous?*" the guard asked. *Habitez.* Szulim recognized that word. Live. "*Où?*" The guard's voice grew louder.

"*Un hotel, s'il vous plaît.*" Szulim fumbled over his words, his tongue dry and course as he tried to remember how to pronounce the name of the street. Finally they seemed to be able to communicate with each other and the guard picked up a telephone. French flew out of his mouth at such a speed that Szulim could not make sense of it, but as the man spoke into the receiver, he stared at the boys and moved his hands up and down, as if indicating their height. He hung up the phone and motioned for them to stand. He placed his hands on their shoulders, much more gently this time, and led them out of the store. On the sidewalk, two policemen stood waiting for them and held open the door to their car. Szulim couldn't look at his brother as they climbed into the back seat; both panicking at the anticipation of Pop's reaction.

A NEW ACQUAINTANCE of their father's who happened to be visiting the hotel understood French and spoke with the policemen, shaking their hands as they left the room. He smiled at Szulim and his brother. "*Zol mir der freihait dinen!*" He laughed at Szulim and Abraham. "You're free men!" He turned to Szulim's father, clapping him on the arm. "Your sons, now that they've been in jail, liberty can serve them."

———

SZULIM AND ABRAHAM stayed close to the hotel after that, but in their minds, they traveled back to Poland.

"I'm a big general in the Russian army, Abraham." Szulim clutched his brother's hand and they walked through the park, lost in elaborate stories of revenge. "You're my second in command."

"Are our uniforms covered in medals?"

"You bet. We've got carbines. One in each hand. We walk into a village…"

"Is it Zelechow?"

"Sure, stop interrupting. We stand in the center of town. 'The Wajnberg's are here!' we shout. Everyone freezes. They're terrified. Well, the Polish are terrified. The Jews dance a hora."

"Do the children throw candy?"

"Oh yes. The Jewish men run through town, dragging bandits and rotten goyim to stand in front of us. There's Wladislaw Turek, Mylech Szarfartz…"

"He's Jewish."

"No matter." Szulim spit on the ground and Abraham did the same. "That farmer in Maciejowice, remember how he wouldn't take us in? The Gestapo, all of them. They line up, shaking in their shiny boots, and you and I raise our guns … *blam blam blam*! Bullets fly everywhere. We just keep waving our guns back and forth across the line. And like that, they're dead. *Toyt*! We don't say a word. We nod at the women and walk out of town."

Szulim and Abraham roamed Paris in disguise. They may have looked like skinny Jewish boys with nowhere to go and nothing to do other than collect trinkets in their pockets, but in their minds, they were heroes. With Parisian taxis and bakeries and mannequins decked in the latest couture as backdrop, Szulim and Abraham took revenge, over and over, on the Polacks and Germans, every shiny boot Gestapo and stupid bandit, the apathetic goyim and torturous guards.

———

"GOD FORBID THEY take him to church!" Szulim's father was anxious. After several months of waiting for a visa, it was becoming clear that papers would be very hard to come by, and the six Wajnberg's could not live for much longer in one hotel room. Plus, it was increasingly difficult to feed everyone without a steady job. Pop either spent his days at the pletzel finding odds and ends to sell, or at the Displaced Persons bureau begging for passage to Palestine. He found little success at either.

An older French couple that lived on a farm outside of Paris had volunteered to take temporary custody of Berish. They would raise him until visas came through, providing food, tenderness and a place to run around. And Szulim's mother, without a young child to care for, would be able to work.

"Oy, Perl. We survived being religious and now we have to send our baby to the goyim?" Szulim's father agonized over the decision. "But I know we have no choice. It's the right thing to do."

Szulim, too, would be sent away. His father had heard at the pletzel about the formation of an outpost of the Chachmei Lublin Yeshiva. Not too long before the *shaddach*, the arranged marriage between him and Szulim's mother, Chaim had been chosen to study at the famous yeshiva in Poland. Only a select few who knew pages of the Talmud by heart would be accepted. But his impending marriage prevented his enrollment. Now, the yeshiva that had been destroyed in Lublin was reforming about 50 kilometers outside of Paris in an old villa named Gastain. And Szulim's father wanted to make sure his son got a Jewish education.

Though Szulim was not happy about leaving his family, he trusted his father. He had learned by now that Pop would never do anything to harm him. But still, they had just gotten back together again. And he'd be going without Abraham who was both not old enough and not learned enough. Only Szulim had really studied with Feter Moshe in the cellar.

"*JAMAIS MANGER DES escargots?*" The groundskeeper of the school at Gastain, a man named Paul, plucked a snail from the garden. He, along with the neighboring farmers who came to look at the Jewish boys, taught Szulim to speak the language. He imparted some culinary wisdom, as well. Szulim stared one afternoon as Paul took a small block of cheese out of his pocket. With a dirty penknife, he cut off a sliver and placed it in the center of his hand. He picked up the snail from the ground and gently lowered the shell onto his palm, next to the cheese. When the snail poked its head out of the shell, sniffing at the cheese, Paul tossed *le fromage* into his mouth and sucked the snail out of its shell, swallowing both in one gulp.

Szulim stared in horror until Paul found another snail and offered it to him, along with more cheese. Szulim didn't wonder whether a slug in a shell might be kosher; instead he looked at Paul for encouragement before devouring the delicacies. He smiled at the groundskeeper as he worked the rubbery animal, still alive, down his throat. He wanted to show his appreciation. But it would be many more years before Szulim could summon the courage to try escargot again. He eventually found that dead, and slathered with butter and garlic, they could be quite tasty.

The several months Szulim spent at Gastain were pleasant enough. He was one of ten boys studying Torah and the Talmud, learning to negotiate among the popular crowd who, in this case, were two brothers, teenagers already, the only boys native to France. They weren't Jews like Szulim and the others; they represented the bourgeoisie, dressed differently in nice clothes, speaking French fluently. Szulim both admired and resented them at the same time.

THE YESHIVA EXPERIENCE was short lived, and just as Szulim got used to the routine and the other boys, he had to go back to Paris. His father was growing anxious. Szulim heard the words "occupation" and "demilitarized zone," the Marshall Plan. It meant nothing to him, but these words were written in lines on his father's forehead and rattled in his mother's deep breaths. His parents spoke of another war, and Szulim began to look to the heavens when he walked outside of the hotel, wondering how low-flying airplanes would look swooping across the Parisian skyline.

"We need to get out of Europe," his father said. Everyone in the pletzel had been talking about *The Exodus* and the plight of those Jews who had headed for Palestine and were now held in Cyprus. They were the lucky ones. Others had been sent back to the very countries they fled, or were stuck in unknown camps. Szulim wondered about his friends from Hotel Beau Site. Pop no longer strolled the pletzel looking for work; instead, he brought Szulim, Sara or Abraham with him to the Joint and HIAS headquarters.

"Look sad," he'd tell them, hoping that the presence of a child would stir up some sympathy and somehow, by another miracle, produce a visa. Thanks to the blockades, Palestine, on its way to becoming the State of Israel, was no longer a dream. Szulim's parents had their eyes set on America. But the Polish quota meant there'd be a long wait.

Finally, towards the end of the month of *Adar*, as trees began to bloom and flowers blanketed the city's gardens, Szulim's father burst through the door of the hotel room waving papers. "I got them! We're going to Costa Rica!"

"Where is that?" his mother asked.

"They said it's America."

"Thanks God!" The entire family, including Berish who had been sent back from the farm, gathered in an embrace.

TELLING: SUMMER 2009

I'M EXCITED FOR tonight's phone call. It has been a few weeks since we last spoke, and in that time, I've taken the bus into New York City to visit the JDC headquarters in order to research the Rescue Children convoy. I found pictures and made copies, wondering if one of the young boys in short pants and long socks sitting on top of a jeep and smiling not at the camera, but off to the side – as if recalling a single pleasant memory among all the other memories that haunted their dreams at night – might have been Sal or his brother.

As I searched through the microfilm, I came across a letter about a man named Leo Weiss. He had been an Alderman in Zelechow and was lucky enough to immigrate to the United States in the 1930's. Once he had settled in Chicago, he joined with five others to form the Zelechower Relief organization, a small fundraising army apart from groups like the JDC or HIAS – the Hebrew Immigrant Aid Society; he had managed to raise a good deal of money. Leo Weiss had realized that sending packages to displaced *landsleit*, or countrymen, wasn't helpful and thought it would be more effective to just get them out of Europe. So he contacted landsleit who had already settled in South America, Central America and Australia, and convinced them to sponsor applications for the Zelechowers stuck in Europe so that they could be admitted to these other countries as well. Leo Weiss, with his relief organization, raised the money to pay for all the fees associated with the visas.

I'm breathless relaying all of this to Sal. "There's an entire diaspora who has this man to thank!"

Sal is amazed. "Let me tell you what I know about Leo Weiss. He had a nephew, Morris, who was born in Chicago, and this Morris worked in a post office. Well, through his connections, Morris started a secondary business where he'd buy sheets of stamps and then take a plate block, do you know what that is?" Sal stops to explain how four stamps that are attached to each other with a circular seal printed in the shared corners are apparently quite valuable. "Anyhow, this Morris would sell these blocks to collectors who were willing to pay top dollar. The rest of the stamps from that sheet, he'd sell individually at a slight profit."

Sandy is on the phone listening silently. She can hear the excitement in Sal's voice and she, too, is anxious for me to send the pictures from the archives. Ever since Andy and Robyn were babies, Sandy would compare their faces to pictures of herself as a child. There had never been any photographs of Sal.

"At the end of the war, Leo created bulletins – probably 30 to 40 pages – written in Yiddish, of course, with Hebrew lettering. And photographs. Anyway, every month, Leo would gather news about people from Zelechow and write of their whereabouts. Like the message boards we set up after the war in Zelechow and then Lodz, these bulletins were the means for families to reconnect. The two of them, Leo and Morris, sent these bulletins all over the world."

Morris must have done really well selling stamps; I can only imagine how much it must have cost to mail these small booklets overseas.

"It's amazing. There we were in France, getting word from Chicago about someone else in France or in Germany. In those days you had two options for sending things – airmail or regular post. The regular post could take from a month to a year!" Sal thinks about his father going every single day, sometimes twice a day, down to the lobby of the hotel in Paris asking if the mail had arrived. "We lived for those bulletins."

"Do you think he was responsible for your family getting to Costa Rica?" I ask.

"I don't know. But it was Leo Weiss who helped us when we were on the boat, the *Jagiello*, headed for Puerto Limon. We were the only family on board with papers for Costa Rica. Well, as it turned out, Costa Rica was in the middle of a civil war and we had to detour to Panama." Sal adds this latest revelation to the list of miracles he began forming in his mind long ago. "Would you believe that a Zelechower who lived in Panama City came and met us at the boat? Somehow, he had gotten word from Leo Weiss that my family was coming and needed help."

I'm blown away. Now with Facebook and email, people think nothing of being in constant contact. But the crudity of the information system back then? I think fondly back to my college days in the late 80's, making a long distance call to my grandmother who would squeeze an entire conversation into a single sentence – "How are you? Good? Good. Your classes? Good? Good. Friends? Good? Good. Bye." – never waiting for a response, always panicking at what the call might cost.

"This continues to amaze me," Sal says. "How families reunited after the war. How all of us from a ravaged shtetl in Poland, scattered around the earth, managed to stay connected. It's like Jewish ESP."

ADAPTING

Panama, Costa Rica

April 1948

Szulim leaned on the railing of the cargo ship. The rocking of the boat no longer turned his stomach like it had in the beginning. He had learned how to walk so that he wouldn't fall. He could stare out at the horizon without bile forming in his throat, watching the vast nothingness tip up to the left and back down again.

When they boarded the *Jagiello*, Szulim had spent the first few days below deck losing his insides. They all did. Eventually they emerged, blinking into the sunlight and wondering where they were; nothing but a vast ocean stretched farther than the eye could see. Szulim had never seen so much water in his life. Between the floor shifting underneath them and plates of funny, stringy noodles covered in a lumpy red sauce, their stomachs had been revolting.

"What is this?" a woman had asked a member of the crew when they were first presented with their dinner.

"Spaghetti and tomato sauce."

"Chaim, can this be kosher?" Szulim's mother moved her fork around, uncovering the bits of red flesh and tiny black seeds. "Look at the worms."

"I've never seen anything like this." Pop muttered into his plate, looking around at the other religious Jews. "Kids, Perl — you eat. God would be more upset if you starved."

Szulim's father pushed aside his dish. "Veyismere," he said to himself, "they don't have chickens in Italy?" Szulim, too, had wondered about this voyage. A Polish boat, operated by Italians, carried Germans and other Eastern European Jews who were no longer considered refugees as the boat left the shores of France. A chorus of languages surrounded him. Varying intonations of Yiddish, French, German, Polish, Italian and Dutch peppered the atmosphere. And of course, Spanish.

Szulim nibbled slowly, working the tangy tartness around his mouth, his tongue forming the word "spaghetti." This foreign food would one day become his favorite meal. When they eventually settled in Costa Rica and tomatoes were plentiful, his mother added them to her sour salt cabbage soup. She had been mocking their new cuisine, and in doing so, stumbled upon something delicious.

Szulim took a break from playing with the other children on the boat and sat on a deck chair next to his father. He listened as Pop read from the Yiddish-English dictionary he had picked up months before in the pletzel, sounding out unfamiliar words, practicing phrases. *I am pleased to make your ack-vaintence. I seek to find a job. I have a pencil.*

"*Tsuhern zikh, fraynd.*" Another refugee, himself heading to Uruguay, had interrupted Szulim's father with a smile. He pointed to the dictionary in Chaim's hand. "You'll need to speak Spanish."

Szulim thought his father would throw up again.

"But, aren't we going to America?"

"Yes and no. It's America, but not the one you're thinking of."

A bubble had burst, showering Szulim with disappointment. He and Abraham had been shouting their dream into the wind, feeling the mist of the ocean on their face and squinting into the sun as they imagined their new life waiting for them in America, another land of milk and honey with streets paved in gold. A house, jobs for Pop and Mama, school. A place they wouldn't move away from every other week. A place to light the Shabbos candles and call home.

What kind of life would they make for themselves in this lesser country, with only $904 in his father's pocket?

Now, LEANING ON the railing, he stared not at nothing, but at the port of some country called Panama. His family was supposed to disembark here in this country he had never heard of, even though they didn't hold the right papers. Szulim stood quietly on the deck with Sara and Abraham, gripping his tote as Mama held Berish, watching his father huddle with a man wearing short pants and a strange hat who, just moments before, had strode up the ramp and onto the boat. His father picked up the Torah that lay wrapped on the crate of life vests and turned to his family. "This is Mr. Altman. He's from Zelechow and will take us to his house until the revolution is over. Let's go."

———

SZULIM THOUGHT ABOUT Gedalia Yosef's bakery, how it felt when he carried the cholent pot across the street and stood in front of the huge oven with a roaring fire, that wave of heat rushing into his face. Now that heat penetrated through his brown jacket and white shirt, prickling his legs underneath his black pants. Sweat collected where his hair met his neck and dripped down his back. He looked at the people walking around the port, amazed at all the skin. No one dressed like his family, covering their arms and legs. Here in Panama, naked limbs stuck out from shirts and pants that seemed to be missing essential pieces of fabric. And all the skin he now saw, like the crust of a loaf of bread, was much darker than his own. Szulim studied the back of his hands, seeing through his pale, pink skin to the blue of his veins. He and his family were like the inside of a challah and he wondered how long it would take baking in the sun to look like everyone else.

Szulim and his family climbed into the back of Mr. Altman's car. His father sat in front with the Torah lying across his lap. He refused to put it in the trunk even though Mr. Altman said he'd be more comfortable.

"What kind of car is this?" Szulim's father asked.

"Not German, don't worry."

Szulim squinted as he stared out the window at the city rushing by. The fields shone a brighter green than in Poland, the trees fanning out over the landscape as if God had commanded them to cover all the animals and people and shade them from the sun.

In no time, they arrived at Mr. Altman's house. Mrs. Altman stood on the grass next to the driveway and the first thing Szulim noticed were her arms. Hinda Altman, their teenage daughter, introduced herself; her eyes glowed and her lips parted to reveal straight teeth. Szulim watched as Sara smiled at this new girl a few years older than herself. Szulim had missed his sister's smile.

"Do you want a Coca Cola?" Hinda walked into the house, motioning for them to follow. Szulim, Abraham and Sara looked at each other and shrugged as Hinda turned her back. What was a Coca Cola? The Altman home provided shelter from the sun, but blocked whatever breeze fluttered through the thick air outside. Szulim positioned himself by an open window hoping for relief. He wondered if Pop would let him rip his pants and shirt to match the clothes he saw all over this tropical city. Hinda called to them from the kitchen.

"Here! It's cold."

She held out three bottles. Szulim stared at the curvy glass. He remembered his cousin Berleh telling stories once about genies that lived in bottles. Szulim held this Coca Cola in his hand, staring into glass the same color as the ocean where it crept up to the shore of this hot land, wondering what magical being resided inside the brown liquid that danced in the bottle. He watched Sara follow Hinda's movements, doing everything she did one beat later, and raised the bottle to his lips. Just like his sister, Szulim took a gulp and nearly coughed the drink all over the floor. He wasn't prepared for the tiny bubbles popping all over his mouth or the iciness of the liquid. He didn't know it was possible for anything in this country to be so cold.

"Sip slow," Hinda said.

Szulim braved the pinpricks on his tongue and tried again. This time, a sweetness filled his mouth and relief from the oppressive heat washed down his throat and into his whole body. He smiled at Abraham and Sara as he gulped down the rest, knowing now what to expect and marveling at the fact that heaven could fit into such an oddly shaped bottle and be consumed.

"Come, I'll take you to the Canal Zone." Mr. Altman grabbed his hat. Not a hittel that Szulim wore, or a black hat like his father, but a wide-brimmed hat that clearly was not made of felt. He stepped into the sun and put on the straw head covering, his face falling into a shadow. As they drove through Panama City, Mr. Altman explained that the Canal Zone was really U.S. territory and anyone could go there. But not everyone could buy there.

"I work in the Zone. I'm lucky. The prices are much better, you wouldn't believe." Szulim stared out the window. What he couldn't believe was his good fortune at discovering the Coca Cola. He couldn't get enough of that drink. Szulim could tell they had passed into the Zone, without Mr. Altman announcing it, just by the cars. Even in Paris, where buses drove through the city, along with taxis and the occasional army jeep, people walked or rode bikes. But here in the Canal Zone, cars of all colors spun around the streets. Luxurious, flashy American cars. "American as in the United States," Mr. Altman clarified after hearing about Pop's confusion over the whereabouts of Costa Rica.

They stopped at a kiosk. "What is that?" Szulim pointed to thin cookies that curved around and stacked on top of each other, with a shape like towers that came to a point at the top.

Mr. Altman laughed. "Ice cream cones! Wait 'til you try it."

This was not the ice cream Szulim remembered from the stand near the marketplace, or even what he enjoyed during his brief stay in Prague. There, a soft cream, always vanilla, rested in a tiny wafer-like bowl. Here, the muscles on the vendor's arm twitched as he scooped a ball of hard, packed ice cream into the cookie cone. Szulim could choose from several flavors. He picked strawberry.

They walked from store to store and Szulim watched as his parents' eyes widened seeing all of the wares. Szulim stopped at a fruit stand. "Ananas! And an orange!"

"*Vos noch!*" Mr. Altman dismissed the magnificent bounty with a wave of his hand. "These things grow on the side of the road. Can you believe?"

Szulim couldn't.

May 1948 – April 1949

SZULIM LOWERED HIS head as he had seen his father do and boarded the plane that would take them from Panama City to San Jose. He thought about all the different vehicles he had ridden in throughout his life. An army jeep, a truck, a train, a boat. But all of those had stayed on the ground, or the water. Now, Szulim would soar up into the sky. That hadn't been part of the original plan; the *Jagiello* was supposed to have taken his family straight to Costa Rica. But it seemed to Szulim that plans didn't always account for much. After a few weeks tooling around Panama, his family received airline tickets from the Joint so they could finally get to their proper destination.

Szulim peered into the tiny cabin and didn't know whether to be jubilant or terrified. Butterflies and lead weights battled it out in his stomach. He wondered if his whole family would fit. Not quite; there wouldn't have been room for Rivka. He sat down and fastened the seat belt across his lap, just like his parents and Sara. As the plane raced down the strip of road, his ears filled with a cottony hum and his heartbeat matched the rev of the motor. His tongue fell back down his throat as the plane tilted upwards and the queasy sensation from the first days on the boat came back. He looked down at his hands gripping the edge of the seat and his heels dug into the floor.

Sara sat like a stone with tears streaming down her face. Abraham cried out loud, stopping only to vomit. Szulim's father pulled the fringe out of his pants, his fingers working as fast as his lips as he rocked back and forth, his eyes closed, psalms streaming from his tongue. Mama held one hand over her mouth and swallowed often, keeping her eyes on the children. Berish, not even three-years-old, slept with his head on her shoulder.

The plane rattled in the air, bumping like the buggy that carried them from

Zelechow. Szulim looked out the blurry window and saw mountains covered in green. He thought it bizarre that they could all be seasick this high up, the ocean so far below them. Before long, the cotton in his ears turned to rubber, stretching and pushing on his brain. He covered his ears with his hands and cried.

"Yawn," his father said, showing him how to open his mouth wide and take a deep breath. "It will help."

Szulim stretched his jaw as far as it would go and could feel his stomach rising into his throat as the plane drew closer to the mountains.

"Look, kids." His mother, still pale, pointed out the window. "See how small the buildings are?"

Like bugs, Szulim thought. He remembered the planes flying over Zelechow all those years ago. Did his house look like a bug then, too? Could those pilots even see him staring up at them in his Rosh Hashanah clothes? The plane sank closer to the ground below, then bumped hard against the earth, shaking Szulim back to the fact that they had reached their final destination. The end of a long and painful journey.

———

ANOTHER CAR. SZULIM didn't understand why everyone drove, especially in these places where it never snowed. He had walked down the stairs of the tiny plane and stepped onto the grass, his knees still wobbly. His parents waved at some people who stood near the building at the side of the field. A sign read "La Sabana." The letters were the same as the ones on buildings in France. Not Hebrew or Yiddish. The stranger shook his father's hand and clapped him on the back the way his uncles used to do at shtiebl.

"No luggage?"

"Just this," his father said carrying the Torah wrapped in a white sheet. The kids each carried their totes, Szulim also holding the one small suitcase his family shared. Szulim wondered how his parents knew this man standing before them now, wearing shirtsleeves and short pants, holding the door open to his automobile.

As they drove, the man spoke. "I guess I was lucky leaving Zelechow before."

"Very." Szulim could tell by his father's short replies that he was still trying to recover from the plane ride.

"How was the flight? Bumpy?" The man stretched his neck to look into the mirror attached to the windshield, smiling at Szulim's mother in the back seat. "I can tell you this now. The mountains, there have been a few plane crashes over there."

Szulim stared out the window. Costa Rica felt just like Panama. Hot. But San Jose appeared greener than the Canal Zone; buildings grew shorter, grass more abundant.

"I have to say, it's pretty amazing how the Joint sent us a telegram letting us know of your arrival. From New York, I get word that you're flying here from Panama. Can you imagine?" The man, Mr. Eisenberg, waved his hands as he drove, as if indicating the arc that the message had taken.

"The Joint is the most efficient institution I have ever heard of," Szulim's father said, regaining his voice. "Here we have nothing, and they set this all up for us — the hotel in Paris, passage to Central America, this flight. Sending messages to the Altman's, you. And to think there are probably thousands of families like us going all over the world."

"Everywhere we've been," Szulim's mother said from the back seat, "there's been someone to help us."

In just a few minutes, they pulled up to an apartment house.

"Well, here we are!" The man turned off his car and led them up some steps into the lobby. From inside, they walked down a flight of stairs. The man pulled a key out of his pocket. "I found this place. It's a basement apartment, so it opens to a little yard. It should work out nicely, I hope." He smiled at them, rubbing his knuckles in Szulim and Abraham's hair.

Szulim dropped the suitcase and his tote inside the small living room. He had never seen a floor like this, hard and shiny, almost like it was made of tiny pebbles, but completely smooth. The kitchen stood off to one side, and along the other wall were two bedrooms.

"Go out back," the man pointed. "See that slop sink? The stairs leading up go to a maid's room. But you can put some kids in there."

Szulim turned to his father. "Can Abraham and I have that room?" He didn't want to sleep in a cellar, even if it did open to a patio.

"Come," the man said. "Leave your things. You'll come to our house for lunch."

————

SZULIM HAD AN easier time than his parents getting used to the new calendar. On the 5th of *Iyyar*, or May 14th, practically everyone had gathered at the Centro, the Jewish community center in San Jose. Nearly 200 families made up the Costa Rican Jewish population, most of them living in the capital, but even those who settled in the provinces came to San Jose on special occasions. Today was a special occasion. Adults and children sat quietly, ears turned to the radio as the votes came in. The State of Israel was being born.

Mazel Tov! erupted throughout the room as the last vote was counted; hugs passing from one person to the next, an offering of congratulations on everyone's lips. Grown men smiled, tears streaming down their faces as youngsters applauded and jumped up and down. Finally, a place in the world, a small strip of desert land, where Jews would be welcome. A place to call home.

But Costa Rica was home now. Szulim looked at the people around him. They looked like everyone he remembered from Zelechow; they spoke Yiddish like everyone he used to know. And in fact, practically all of them had come from Zelechow, the only difference being that they had left Poland before the war. Yet there were some who came afterwards, like his Feter Moshe and cousins Berl and Herschel. They had fled Poland and made it to Costa Rica a few years earlier. And by the time Szulim's family had arrived, Feter Moshe had already left for New York. Berl and Herschel stayed in Costa Rica, though, and began to put down roots. They opened a store and even changed their names to Bernardo and Enrique. Szulim's parents were surprised to learn that their nephews were living amongst them; Szulim wondered why they hadn't come themselves to meet his family at the airport.

To the rest of Costa Rica, to all the non-Jews, these former Zelechowers were known as *Polackos*. In Poland, Szulim never felt Polish. The Jews there were citizens in name only; viewed as other, foreign, by those who were born and lived in the same place as Szulim. Yet now, here in Costa Rica, they finally became Polacks. When the first Jews had settled in the tiny Central American country, they had been afraid to call attention to their religion, so they referred to themselves not as *Judio*, but as Polish. Szulim wondered if there'd ever be a place where he could be exactly who he was supposed to be, the same as everyone else.

———

"You need a real name." The head of the public school looked down at his file and up at Szulim who stood in his office waiting to be assigned to a classroom. The process of assimilation would begin at *La Escuela Republica Argentina*. Szulim didn't understand why the school in Costa Rica was named after a different country, but he didn't ask. The principal narrowed his eyes in thought and said, "We'll call you Salomón."

Szulim sounded out the new name to himself, putting the emphasis on the 'mon' just as the principal had. He was more than fine with the change. After all, it wasn't the first time he had taken on a different name. He thought about Sokol's daughters and how they called him Mietek. He would do anything now to fit in.

"And we'll put you in the 6th grade. There are three other Polackos in that class." Szulim did the math in his head. He hadn't had any formal schooling since Lodz when he was in the third grade, but at twelve years old, that seemed about right. He'd be among his peers. The principal turned to Abraham. "Abe, you'll go in the third grade. There's a boy like you in that class."

Sara stood quietly, waiting for her assignment. She was 14-years-old already. "You, my dear," said the principal, "will go to a different school. *Escuela America*. There's a girl in the fourth grade you can be friends with."

Szulim looked at his sister who would be at least four years older than the rest of her classmates. None of these other Jewish students, however, spoke Yiddish. So selecting a classroom based on their presence didn't make much of a difference. No Hebrew lessons, as this was a public school. All subjects would be taught in Spanish with great emphasis placed on handwriting and discipline.

————

"*VECH OYF, YINGALEH!*" Szulim heard his father's voice calling to him from a great distance. "Wake up, Szulim. I need your help."

Szulim slowly opened his eyes, bracing against the light that streamed in through his window every morning. He still hadn't gotten used to the strength of the sun so close to the Equator. But darkness filled the room. "What time is it?"

"My legs are hurting again." His father sat on the edge of his bed, rubbing his calf. "You'll take off from school this week and go with a *peon* to make my collections."

Szulim's father had begun to make a living as a *klapper*, a peddler. All of the Jews who had immigrated to Costa Rica started out this way, picking up odds and ends on credit from the local stores and then selling the wares out in the provinces. When the merchants of San Jose heard about Szulim's family and the horrors they had lived through, they were all too eager to help.

"Even the Arabs!" Szulim's father, who had changed his name to Jaime, said proudly to his family over dinner one night. "They don't know me from a hole in the wall, yet they're extending me credit."

"And your nephews?" asked his mother. "What have they done for you?"

"They're good to our kids."

Szulim had to agree with his father. On Sunday evenings, Berl and Herschel, or Bernardo and Enrique as he tried to remember to call them, took Szulim and Abraham to the movies, and afterwards to the Parque Central where the girls walked in *vueltas* or circles, going one way, while the boys walked in another, each checking out the other. Sara had joined them, as well, until the Jewish community began talking, suggesting that she should marry one of her cousins. After the first insinuation, she stopped joining her brothers on their familial outings. Sometimes, the Boruchowicz boys would treat Szulim and Abraham to a Coca Cola or ice cream soda. The older cousins had money now and knew that Szulim's family was still struggling to put food on the table, so they were generous with the children. Szulim's mother, however, could feel the strain in the relationship. "*Zey zeinen zeyer momma's kinder*," she had said more than once. They're their mother's children. "Laicha was not such a charitable woman, either."

But Szulim wasn't thinking about his cousins or who extended credit to whom as he tried shaking himself awake before the sunrise. He yawned in the darkness and began to get dressed, careful not to wake Abraham. He wasn't upset about missing school. In just a couple months time, he had already surpassed his peers in math and geography. The Jewish kids were coming to *him* for answers. Spanish still gave him trouble, though. And he couldn't ask his parents for help. His mother barely got by speaking the native language as it was.

"There's a bus coming in 20 minutes. It'll take you to Rio Jiménez. You'll meet a fellow, Pablo, at the bodega across the street." Szulim's father hobbled into the kitchen and poured a glass of milk. He tossed an orange, a banana and a cheese sandwich into a small sack and handed it to Szulim. "Oh, here's something I need you to deliver," he said, folding two pairs of trousers and adding them to the sack. "Don't worry. You're not doing the selling. Just collecting some pesos. Pablo knows where you need to go."

Szulim leaned against the window of the bus and tried to doze, but his head continually tapped the glass as the bus bumped through the countryside. The ride took over an hour, but Szulim kept one eye open, afraid to miss his stop. The fields seemed smaller than in Poland, the landscape thick with trees and bushes whose leaves were the size of umbrellas. He had read something in school about dinosaurs, and how they roamed the Earth before people. The plants he stared at through the streaked windows of the bus seemed prehistoric; oversized, like the animals they must have sheltered millions of years ago.

For weeks, Pop talked about his business over dinner, explaining to his family how he was going to do things different than the typical klepper. He'd sell good items to the farmers.

"Everyone's afraid they'll run away. Where they going to run to?" They had learned quickly of the relative honesty among Costa Ricans. "Don't worry," fellow Jews had said at the Centro. "If the Costa Ricans steal from you, they don't steal much." That was confirmed years later when a crook came into their home and took only a light bulb from the ceiling.

Szulim's father figured he could make more money with higher quality wares. Pop extended credit on his items and the farmers paid off their purchases over time. Every week, he'd travel to the provinces; meeting a different peon in each village who would carry on his back all of the goods Pop had to offer – denim, fine fabrics, ready-made shirts, blankets. They'd walk from one farmhouse to another, the distance between each customer varying between a kilometer or two, sometimes more, trying to sell the items he carried and collecting payment on the things they had already bought. "If I'm going to walk all that way, I might as well make it worth my while. Why sell 20-peso trousers when I can get better pants and sell them for 30?"

He had come to understand that the farmers in Central America, while still goyim, were not like the farmers in Poland. If they couldn't make payment one week when his father showed up for collections, they were ashamed. Some would even hide when they saw him coming. Then again, Szulim's father was such a good salesman that he talked them into buying things they probably knew they couldn't afford in the first place.

Looking through the windshield of the bus, Szulim saw the sign for Rio Jiménez hand-written on a piece of wood and nailed to a stake driven into the ground. He threw the sack over his shoulder and walked down the aisle, stepping out of the bus and onto a dirt road. Across the street was the bodega his father had described. A woman walked by holding onto the collar of a mule. As she passed, Szulim saw a man leaning against the side of the stucco building, a shack really, smoking a cigarette.

"*Eres Pablo?*" Szulim asked.

The man looked down, and with his cigarette still dangling from his bottom lip asked, "*Quien eres tu?*"

"*Salomón. El hijo de Jaime,*" Szulim said, remembering the Spanish name his father had taken.

Pablo took the sack off of Szulim's shoulders, shook his head and said, "*Tu papa es loco!*"

"My father is sick. I may look like a little kid, but I'm tough. C'mon."

"Is this all?" Pablo asked, holding up the sack.

"Yeah. He doesn't trust me to sell yet."

Pablo pointed in the direction of the first farmhouse and they walked along, kicking up dust that stuck to the sweat beading around their ankles. Szulim was grateful for the wide-brimmed hat his father had given him earlier that morning. The school day hadn't even started and the sun already burned bright. They turned down a smaller road, a footpath, really, that led to a one-story house with a single sheet of ruffled metal forming the roof. The farmer's wife looked at the little boy standing on her doorstep and back to Pablo.

"*Quien es?*"

Szulim sighed and offered the same reply he had given to the peon earlier that morning. He asked for two pesos, just like his father instructed.

"Why aren't you in school?" Szulim would learn that even in the provinces, education was held in high esteem. In fact, Costa Rica had the highest literacy rate in the world.

"Don't worry," Szulim smiled at the woman. "I work hard and will make up my studies in the evening."

SZULIM WAS STARVING by the time he got home; looking forward to eating anything, even those red beans with rice everyone in this country seemed to love. Most of their meals had been chicken, never meat, since the kosher butcher was only qualified to slaughter fowl. Years later, when the San Jose shochet finally traveled to Mexico for proper training to slaughter meat, Mama tried making cholent again, adding the Costa Rican beans. They learned the hard way, after bouts of diarrhea, why no one – not even the rich people – ate fatty meat in the tropical climate. But without fatty meat, the cholent could never be *zoftic*, thick and rich and tasty, the way it used to be when Mama carefully unwrapped the pot every Sabbath and pronounced the meal, and their life, 'good.'

———

"HEY, *MARICÓNS!*" SZULIM held Abraham's hand and began walking faster, drawing his chin inward and looking down, hoping they could get home from school before even more kids joined in the jeering.

"Szulim," Abraham whispered, matching his brother's hurried steps, "what's a *maricón?*"

"*Faigelehs.* You know, boys who like each other."

"But we do like each other. We're brothers."

Szulim squeezed Abraham's hand without stopping. "Just ignore them. Those kids are stupid."

"*Beso, beso, beso!*"The taunts and exaggerated kisses followed them up and down streets and around the corner.

He tried to comfort his brother by telling stories of how the two of them were the greatest soccer stars in the world. And baseball, too. When these kids saw them step up to the plate and knock the ball not only out of the park, but all the way into the ocean, hundreds of kilometers away, they'd be sorry they ever called the Wainberg boys anything.

The Lebanese kid from Szulim's class was certainly sorry now. Every Friday, it had become habit for the boys to go to the plaza after school and fight, reenacting world struggles like the Arab-Israeli war on a much smaller stage through the antics of typical young male aggression. They followed the unspoken rules; no wounds, fight for fun not for pain. Szulim got sweaty and dirty every week, but never roughed up. One day, this boy's older brother rode his bike to the plaza and jumped in on the fray. The bystanders saw that the rules had been unfairly changed and tried pulling the big brother off. When Szulim broke free from the older boy's grip, he grabbed the kid's bike and rode away, pedaling furiously through the streets of San Jose. Szulim heard afterwards that the brothers looked all over town trying to find the two-wheeler that he had left lying on the side of the road, after he got far enough away from the plaza. That ended the Friday fights.

Szulim was used to taunts. Living in Zelechow, the Germans delivered verbal assaults almost daily. And even before Zelechow became a ghetto, the gentile kids who lived in his village threw stones at old men with beards or made faces at boys walking to cheder. But it wasn't the goyim now. The Jews themselves poked fun at Szulim and Abraham simply for holding hands. The very kids who were supposed to welcome him and take him in like family, whose intelligence or kindness didn't matter to Szulim's parents nearly as much as the fact that they were Jewish, picked the fights. It was one thing to throw punches at a boy whose background was at war with your own. But to be treated horribly by another Jew? This was new to Szulim, and very unsettling.

"What can I say?" his mother said when they got home and cried to her. "They're brought up differently."

———

"I KNOW YOU."

Szulim looked up from the book he was reading in the lounge at the Centro late one afternoon. A man spoke to him in a voice that was neither Polish nor Costa Rican.

"You studied at the Chachmei Lublin yeshiva in France, didn't you?"

Szulim eyed the man for a moment and then recognized him as one of the rabbis who had been involved in revitalizing one of Poland's most prestigious and well-known yeshivas after the war by creating an outpost of the school in the outskirts of Paris.

"Rabbi Hershberg!" Szulim stood up to shake the man's hand. "What are you doing here?"

"I'm traveling around Central and South America raising money for a new yeshiva in Detroit. In the United States."

"Will you be here for a bit? I know my father would love to meet you."

"Go, take your time." Rabbi Hershberg smiled at his former student and Szulim ran home to get his father.

Half an hour later, when the two men shook hands, Szulim stood to the side and listened as they spoke.

"There's not even a real school here," Szulim's father said quietly to the rabbi as he waved his hand around the room, indicating the rest of the Costa Rican Jewish community. "We survived everything being Jewish, and now we come here and I worry they'll grow up to be goyim."

"It'd be a waste for your son to stay here," Rabbi Hershberg agreed. "Let me extend a scholarship so that this young man can study in Detroit." He patted Szulim on the back.

"How can I send only one son?" his father said. "There's Abraham."

"Of course. We'll take him, too."

Two months later, at the end of May, a letter would arrive from the consulate with visas for the boys to study in America.

———

SZULIM STOOD ON the bima clutching the silver *yad* in his right fist. Bare hands could not touch the sacred parchment, so he drew the slender rod across the lines of Hebrew text as he chanted the week's Torah portion. His adolescent voice cracked as he performed the proper cantillation, not missing a single trope. The melodies came easy after hearing them sung at shtiebl every week for the first six years of his life, and after that, by Feter Moshe in the cellar. Szulim already knew the *maftir*, the concluding Torah portion; he didn't have to study for the occasion.

The event of his Bar Mitzvah felt unremarkable. Not because it was just another Saturday spent in synagogue without even a modest celebratory feast. Or the fact that his father organized a minyan just so Szulim could be given an *aliyah*, the honor of ascending to the bima to read from the Torah. Rather, the event itself marked the rite of passage from something that had never really existed for Szulim in the first place. His childhood. *Today I am a man*, he thought. But it was just a public declaration of what he already knew, and what he had been for some time already. If he was now, in fact, seen as an adult in the eyes of the Jewish community, did it mean that prior to this day, he had been merely a boy? Months before, he had walked from farm to farm in the provinces, doing a man's job, asking for pesos from people who were shamed by their poverty. And five years ago, back in Zelechow, he took over as the man of the house when his father lay frail in the Russian hospital. Certainly it was not a child at the tender age of five who saw death poke through the snow, or a boy of eight, with milk teeth still, who dug a grave for his sister.

Normally, a Bar Mitzvah would approach the Torah for the first time at the age of thirteen. But Szulim had travelled the world clutching the ancient scroll to his chest when his father's arms grew tired. And who might have watched him slip into adulthood with tears of pride? His Mimehs Gitel, Foigel, Tertza and Sara. His little cousin Berl. Rivka and Havah. Gedalia Yosef and Mimeh Yehudith. His Bubbe Wajnberg from Maciejowice. The boys from cheder with whom he played Comme Comme Tir on the streets of Zelechow. Even the children from Lodz and the Hotel Beau Site, Jewish kids whose kindness and friendship extended beyond the walls of the synagogue. *Today I am a man*, he thought. *Just like the day before.*

STUDYING
Detroit, Michigan

SUMMER 1949 – SUMMER 1951

SZULIM STEPPED DOWN from the Lacsa 340, a two-engine plane that didn't shake nearly as much as the one that took him to Costa Rica. He and Abraham each carried a small suitcase into the Miami International Airport. They were finally in America. The real America; the United States.

Szulim didn't realize the man shouting "Sal! Abe!" was calling to him and Abraham until he saw the sign with "Wainberg" scrawled in thick black marker. Rabbi Hershberg was standing in the crowd, holding up the placard and waving to the brothers. "How was your flight?" he asked when the two boys approached.

Szulim and Abraham looked at each other and shrugged. Uneventful. No one got sick; they knew to swallow as the plane descended. Eager to leave behind the constant teasing from Jews who weren't really Jewish, Szulim had stared out at the clouds and the ocean below, focusing only on the better life that lay ahead. America, the place where he could really learn; the land he had dreamed of after the promise of Palestine faded. After Costa Rica failed to open its arms and welcome him the way he had once hoped.

And now that he was in a new land, Szulim figured it was as good a time as any to truly take on a new name. Granted, he had become Salomón in the Costa Rican school, but here in America, he and Abraham could reinvent themselves. Sal. It seemed distinguished. He'd eventually learn, years later when he had his own accounting practice, that the vowel sound would lead to some confusion. Clients would say, "What should I call you?" Sal would answer, "I don't care what you call me. Just call me!" Sal pronounced his name rhyming with 'wall,' but found that English speakers would either spell it 'Sol' or pronounce Sal like 'pal.' But Szulim's passport said "Salomón," and it seemed silly to go through so much paperwork just for a vowel. Besides, Szulim – now Sal – knew how hard it could be to get papers. After a few years in Detroit, Abe would take on a new name himself, one that felt more American and would prove to be much simpler — Alan.

But on their first day in America, standing among the crowds in the Miami airport, Sal and Abe were surprised to learn that they wouldn't leave for Detroit right away.

"I want you should meet some people," Rabbi Hershberg had said as he helped them into a car. They went to Miami Beach and met Jewish families who lived in enormous houses filled with fancy furniture and wall hangings. After a few days in Miami, they took a train, not to Detroit where the yeshiva was located, but to Chicago. "I have a few more people I want you to meet."

The first few months of their studies, Sal and Abe traveled around with another rabbi, Rabbi Frankel who was the brother-in-law of the head of the yeshiva. "We're going on an excursion," he had said as he ushered the young immigrants through Toledo and Cincinnati. "Remember your accent," he'd remind the boys before introducing them as the *Yiddishe Kinder* he had saved from Europe. Sal never knew there were so many rich Jews, and by the third or fourth excursion, as his English improved and he had a better understanding of the trip's purpose, he refused to go along.

AFTER SPENDING A year in the 3rd grade in Lodz, and then a year in the 6th grade in Costa Rica, Sal was placed in the Yeshiva's 8th grade. He enjoyed the first half of the day — 7am *shacharit*, or morning prayers, followed by breakfast, then Talmud study for four hours, followed by lunch. Yet after Hebrew and *minchah*, the afternoon prayers, Sal grew frustrated. That's when Mr. Rosenberg, the principal and teacher of history and current events, taught the boys secular subjects until dinner. Sal struggled with the language and was completely lost. So the school found him a tutor, a kind man named Mr. Teddy Hollow from Hungary. Mr. Hollow spoke English, but with a French accent. Fortunately Sal found other ways to learn, mostly outside the classroom. He worked hard, attending classes and prayers during the day, staying up late to do his homework. And within a couple of months, he was at the head of his class, just like in Lodz and Costa Rica.

———

FRIDAY AFTERNOONS, BEFORE the start of Shabbat, was considered free time and Sal looked forward to those precious hours when he could hang out with his newfound yeshiva friends — Ed Kraus, Jaime Neuman, Shlomo and Maxie Rotenberg, Nate Steiberg and Moshe Finhendler. The kids didn't tease him; they could care less that he wasn't from the United States, as they called it. They were just eager for Sal to learn how to play sports, to be American like them. Almost every Friday, they met up with another group of yeshiva boys, the Bet Yehuda crowd – Jack Zwick, Meyer Segal, Joel Sperka and Eddie Traurig. They broke into teams and rechanneled their zeal for Talmud onto the ball.

"Sal, you just stand here."

"That's it? I don't swing?"

Shlomo handed Sal the bat after pointing to each of the four corners of the field. "Nah, just stand there. Jack'll throw four times and then you'll walk to first. We'll tell you."

Stand and then walk. It sounded simple enough. Much easier than fitting his hand into the unwieldy mitt and trying to grasp something small and round. With tutelage from the other boys, Sal had been keeping up with professional baseball, but when it came to actually playing the game, he couldn't understand the thrill. This opinion, he kept to himself. Soccer made much more sense, despite the fact that they didn't call it football when clearly it was a ball that was played with the feet. And that thing they call a football ... it still confounded him ever since he first held the misshapen lump of leather in the orphanage.

———

THE SCHOOL WAS closing for the High Holidays but there was no way Sal's parents could afford to fly him and his brother home. Sal was grateful that his friend Ed invited him to be with his family for Rosh Hashanah. Nate Steiberg's family was also from Detroit and he invited Abe to his house. Sal packed a small bag with his toothbrush, change of clothes, and his tefillen. They didn't have to walk to the bus station; Ed's father drove in from the suburbs to pick them up.

"Thank you so much for having me." Sal held out his hand to Mrs. Kraus as he walked into their large house, but her hands remained clasped together in front of her apron.

"Well," she said, "Costa Rica is so far, you know."

Sal looked around, noticing the heavy drapes, the frames covering the walls filled with photographs of Ed and his younger brother and sister, grandparents, aunts and uncles. The dark wooden furniture shone underneath lace mats covered with vases and curios.

"You have a beautiful home." Sal smiled at Ed's mother. She blinked several times as she smiled back.

"Hannah, Ira," Mr. Kraus said turning to the kids coming down the stairs, "Come meet Ed's friend from Costa Rica."

"Actually, I'm from Poland."

"Yes, well, you know," Mr. Kraus smiled, "that's the past."

"You have an accent." Hannah stood on the bottom step and stared.

"Let's sit down and eat," said Mrs. Kraus.

Ed's family was gracious, but Sal could see the word "greener" written on their faces as they looked at him, and for the first time, he felt like a foreigner. A stranger in a relatively normal land. They didn't ask him about Poland, or the war. Sal wouldn't have minded sharing some of his experience, being the center of attention. But no attention was paid to the Holocaust, and at that moment, Sal sensed that Americans just wanted to forget about the whole thing. "Who needs to talk about these troubles?" he'd hear in years to come. "It's over. Let's focus on happier things."

———

SAL AND ABE weren't the only Survivors at yeshiva. Mordecai and Aron Katz, too, came from Poland. They were several years older and had never pretended to be orphans; they truly had lost their parents.

"Stupid yid," Mordecai muttered often to Sal or Abe.

"You're stupid." Sal and Abe always returned the pokes, never taking an insult without giving it right back. The rest of the boys at yeshiva knew where to find the Katz and Wainberg brothers. They were constantly fighting in some corner or another.

"Come." Rabbi Rotenberg, the head of the yeshiva, put his arm around Sal's shoulder after a particularly rough scuffle and led him down the hallway towards his office. "I'd like you to join me for Shabbat dinner tonight. I have a *muser* for you, a little story. You may learn something."

LATER THAT NIGHT, lying in his room — the first bedroom he ever had to himself — Sal thought about the rabbi's admonition. "Mordecai and Aron, their experience was different," he had said. "Their suffering was different." Sal listened intently to the rabbi as he explained human behavior. "You have to understand that it's not about you," he said. "They're fighting their own demons." Sal turned these words over and over in his head, anxious to share them with Abe. He heard the wisdom, coming to the realization that when people yell at you, they're not really yelling at you. They're yelling at themselves.

"So why fight?" Rabbi Rotenberg had smiled at Sal before tearing off another piece of challah and handing it to his student. Sal had thanked him and carried this lesson into adulthood.

———

MILTON BERLE PICKED up where his English tutor failed him. After Shabbat services on Friday, when they didn't study because of the Sabbath, Sal walked with Moshe, Shlomo, Maxie, Ed and Abe ten blocks from the yeshiva to Dexter Avenue. A television sat behind the glass window of an electronics store, and even though the store was closed for the night, the television flickered in the dark, broadcasting the evening's entertainment to the entire neighborhood. Uncle Miltie and Ed Sullivan, their faces and voices both, came through the glass thanks to a speaker set up outside.

"But, it's Sabbath." Abe looked at Sal, then at the other boys whose faces glowed blue under the streetlamp.

"Yeah," said Maxie. "But we didn't turn the TV on. We just walked here."

"He's right," Sal said.

The free entertainment was a *mitzvah* and the boys jockeyed for position in front of the television set. Sal wondered if a Shabbos goy would come late in the evening to shut it off.

———

THE DOOR OPENED to Sal's room and Nate poked his head inside.

"C'mon, you ready?"

Sal grabbed his cap and felt for the change in his pocket. "Yeah, coming."

"*Rocky Jones Space Ranger* is playing at 4," said Ed, hunching into his overcoat as the group of boys headed out into the cold. Rather than play ball on this wintry Sunday, they walked to the Avalon Theater. "At 6:30 we'll see *From Here to Eternity*."

"Deborah Kerr..." Moshe sighed. Sal punched him in the arm. A block from the theater, they put on baseball caps and peeled off their long pants, revealing the shorts they wore underneath. They rolled up their trousers and stuffed them in their totes, along with their winter hats.

Sal approached the ticket booth first, slumped his shoulders and spoke in an octave or two higher than usual. "One ticket for Rocky Jones, please. I'm under 12."

He handed over his 25 cents, a reduced rate for children, and waited for the other boys before walking past the concession stand and into the theater. They didn't have money for popcorn. Besides, it probably wasn't kosher. They had a system. When the movie ended, they'd go into the bathroom and change back into their long pants, stuff the caps into the bag and put on their hats, button their shirts all the way up to their necks and then walk with shoulders back and heads high into the theater for a movie geared towards a more mature audience; the yeshiva boy double feature. *Little Boy Lost*, *Houdini*, *The All American*, *War of the Worlds*, *Flight to Tangier*. Practically every weekend, Sal lost himself in the big screen.

———

SAL CAME BACK from his job as a busboy at Lacher's, one of the kosher restaurants on Linwood Street. When the scholarship letter had first arrived, back in April of 1949, the yeshiva had promised to give the boys stipends; but as it turned out, funding hadn't come through. Sal didn't want to write to his father and ask for help. Not only could his parents not afford it, Sal didn't want his father to be upset with the yeshiva. So he and Abe took odd jobs in order to earn some pocket money.

"Hey, Sal!" Maxie stood in the common area of the dormitories on the third floor where the boys often congregated after dinner, or during breaks from studying. He was waving an envelope. "You got a letter."

No one got phone calls, they were too expensive. Sal remembered when Moshe Finhendler had gone to New York and had forgotten his suitcase. He called the yeshiva collect, and when the operator asked, "Who's calling?" he said, "Mr. *Shik mir thi valske*." Mr. Send me the Valise. Whoever answered the phone understood the message and answered, "He's not here but will arrive in two days."

Letters from home were special, so even though Abe was still at his job, Sal grabbed the envelope and ran to his room to read it. He looked at the Hebrew letters scrawled on the thin piece of paper. He recognized immediately from the handwriting that the letter was from his mother. He remembered the first letter he had gotten from Mama, how he had realized then that he had never seen her handwriting before, aside from a few numbers scribbled in the margins of a newspaper that lay on the counter of the store in Zelechow. Now, correspondence from his parents came monthly. His mother's Hebrew letters were flowy, dipping and dancing all over the page, unlike the tight, blocky manner in which Feter Moshe wrote in his makeshift siddur. When Sal first arrived in Gastain and studied from an official siddur, he had trouble recognizing the words printed in the standard script since he had learned to read from his uncle's scribbles in the cellar.

Dearest boys, the letter began. *May this correspondence and God find you well. All is good here, though it is hot! Oy veyismere. I trust Mrs. Greenspan has paid you a visit?*

She's been in Detroit for some time visiting Rachel. Sal knew the Greenspan's. Their oldest daughter had married a man from Detroit. Sal had never met this daughter because she had already moved to the States when he and his family arrived from Panama. *We were able to buy a ticket for one of you to come home for a visit and Mrs. Greenspan has graciously offered to accompany you on the plane in a few weeks. Pop thinks Szulim should come home first since he is farther ahead in his Hebrew studies. Abraham, I'm sorry we couldn't afford to bring you as well, but we are working hard to buy another ticket soon.*

It had been two years since the boys had seen their parents, Berish and Sara. Though Sal found life in America far more preferable to that in Costa Rica, he missed his family and was eager to pay a short visit. Sal didn't know as he boarded the plane with Mrs. Greenspan that Abe would have more than enough time to catch up to his big brother with his studies, as well as change his name. No one could have foreseen the bureaucracy in immigration that would keep Sal stuck in Costa Rica for 15 months waiting for another student visa.

TELLING: SUMMER 2009

THE PHONE CALLS have gotten easier. I don't feel the same heaviness leading up to them as when I had to probe painful memories, draw out heart-wrenching details. But the conversations are no less revealing.

"It was then, in Detroit, when I first realized there was something wrong with me," Sal begins. "Something had happened to me that I had never accounted for. Something unresolved. Can you understand that?"

I nod, then realize Sal can't see my gesture. "Of course," I say. "It was when you had time and freedom to ruminate. Plus, you were maturing."

"I suppose, but I wasn't smart enough to try to find a way to resolve it; instead I fought it out within myself. I tried to come up with a reason. Why did this happen? Why couldn't I have been a normal person?" Sal pauses. "It still bothers me. To this day, I do things ... I behave in certain ways, and don't give it a second thought. But when I reflect on it, I realize it's a reaction to my experience."

Sandy inhales quickly and holds her breath. She never thought Sal could admit to his differences, his eccentricities. There's been a whole lifetime of them. She had told me about being in Gainseville the night of the moonwalk; she was pregnant with Andy. They were with friends, transfixed by what they were watching on the television set. The entire world sat transfixed. But Sal sat off to the side as if they were watching a sitcom. "Sal, don't you want to see this?" Sandy had asked. "Aren't you excited?" He said, "When am I ever excited about something? I've seen amazing things before."

Sandy sits in the kitchen tonight, holding the phone, as Sal speaks from the living room. She runs her free hand across the table and thinks back to all the family dinners they shared when the kids were growing up. Even during tax season, when the rest of Sal's accounting firm worked late into the night, he never missed a meal with the children. But there were moments at that table when he seemed so far away, like that whole business with the butter and the bread. There'd be an entire stick of margarine, but Sal would take just a tiny bit onto his knife and spread it on the roll, working the small bit over the entire surface, until there was barely anything left on the knife. "Sal," Sandy pointed to the table, "there's more butter right here." But it was like he didn't hear her. Or see Robyn, rolling her eyes. Sal just kept working the knife over the bread, until he had one bite left. "*Dinstig!*" he said aloud, before popping it into his mouth. Andy would stare and ask, "What's 'dinstig'?"

This would shake Sal back to the present and he'd say, "Oh, it means 'Tuesday.'"

"But that's a roll, dad."

"Oh, it's just something Alan and I used to do when we were little."

Sandy still can't understand how Sal and Alan could have both lived the same life, shared the same horrible experiences, yet react to them so differently. For years, Sandy has tried to maintain a social life with the couples they are close to. When they go out to dinner, however, it always has to be at a restaurant of Sal's choosing. Their close friends have accepted this about him. But it's been hard to maintain the friendships when she keeps saying 'no.' No to movies; no to shows. Sal won't go to any of it. Yet Alan does. Sandy had asked, long ago, "Why can your brother enjoy himself this way but not you?"

Sal had simply said, "He's crazy for spending the money."

Sandy knows it's not the money; Sal was a very successful accountant. Maybe it was Survivor's guilt? She got tired of psychoanalyzing. I had asked her a few weeks ago, when we spoke privately, if Sal can experience joy. "Yes," she had said, "but it's tempered." Sandy spoke of Sal at the granddaughters' birthday parties, how he'll look around at the balloons and cake and say, "Do they need to throw out all this money?" She always tells him to relax, enjoy the moment. But she's gotten used to it by now. They call it 'the sickness'; Sal's fully aware of it, and to some extent, Sandy has contracted it, too – this fear of spending money, of letting anything go to waste. Their garage is like a mini-Costco, filled with extra rolls of paper towels, batteries, flattened cardboard boxes. They can barely fit the car inside.

Still clutching the phone, Sandy walks over to the fridge and repositions the drawing that has fallen loose from the magnet. It's a crayon portrait of their granddaughters – Lanie, the 8-year-old artist, is in the middle, right between her big sister Marlin and the youngest, Sadie. The girls' parents, Robyn and Noah, float above them, along with their Uncle Andy. Meht Meht and YaYa (both terms of endearment born from mispronunciations, the first of 'grandma,' the latter of 'zayde') are included in the drawing as well, positioned on either side of the girls. Sandy and Sal had been touched to be included.

Sandy has spoken of the bond between her children, the incredible closeness of the three generations. She knows how lucky she and Sal are to live near their kids and the girls. The intense loyalty Sal has with his own siblings, that he had with his parents, Sandy sees in her own offspring. She knows they get that from their father.

Robyn jokes that her dad didn't become fun until he retired and had grandkids. Sal is crazy about her girls, totally *meshuggenah*. When they learned that Ya Ya means grandmother in Greek, Robyn began calling Sal their Big Fat Greek Grandma. He loved it.

Sal is talking about their grandkids now. "Just the other day, Sandy and I were driving and two of Robyn's girls were in the backseat, making up stories. I said to Sandy, 'That's just like Alan and I. We used to tell each other stories.' Sandy, you remember what you told me?"

"Yes," she says. "I said that's called play therapy."

"I'm not up on all this psychological what-have-you," Sal says. "But, you know, I think she's right." Sandy is happy to hear Sal acknowledge her in this way. "Through play, as Sandy says, I was able to exorcize my demons. Alan and I both. And who did my sister Sara have to share in that intimate act of healing? No one. So there you have it. It may explain things somewhat."

"Was it hard to leave Sara when you left for Detroit? And Berish, your parents?" I ask.

"Perhaps to some degree, after all, we were finally together again as a family. But I knew Costa Rica wasn't where I ultimately wanted to be." Sal pauses to reflect a moment. "It was hard leaving Bernie – that's what we called Berish when we changed names – he was so young still. Sara, I felt she would be fine. I guess I was a typical adolescent at the time, worried only about myself. I didn't think about the fact that we were moving on and she would be stifled. If anything, I thought she was content."

"Was she?"

"I thought so. That first year in Costa Rica, my family would go to synagogue every Saturday. But in the afternoons, Alan and I would sneak out and go to the movies."

"So, you do like movies!" I laugh.

"I did. But the movies today are not worth paying money for. Anyway, Sara knew we snuck to the theater and asked us once why we never invited her to come along. So we did. But then she kept saying things like 'you shouldn't be spending the money.'"

"The voice of reason," I say.

"Exactly. The good angel on our shoulder. We started to grow apart. Sandy and I have talked about this many times, but it was like Sara, only a year and a half older than me, was of a different generation."

"You each reacted to your experiences in such different ways," I suggest. "You all lost the innocence of childhood…"

"Yes, but I sometimes think that it was that innocence, that lack of a greater worldview, that saved us." Sal shares something he has read recently, a study on who survived, who didn't and why. He wasn't surprised to learn that babies and toddlers perished outside of the camps, unless they were raised by gentiles, but teenagers, too, did not survive in hiding.

"Why is that?" I ask.

"Probably the same reason they're so hard to raise today!" Sal knows. He raised two. "That feeling of invincibility they possess, combined with poor judgment. Young children, like my siblings and I, were scared. We were obedient. Teenagers challenged authority and took risks."

This makes sense to me. But still, how could a child of five or nine, kids the age of my own sons, survive such horrors?

"Maybe it's because we didn't fully understand what there was to worry about." I listen to Sal's explanation and remember him talking about the curfew, how at the time he didn't think much of it. "When we were in Paris, waiting for a visa, what did I know of the Berlin Blockade and immigrant quotas? The worrying alone is enough to make you give up. It's like kids in car crashes. They fare better because they're looser, more relaxed. This is just my theory."

"Is that why you survived?"

"I have no idea why I survived." Sal sighs. "I certainly don't take any credit for it. If anything, it's my father. But what makes us, any of us, survivors?"

It's a question my friend had brought up a few weeks before when she mentioned an article that had run several years ago in some business magazine. It had profiled a handful of big time success stories, people who created companies that made millions. One thing they all had in common was that they were Holocaust survivors. I did more research after that conversation and discovered that Dr. Ruth, Roman Polanski, U.S. Representative Tom Lantos — all had been through the Holocaust. Which begged the question: is the character trait that enabled these people to survive the same trait that made them successful?

I mention this article to Sal and ask, "So, are they natural-born leaders, risk-takers, what have you, and it was this inherent gift that kept them alive? Or, are they successful because their earlier experiences taught them something they could then apply to other parts of their life?"

Sal thinks about this for a moment. "Perhaps a little of both. I can tell you that my experience had a direct impact on the trajectory of my career. When I first started in accounting, I went to work for a guy — I won't mention his name in case you should know him — but he was a real taskmaster. Yelled constantly, had no respect for his employees. No one lasted more than a year or two."

"And?"

"Well, two things I understood. He wasn't yelling at me; he was yelling at himself. Remember that lesson from Rabbi Rotenberg? He had his own issues and they weren't mine and if he needed to take it out on someone, fine. The other thing was, he didn't scare me. What was the worst thing that could happen? He'd fire me? Big deal."

I understand. After everything Sal had been through as a child, losing a job paled in comparison. "So, how long did you last with him?"

"Five years and then I started my own practice," says Sal. "I lasted longer than anyone. I'll tell you, I actually learned a lot from him."

Sandy knows exactly who Sal is talking about. She had been so impressed with her husband, all those years ago, and how he had handled himself in that office. In fact, Sal had impressed her when they first met back in 1961. She thought he was unlike any other man she had ever gone out with. Worldly, mature, incredibly serious – a grown up, completely committed to his family. *You watch how a man treats his mother and sister*, her mother always said. *That's how he'll treat you.* Sal had worshiped his parents and was completely devoted to Sara and Bernie, always writing to them. The bond he had with Alan was remarkable. Sandy could see that Sal was a man who took care of people and she felt very safe with him.

"So, tell me," I say. "How else has your experience shaped you?"

"Oy." Sal takes a moment to think. He told me recently that so many of my questions make him stop and really dig deep. "You know that book you gave me to read? About the Lost Boys in the Sudan?"

"*What is the What* ... did you like it?"

"Not so much. Sandy and I both read it, and the whole time Sandy's reading it, she's commenting on how sad this and horrible that. I read it and all I could think is that it was nothing compared to what I went through."

"Really?" I am incredulous. "A boy gets torn apart from his family, wanders through the jungle for years, sees his best friend get eaten by a lion..."

"I know. And I'm not so impressed. What's wrong with me? Why shouldn't I be able to have normal feelings and reactions to something like that? It's a major character flaw."

I don't see it as a character flaw, necessarily, rather, a response to his own suffering. I venture out on a limb. "You know how when a person suffers nerve damage, they'll feel nothing attached to that nerve? Do you think it's possible that you had emotional nerve damage, and maybe lost some of that ability to empathize?" I hold my breath, not sure how Sal will react.

"I think in a way that makes sense. I have an incredible tolerance for physical pain, so who knows? I don't beat myself up over it, or lose sleep."

Sandy has never seen Sal beat himself up over anything, ever, always so certain and sure of himself. When they were raising the kids, he was the husband who could do it all. He was certainly more hands-on than most of her friends' husbands who panicked at the thought of a dirty diaper. Dressing a wound, building a model, he was the one who made breakfast every morning for the kids. Sal attended every one of Andy's baseball games, every one of Robyn's dance recitals. He never wanted to miss a moment from the kids' lives. He just didn't know what those moments were supposed to be. He could take care of all of their physical needs, but it was like he was unable to help them emotionally. As Sandy described it, he was at a loss with the *coochie coo*.

Sandy remembers Sal standing in the backyard with Andy, holding a mitt. He had no idea what to do and she'd ask, "Didn't you throw a ball when you were a kid?" Or they'd all be in the den watching *I Love Lucy*, and he'd be the only one who didn't laugh. At the time, Sandy attributed it to his rural upbringing, his piousness. But now she knows it's so much more than that. She thinks back to when they first started dating and getting serious, when she imagined how a life with Sal would be an easy one. *How ironic*, she thinks now. Life with Sal has been interesting, fulfilling, complicated and intense. But not easy. She can see their marriage mirrored against those of their friends. And while it's true that one can never know what goes on in another couple's bedroom, Sandy knows. This is not normal. She and Sal are not normal.

Sal is getting tired. We've been on the phone for three hours. He has only one more thing to add. "This time in Detroit – and then the year-and-a-half I spent in Costa Rica for what I thought would be a short visit – it was a time of great reflection. As any child who suffers something, I dealt with it after the fact." Sal thinks for a moment. "No, let me restate. I'm still dealing with it."

LEARNING

Detroit, Michigan

Winter 1953 – Summer 1953

January 20, 1953. The day Dwight D. Eisenhower took the oath of office and became the 34th president of The United States, Sal flew back to Detroit from an 18-month visit with his family. During social studies class the next afternoon, Mr. Rosenberg, the principal of their secular studies, welcomed Sal back from his "sabbatical" and led a discussion about the election. Sal stared at the mimeographed newspaper article and pored over the words of Eisenhower's inaugural address.

> At such a time in history, we who are free must proclaim anew our
> faith. This faith is the abiding creed of our fathers … This faith
> defines our full view of life. Here, then, is joined no argument
> between slightly differing philosophies. This conflict strikes directly
> at the faith of our fathers and the lives of our sons.

Sal read it over and over; talk of faith, commitment and war. What did any of these Americans really know about war? He hadn't seen foreign soldiers patrolling the streets of Detroit. His friends played ball as if that was the only care in the world. He envied them the lightness in their steps, feeling for the first time how he stood apart in a way that he could not yet define. He thought about the notion of faith, of fathers and sons, of what it meant to be an American. The Talmud, the movies, his friends, his past – all churned together inside him, playing on a never-ending reel in his mind. The whims of others, the direction of his own choosing; understanding and reconciliation.

———

SAL AND ALAN walked around Sam's Department Store during one of their free Friday afternoons. Sal was eyeing the various discount merchandise, comparing it to the dry goods his parents sold in La Perla, the store they had finally been able to open in the marketplace in San Jose. Pop had continued klepping; he wasn't sure how business would go in their new store, and he had to ease out of the peddling business slowly. After all, if he didn't bring something new for the farmers to buy, they'd have little incentive to pay him what they already owed. But the store did well; well enough that his parents had been able to buy their oldest son a plane ticket. Sal worked in the store during the year he had spent in Costa Rica waiting for another visa. He had seen firsthand his mother's sales skills. Her Spanish was still pitiful, despite having lived in the country for several years already, but the Costa Ricans were charmed by her efforts at communication, and somehow, with smiles and gestures and a few understood words, Perla (for she too had changed her name in their new country) convinced people to buy the stuff on her shelves. Everyday for a year, Sal had helped his parents open their stall, hanging items outside, placing others on the shelves towards the back. And every evening, when it was time to close, they'd pack it all up.

Now, wandering through the aisles in downtown Detroit, Sal was simply a customer, unidentifiable as a yeshiva boy with his *yarmulke* tucked into his pocket. He had mixed feelings about wearing the skullcap that was required of him. He never took it off on the grounds of his school, not just because it was mandatory, but out of respect. Yet as he had begun delving deeper in the Talmud and studying on his own, he found himself trying to reconcile logic with faith.

Sal kept his head covered as a child, but never with a *kippa*. No one in his right mind wore a yarmulke in Poland. The gentiles would never have tolerated such a provocative display of religiosity. Even the *payot*, common before the war, grew shorter and shorter when things changed, when life became too difficult for curls of hair to hang in front of the ear. So the Jewish men wore the same hats as the goyim and tucked their *tsitsit*, the fringe of their prayer shawls, into their pants. The women and girls covered their hair with babushkas while Sal and Alan, along with all the boys their age, wore hittels – felt caps, like berets with a visor. When he and his family immigrated to Costa Rica, the head coverings traditional to Europe and appropriate for the cold were replaced with straw hats that shielded their faces from the sun. The same hats everyone living in a tropical climate wore. Besides, the Costa Rican Jews, like the goyim in Poland, would have had a field day if Sal or his father wore a yarmulke. Only in Detroit had the kippa been customary.

Sal and Alan left the shop, and as they strolled towards the fancier department store a few blocks away, they ran into Rabbi Rotenberg.

"Sal?" The head of the yeshiva stopped and stared. "Where's your yarmulke?"

"In my pocket."

"And why is it not on your head?"

Sal looked at the rabbi and shrugged. "I'm not at the school, so I didn't think it was necessary."

"What's not necessary? God? Is God not necessary?" A strand of saliva vibrated in front of the rabbi's teeth, like the string of a harp, and he paused to pucker his lips.

"Well, in the Talmud, I thought …"

"Come, I'd like you to join me for Shabbos dinner this evening. We can talk."

As SAL WALKED side by side with Rabbi Rotenberg, a kippa resting at the back of his head, he tried reasoning with the director of the yeshiva. "Nowhere in the Talmud does it say we have to wear a yarmulke. In fact, there was a portion we read last month that talked about the value of the yarmulke, and how a particular rabbi thought it was valuable, but it was noted that he never went without a head cover." Sal held out his hands. "So I figured, if the Talmud talked of this rabbi who never went without, then there must have been others that did. That it must not be required."

The rabbi stopped walking and turned to face his student. "*Emunah*, Sal. Believe, even if it's not logical. We study the Talmud so we can be Jews. We wear a yarmulke and refrain from traif so we can be Jews." Rabbi Rotenberg shook his finger at Sal. "You can't reason your way out of who you are."

"But, the whole point of studying Talmud is to question."

Rabbi Rotenberg faced down the street and began walking. "You shouldn't question God, or your father."

———

SAL WALKED PAST the drugstore across from the yeshiva where he and his friends would stop in on Friday afternoons. Summer had come early to Detroit and he thought how wonderful a milkshake would taste about now. The only thing he ever consumed from this drugstore was a milkshake or a soda; nothing else was kosher. But oftentimes, Sal eyed the hamburgers as they passed through the window between the kitchen and the counter. He'd watch the kids from Central High talking and laughing in between bites, wistful of their freedom to sit at a table and not be conscious of what went into their mouths. Not that he didn't feel free. He and Alan spoke often about their independence. About how wonderful it felt to be living without the weight of the world on their shoulders, with hours on the weekend completely unstructured and theirs alone to make of it what they will. These free hours, however, had begun to be filled with work.

Sal hurried his pace so that he wouldn't be late for his job. He and Alan planned a weeklong trip to New York at the end of the summer, stopping in Charleston, SC along the way for a visit with a distant cousin of Pop's. But in order to travel, they had to come up with the bus fare. So Sal spent a month at the JCC working as a lifeguard. Sal was grateful to Marty, an engineering student he met there when he first arrived in Detroit. Not only did Marty teach him to swim, he also taught Sal to be a lifeguard, and then gave him a water safety instruction test so Sal, too, could eventually teach others to swim.

Sal earned the bus fare in a variety of other ways as well. When he wasn't at the pool, or studying or praying, Sal bussed tables at Lacher's. He didn't have a social security number, so he got paid in tips. Then, as the weather turned warmer, Sal rode around the streets of Detroit on a bike with a freezer attached to the front selling Good Humor. And when the quiet Jewish fellow came by the yeshiva to pray, he pulled Sal aside and offered odd jobs, like making chicken coops or moving furniture. In the same hodge-podge manner, Alan, too, managed to scrape together some savings.

FINALLY, IN AUGUST of 1953, Sal and Alan boarded a Greyhound that would take them on a roundabout route from Detroit to New York City, via Charleston. As they rolled down the highway, watching fields become farmlands and then wooded areas, Sal turned to Alan. "I want to live here. In America."

"You do. We do, at yeshiva."

"No," Sal said. "I mean really live here, with a resident visa. So we can work real jobs. Make a life for ourselves."

"That'd be nice." Alan agreed. "You can't work with a student visa. Not for real wages."

"It's not just that." Sal shook his head and looked out the window at the vast fields. "You don't know what it's really like in Costa Rica. You were only there for a year."

Sal turned back to Alan and tried to explain. "The Jews there say they're Jewish. But I felt like we're constantly being judged for being more observant." Sal spoke of how he'd go to synagogue with Pop every Friday night and Saturday during the year he had been home from yeshiva, yet the other Jews spent the Sabbath working in their businesses.

"Remember that Herschel Raifer?" Sal asked Alan. "The gabbai who acted like the rabbi? He has an illegitimate kid in some village."

"No way!"

"I'm telling you. And he beats up his wife." Sal shook his head. "This, our spiritual leader."

"What does Pop say?" Alan asked.

"Ach, Pop." Sal sighed. "I don't know if he truly doesn't see it, or if he doesn't want to see it. It's all so hypocritical."

"I feel bad for him."

"Me too. It's the only world he has now. Anyway, we need to get out."

So they made a plan to graduate early from yeshiva, leaving Detroit in January, which was only four months away. They'd return to Costa Rica and immediately apply for a resident visa so they could come back to America as legitimate Americans. The sooner they could begin their new life, the better. On the bus, they wrote a letter to their parents informing them of their intentions.

AFTER FOUR HOURS, they pulled into a Greyhound bus stop in Toledo, Ohio. Sal and Alan got off, happy to stretch their legs. They followed the rest of the passengers across the parking lot and into a small restaurant filled with sunlight.

"Hi, hons." The waitress barely looked at them from behind the lunch counter where they sat, a ballpoint pen poised to take their order, her mouth working on a large piece of gum. "What'll you have?"

Sal glanced at the menu and quickly surveyed the room, taking in what others were eating. He looked up at the waitress, still chewing her gum and scratching her frizzy hair with the bottom of the pen.

"I'll have a burger and some tomato soup." He closed the menu and looked at his brother. Alan stared at Sal, his mouth agape, until he closed his menu as well, looked to the waitress and said, "The same, please."

TELLING: SUMMER 2009

"I DIDN'T EVEN think about it," Sal says of the time he broke the laws of kashrut. "No, that's not true. I had done plenty of thinking already. Eating that food was purposeful. I knew what I was doing, and more importantly, deep down in my heart, I knew there was no reason why I shouldn't enjoy it."

Sandy's ear is growing hot from pressing it against the phone, but she is absorbed by Sal's explanation of how he reconciles faith with logic.

I, too, am fascinated. "Was this like stage two – first the kippa, then the food?"

"Yes, I suppose." Sal pauses for a moment. "But eating non-kosher food was much more than taking off my kippa. The business with the yarmulke belonged to the yeshiva only."

"What do you mean?"

"I honestly felt that wearing a yarmulke wasn't necessary. I wore it at yeshiva out of respect, not conviction. Had Rabbi Rotenberg tried to engage me in a discussion about it, made an effort to seek common ground, my whole outlook may have been different. But on that walk to dinner, after he caught me without a yarmulke, he laid down all the terrible things that would happen to me if I didn't obey." Sal laughs. "I guess you could say that started me, at the age of 17, on my 'road to perdition.'"

"Do you think this was some sort of teenage rebellion?" I ask.

"I wasn't trying to be subversive. But the fact that this rabbi couldn't argue – no, that's a terrible word – connect with me on any kind of logical plane, it felt indoctrinating. That sealed the deal."

"So, what about the food?"

"That was all about my faith. My faith and my family," Sal says. "I remembered my father's parting words at the train station in Lodz."

I remember them too. *Don't ever forget who you are. Don't ever forget that you're a Jew.*

"But that's the thing! I never forgot I was Jewish." Sal tries to find the words to help me understand. "I just couldn't come up with a reason why I needed to keep kosher; I couldn't reconcile this practice with everyday life. It wasn't a matter of turning against religion, just finding a different way to be Jewish. Once I came to this conclusion, it was simply a matter of finding the proper time to put it into practice. And the proper time came when I was no longer in the yeshiva environment."

Sandy listens to Sal and understands now why he never asked her to keep a kosher home. She hadn't grown up keeping kosher herself, but she would have done it for Sal. She had always felt bad that his parents could never eat at her house.

"What about Alan?" I ask. "Was he on this same journey?"

"He wasn't as knowledgeable about Talmud." Sal thinks for a moment. "We never really discussed it. But I guess he figured if his big brother was doing it, then it's okay. He was content to let me be the leader."

"Did you think about your father at this time? Were you at all concerned with what he might think?"

Sal thinks about his father still. "He was a very religious man, as you know. But he was also extremely tolerant. He always said religion is a good thing, for the religious. He wasn't offended by non-religious actions. I knew he trusted me, that he believed I was a good person."

"And I guess he was smart enough to accept you rather than alienate his child."

"Absolutely. He was never going to be able to convince me to do something I didn't want to do, or didn't believe in." Sal remembers the time his father first caught him with a cigarette, when he was 15 years old and stuck for a year in Costa Rica. His father had just looked at him and said, "What are you smoking? Mind if I try one?" Then he told his son not to smoke on Shabbos.

"When did your parents find out you stopped keeping kosher?" I ask.

"When Alan and I returned to Costa Rica after graduating yeshiva, and realized it would take longer than we had anticipated to get papers to move to the States, we organized Red Cross water safety lessons in a place called Ojo de Agua." Sal explains how it was a really long drive out to the provinces, so his mother used to pack their lunches. There were no kosher restaurants, so the only way to keep kosher was to eat food that came from their kitchen at home. "One day, Alan and I forgot to take the lunch. When we got home late at night, my mother was so upset that we hadn't eaten. I told her not to worry; we ate in a restaurant. Well, you can imagine."

"Oh my gosh!" I think about Sal's father refusing soup in the cellar when he feared it wasn't kosher. "How did they react?"

"They knew enough not to ask where I ate. But the understanding was there. It wasn't that I accidentally let it slip; I had thought about my response ahead of time. You see, I wasn't going to tell a lie, and there's only so long you can carry on pretending."

"Did you feel like you were betraying your parents in some way?"

"No. I honestly had no sense of guilt." Sal says this with conviction. "I live my life where I do my worrying before I act. Once I finish worrying, I do what I set out to do and I don't look back. I live now and in the future."

"Your parents had such a different reaction than that rabbi," I say.

Sal tells me about the time Rabbi Rotenberg came to Miami, sometime in the 1970's when Andy and Robyn were little. Sal wanted to see him.

"Really?" I'm surprised. "After everything with the kippa?"

"Well, remember. He did teach me something valuable, that whole business with the Katz brothers," Sal says. "He was a very intelligent man. He just dedicated his life to religion and that was where we parted ways. But would you believe, when I visited him some 20 years after I left yeshiva, he says to me, 'What a shame you got lost. You could have been an asset to the Jewish community.'"

"You're kidding!"

"No. All I could think was how different he and I were. To me, observance and proselytizing don't make you a good Jew. It's doing good deeds. And I have dedicated my life to that. You know what is *Tikkun Olam?*"

"Of course," I say. "Repairing the world. It's one of the tenets of Judaism."

"Yes. My father always said you have to give tzedakah 'til it hurts and you have to do it anonymously." Sal thinks about the lessons he learned from his father, the value of money. His parents were one of the richest people in Zelechow, yet arrived in Costa Rica with practically nothing. "What good did the money do, really? You can't take it with you. Want to laugh? Here I am a CPA, and in the early '80's, I was audited three years in a row. Why? I gave so much to charity."

I wonder if Sal feels a need to give so much of his time and money as some sort of payback to those who perished. I think about the last line in the movie *Saving Private Ryan*, when the elderly James Ryan stands at the grave of his fellow soldier and asks his wife for confirmation that his life had been worthy, that he had indeed earned the right to live. I wonder if Sal is still trying to earn that right to have survived. But I don't ask him this.

"Really, that's what I want my kids and grandkids to understand," Sal says. "It's not about owning a nice house or car. It's the legacy you leave – that's the real value. I may have my faults, but have I been an asset to the Jewish community? Yes, I believe I have."

"And do you still question your faith?" I ask.

"It was never so much a matter of questioning my faith. That was, and still is, strong," Sal explains. "It was just the interpretations of it; that's where I had my doubts. And as I questioned some of these practices and made my own way, my wings started coming out."

I think about the story of King Solomon in the bible. Not that I ever knew it before writing Sal's story; rather, I looked it up out of curiosity, trying to get a better understanding of the Salomon who was born in Poland, and became a CPA in Miami. King Solomon was known as a man of wisdom, wealth and power – who sinned by turning away from God.

"Today, I am a very happy conservative Jew," Sal continues. "Some may drive on Shabbat and feel guilty. I do it, but I don't feel any guilt. I know there's nothing wrong and that's just how I am." Sal tells me how his father used to answer the question that so many people asked after the Holocaust. *Did the experience make you more religious or less?* Sal never had his own answer, but his father used to say it was a little bit of both. That for some who were very religious, they'd ask, *How could there be a God if he allowed this to happen?* And then there were those who had never been particularly religious and they'd say, *Well, if there's no God, how did I survive?*

But he doesn't want to preach. "I'm not the world's policeman," he tells me. "There are things I believe for myself, but it's my *shtick*. You know how they say don't ever discuss politics or religion? Lately, I've been discussing too much politics. I don't want to discuss religion."

BIDING TIME
Costa Rica

DECEMBER 1953 – FEBRUARY 1959

THE MARKETPLACE IN San Jose bore no resemblance to the one in Zelechow, which Sal had last seen at the age of eight, on the day of the pogrom over nine years before. In Poland, the large square remained empty, except on Tuesdays when people would arrive early in the morning and set up a cart or a blanket to display their wares. By nightfall, the market would disappear. Here, in Costa Rica, every stall had a permanent owner who paid rent, obtained a license from the city, and opened his kiosk daily.

It used to be that stores would close on Sundays, until officials realized shopkeepers were losing business. But Sal's parents closed their store on Saturdays to observe the Sabbath. "You're crazy!" their friends said. "That's the busiest day!" Pop just smiled and shrugged. Sal and Alan convinced him to let them open after sundown during the winter months when Shabbat ended around 6pm. Normally all of the stores would close then, but in the months leading up to the Christmas holidays, the shops stayed open until midnight or later. Sal and Alan conducted business until 2:00 in the morning to make up for lost time, and when Sal kept records that second winter in late '54, he noticed that nearly 50% of their business came during those hours after Sabbath.

Unlike other stores, which specialized in a particular item, La Perla carried a little bit of everything – piece goods, shoes, watches, sewing machines. Sal put the sewing machines to use when business was slow after the holiday season and he became known for making aprons. People came in to place special orders, requesting a particular color or design.

"Come back tomorrow," Sal would tell his customers, "and I'll have it for you."

The only thing La Perla didn't carry was food. "Never again," his father said pointing his finger, "will I sell sugar."

CATCHING HIS BREATH after that first Christmas shopping season, Sal couldn't believe it was only a month since he and Alan had left Detroit. He was grateful that Mr. Rosenberg had understood their situation and worked out arrangements. Sal recalled the day five months before, early in September, when he and Alan had returned from New York with their plan to graduate early and sat in Mr. Rosenberg's office seeking guidance.

"We want to go back to Costa Rica in January," Sal said. "But we just got a letter from our father asking if there's anyway we can come home a bit earlier, in mid-December. They have a small store and the last half of December is when they make the bulk of their annual sales."

"I don't see that as being a problem for you," Mr. Rosenberg said to Alan. He turned to Sal and said, "but you, we'll have to figure out how to make this work." The principal was a kind man who understood how hard their father had struggled, and continued to struggle, and he wanted to find a way to help the Wainberg family.

"How many credits am I missing?" Sal asked.

Mr. Rosenberg looked through the file on his desk. "Well, according to everything here, if you pass all of your classes this semester, you'll still need two more courses."

"What about night school at Central High?" Sal knew of some boys who had taken a class or two at the public high school down the road.

"Yes, that's definitely a possibility." Mr. Rosenberg punched in some numbers on his calculator. "But you'd still be short two credits. Sal, there's no way you can handle a full course load here and more than two classes at night."

"What about a correspondence course? I heard about something through the University of Florida. An accounting class." Sal had one goal – get the credits to graduate, get home for the holiday season, and get on with his life. He didn't care if he'd be studying and praying at yeshiva morning 'til evening, and then running a mile to Detroit High for night school. Let Alan go out with the girls that semester; Sal would hang out with his books.

Mr. Rosenberg stared at his student and saw that he was serious. "Let me look into it."

NOW THAT SAL was back in Costa Rica working at his parents' store, he saw how the correspondence class came in handy. He set up a notebook labeled 'accounts payable' – 30 days, 60 days and 90 days each on a different page. He set up another book to record the sales. Pop's accountant Guillermo would come towards the end of each year and ask, "How much do you want to pay in taxes?" Sal would work backwards through the books and give Guillermo the numbers.

Mr. Pleasant, Sal's math teacher at yeshiva, had taught him bookkeeping as well, which Sal had found incredibly appealing. He liked the order of it all, the logic. The principle of bookkeeping, Mr. Pleasant taught, was that for every figure, there is a counter figure. If something didn't balance, it meant that Sal had done something wrong, and he'd rework every problem until he got a perfect solution. Finally, there was something in his life he could control, something he could account for. Something that made sense.

"WHAT'S GOING TO be the *tachlis*?" Sal's father looked at his oldest son while his mother sat at the kitchen table next to her husband, her hands wiping invisible crumbs off the cracked wooden surface.

Sal considered this. What *was* his goal? To get his visa; to leave Costa Rica and its ancient ways. He and Alan had only been home a few months when the *shattchan* came knocking. Any time he wanted to ask a girl out to a movie, his mother had to check with this matchmaker to see if she was available. It wasn't like in Detroit where you could go out for fun. Here, if Sal wanted to go on a simple date, it meant he was serious. At least in the eyes of others. Sal was barely 18 years old, and biding his time until real life could begin. He and Alan assumed their visas would arrive at any moment.

Sal often came home from the store and found some girl's mother sitting in the living room with a beseeching look on her face. "What's wrong with our family?" this woman would plead with his parents. "Don't you want something to happen?"

"What can I tell you? Talk to my kids, not me," his mother would reply.

Sal couldn't date the Jewish girls without an assumption of marriage, even after a single outing. It got to the point where the girls began turning them down. "My mother says I can't go with you," they'd say, "because nothing will come of it." Sal knew this was true and tried convincing his contemporaries to go out in groups – three boys, three girls. But still, the parents got involved. Non-Jewish girls were simply out of the question, though the boys did sneak out every now and then to meet a *shiksa*, worried that it would kill their father if he ever found out.

THEY'D STROLL DOWN the Avenida without a care in the world, Sal and Alan, the midnight moon following as the breeze blew through the large palm fronds, dancing along their arms. They had stopped looking over their shoulders long ago, even before they had gone to yeshiva. It had taken some getting used to at first. Sal remembered arriving in Costa Rica at the age of 12 and walking with a rounded back, his head twisting from side to side. But no soldiers roamed the streets. Only the cats watched their movements, jumping down from stucco walls or rubbing their backs against the trunk of a palm tree. Sal and Alan conversed in English, now, even though they were living in a Spanish-speaking world; they told everyone they met that they were American. "It can't be much longer, right?" Alan looked at Sal. "We'll be back there soon."

––––––

TWO YEARS HAD passed since they graduated, but still, no visas. Business had been growing steadily, yet one store could not support the five people who worked there. Sara had left school after the 5th grade, while Sal and Alan were in Detroit, and worked alongside her parents; early on, she had a much better grasp of the new language. Sal realized that his dream of living in America was taking longer than he had ever expected, so he and Alan opened a second store and named it Bazaar Detroit. They also developed a new business plan.

"Pop," Sal sat facing his father. "Alan and I are working on Saturday."

"It's not right."

"It's the only way we can be successful," Sal said. He had done the numbers and knew the vast majority of the weekly sales occurred on Shabbat. In addition to opening a second location, they enrolled in night classes at the Colegio Commercial Minerva, a trade school. They took courses in bookkeeping, all the while waiting for papers, and struggling to maintain a social life without getting a bride.

––––––

SAL'S FAMILY HAD just received a new letter from Feter Symcha. He, along with his wife and baby daughter, had gone from Germany to Palestine after the war. When Israel had become a state, the government took care of the refugees from Europe, but only on a temporary basis. Symcha had no trade and was trying to learn diamond cutting. The letters they received from him – now a father of two girls, one Polish, one Israeli – were filled with details of a bitter life in the Promised Land. *I'm living in a toilet*, he'd describe as he begged Sal's parents to help him and his family immigrate to Costa Rica. As it turned out, Sal and his family were the last Jews admitted; after 1948, the Central American country would not give visas to anyone but farmers.

Sal's family sent packages to Symcha; mostly coffee which was a precious commodity in Israel. Even the very rich could barely afford it. Symcha would sell this Costa Rican coffee and use the money to buy food for his family. Sal's parents rarely sent packages to Feter Yehuda, his mother's brother who moved to Palestine before Sal was even born. Feter Yehuda was a proud man who wouldn't ask for anything. To ask was to admit that the land of milk and honey could not provide, and that would have been a sin against Israel. Besides, Feter Yehuda lived on a kibbutz, so his needs were met. The few packages of coffee he had received from Costa Rica were probably just shared amongst all the kibbutzniks.

———

"Where you going?" Alan stood at the counter of their newest store, the third location opened in Alajuela, as Sal patted the front right pocket of his shirt, swinging the keys to his father's car.

"Meeting a friend of Campos."

"That the guy you helped all the time with his homework?" Alan straightened the aprons hanging behind the cash register, remembering Mario Campos from the University. "Who became the head of the Bank of Costa Rica?"

"Yeah," Sal said. "I guess I'm a good tutor."

"His friend a woman?" Alan asked.

"No," Sal laughed. "Some guy named Mario Solano. Used to be in the army and now he's the head of Immigration."

Sal drove to Solano's office, which was getting ready to close for the big midday meal. He went upstairs and stood in front of Solano's desk. As Solano turned his back, Sal left an envelope on top of a pile of papers.

"Mario, I know a great restaurant a bit of a distance from here."

Mario Solano turned around and smiled. "Fantastic. There a full bar?"

"Of course." Sal didn't drink but knew Mario as a man who enjoyed his liquor. Sal was hoping Mario would enjoy a drink or two at lunch, which might relax him enough to listen to stories about an Uncle Symcha in Israel.

No sooner had Sal returned to the store after lunch with Mario, than the phone rang. "Wainberg, you left an envelope here. On my desk."

"Mario," Sal said, "I don't know what you're talking about."

"C'mon, Sal. It looks like 10,000 pesos!"

"No, it's not mine. It must be yours."

"Perhaps you're right." Mario's pen tapping against his desk could be heard through the phone. "Well, thanks again for lunch."

"My pleasure." Sal hung up the phone and smiled. Alan just looked at him with one eyebrow raised, the same face he used to make as a little boy, when their aunts chuckled and called little Abraham a lobus.

One month later, an envelope arrived for Sal. In it, a tourist visa for a Simon Wainberg. Feter Symcha, who would change his name to Simon, came alone from Israel and worked in Alan and Sal's store, continuing to send coffee to his wife and daughters until they, too, could reunite in Costa Rica. Sal had other lunches with Mario Solano – leaving envelopes, pouring drinks and regaling him with stories about an aunt and cousins in Israel, and at a the behest of family friends with a son still in Europe, a young man named Mendel Fishbaum.

———

"IT's A FEAST!" Sal couldn't stop staring at the suitcase filled with salamis. "Who needs to cook anything else?"

Sal's mother had been spending entire days at the Centro along with many of her friends preparing food for Sara's wedding. Kugels, chicken, fish – platters for over 400 people, since it was custom for the entire adult Jewish population of Costa Rica to celebrate a simcha in the community. The elderly gabbai would walk from house to house, store to store, hunched over, extending a personal invitation to every single Jew. Sara wasn't marrying a boy from Costa Rica, though, which made the preparations even harder. Only one family was to be responsible for organizing all that cooking.

Though many men had eyes on Sara, she did not find any of the bachelors suitable. They were either too old, or not of good stock. "She shouldn't marry into a family with a shonda," Sal's mother had said. Sara's groom was a young man named Sol, another Survivor, who she had met the year before while on a buying trip in New York City.

Sara had traveled to America for almost two months in 1955, staying with various cousins. Sal never knew he had so many cousins in New York; it was as if any personal connection between two Jews somehow became familial. And these cousins were on a mission to make even more connections; women from Hadassah introduced Sara to nephews and friends and sons of friends. So Sara met Sol and kept up a correspondence even after she left New York to return home. Four months later, Sol showed up in Costa Rica.

In the eight months that Sol lived with the Wainberg's, leading up to the wedding, Sal became very close with his future brother-in-law, to the point where those who didn't know Sal's family very well assumed that there were four Wainberg boys, two with the same name.

The fact that the guests all came from the bride's side didn't diminish the size of the affair, and Sol's brother Jon flew in from New York. He had been instructed to stop at Katz's deli on the Lower East Side and grab what he could before heading south since kosher salami was not available in Costa Rica. Jon took his orders very seriously, arriving with two bags – one holding a suit, some socks and a toothbrush; the other, filled with dozens of salamis swaddled in grease-dotted paper. That second and larger suitcase no less valuable than if it was filled with gold.

———

THE YEARS SAL waited for a visa in Costa Rica was the longest time that the Wainberg family had ever spent together in one place. Almost every day, they'd close the stores in the middle of the afternoon and come home for lunch. Even Bernie's school closed for the big midday meal. Though they had a maid, Sal's mother left the store early to do the cooking.

Sal noticed an improvement in their meals since he had come back from yeshiva. Their maid Juanita had taught his mother how to prepare foods the Costa Rican way. This was when Juanita wasn't crying on the stoop, pouring her heart out to Sal with tales of her rotten boyfriend. "So why do you stay with him?" he'd ask. "Because," she'd wail, her thick dark hair shaking as she lowered her pretty face into her arms, "I love him!" Sal just rolled his eyes.

Red beans and rice with onions. Plantains fried in oil. And on special occasions, after the shochet took a trip to Mexico and came back certified to slaughter cows according to the laws of kashrut, Mom would make cholent with lean meats. Like everything else about Costa Rica, they got used to it.

———

IN FEBRUARY OF 1959 the immigration papers finally arrived from the United States granting resident visas to the two young men who had been waiting five years for their lives to begin. Sal and Alan celebrated and immediately began making plans. Alan had already taken a vacation, traveling to New York earlier that year and stopping in Philadelphia to meet the Siegel's, the kind family from long ago who had sent some chewing gum and an odd-shaped ball to two strange and frightened boys in France. Sal decided to travel to Mexico for a few weeks in order to see the Pan American championship football games. Sal's parents were happy that their sons could finally lead the lives they had dreamed of, but anticipated the pain of not seeing them for a long time. They already knew, all of them, what that felt like.

It was as if Sal and Alan's departure, however, set the clock ticking for everyone else. Sara's husband Sol was already an American citizen, and no sooner did his brothers-in-law leave, than he and Sara began making plans to relocate to the States with their toddler Samuel. Bernie would follow as soon as he graduated high school.

"You pave the way for us," his father said as he helped his sons pack up the merchandise in their store. "I've got a feeling there's a better Yiddish community in America."

LIVING
Miami, Florida

MARCH 1959 ...

FROM THE MOMENT Sal landed in Miami, he got busy – finding a job at J. Byrons department store where he sold suits, then at Washington Federal Bank where he cashed checks – all the while attending night school at the University of Miami. Occasionally he and Alan would go out on a date, like the time he took his landlady's granddaughter to a high school prom. But the tuxedo rentals were too costly, the dancing too awkward. So Sal put off dating until he felt more settled.

A few years later, in 1961, Sal and Alan moved from Miami Beach to Coral Gables where they could be closer to the university, hopefully meet more people. Their roommate Cliff Gordon seemed to have no trouble at all meeting people. Like that girl named Sandy who Sal noticed immediately when Cliff brought her round the apartment to meet his friends. She was cute, with an engaging smile and an unpretentious air. After a few weeks, when Cliff started dating other girls, Sal asked him about the brunette.

"I guess we didn't hit it off," his roommate said. "Feel free to ask her out."

———

"So TELL ME about Costa Rica." Sandy moved closer to Sal, intertwining her hand in his, hoping get to know him better through his description of a place. "What's it like?"

"Ach, I was so happy to leave." Sal looked away. "The social scene was too stifling. You go out with a girl once and her family has you married off."

Sandy counted in her head the number of times she and Sal have gone out. Three years ago, after she stopped dating Sal's roommate Cliff, she and Sal went on a handful of dates. But Sal was so busy — going to school at night, working various jobs during the day. She had never seen anybody work harder than he and his brother — studying, keeping house, earning a living. It had only been in the past few months, since the beginning of 1964, that things between them had gotten more serious. Though what would come of it? In just a couple of months, she would leave for New York to get her Masters in Teaching at Columbia.

"Who wants to be married at 18?" Sal said.

Sandy didn't want to get married right out of high school, either. But she had known then, at the age of 18, what she wanted — to meet a nice Jewish boy and eventually start a family. She figured teaching would be a good career until the kids came.

"So," she probed, "is that why you went to Detroit? To avoid early marriage?"

"No." Sal laughed. "My father wanted me to study Talmud. I don't know that he wanted me to be a rabbi, necessarily. Just Alan and I should know how to be Jewish. Jewish like him."

"You couldn't learn that in Costa Rica?"

Sal sighed. "The Jews in Costa Rica call themselves Orthodox, but they're not. You know, working on the Sabbath. The shochet wasn't even certified to do beef until '55 or '56."

"What's a shochet?" Sandy asked.

"A kosher butcher. They sent him to Mexico to learn how, can you believe? These Jews were not the intelligentsia by any means, but they behaved like it. I'm telling you. Not Jews the way we were."

"So how was your family so religious?" Sandy looked at Sal. "If no one else was, if there was no kosher meat?" This had happened before, where his answers to her questions don't quite match up.

"The Jews in Costa Rica left before we did and never observed like my family. Even before."

"Before what? Left where?" Sandy pulled away and looked at him. "I'm so confused."

"They came to Costa Rica years before we did. For different reasons. They were fleeing something, how do you say, illicit. Bankruptcy, or doing something against the government. They owed money, or maybe they didn't want to go into the army."

"I thought you were born in Costa Rica." Sandy turned to face Sal.

"No." Sal squeezed her hand and looked away. "I was born in Poland. But, you know, the war. We moved."

———

ON MAY 1, 1964, Sal surprised a man named Mr. Truman who had never in all his years of administering U.S. citizenship tests seen anyone get a perfect score. But Sal, who had walked into his citizenship exam like it was nothing, knew that a couple of history questions would never pose a challenge. He had lived history. His upcoming CPA exam, on the other hand, was of great concern; for that he had to study. Sal had since graduated from the University of Miami and had begun working in an accounting firm, but because he wasn't a U.S. citizen when he joined the firm, he hadn't been able to sit for the licensing exam. Now that he was officially an American, it was time to focus on the much harder test.

Also on Sal's mind was his upcoming trip to New York. Pop's second cousin Karola Filowitz and her husband Leo lived in the suburbs, and their son Mark would be called to the Torah as a Bar Mitzvah in October. Sal was looking forward to representing his family at the simcha, but even more, he was eager to see Sandy after several months apart. They had kept up a correspondence since she had left Miami in June to go to graduate school at Columbia. When Sal wrote to her of his plans to travel north, he wondered if Sandy spent as much time thinking about him as he did about her.

When they became engaged over Thanksgiving, Sal knew that she had.

IT WOULDN'T BE for another decade until the entire Wainberg family would once again come together every week to usher in the Sabbath. No, not the entire family. The early fall of 1942 was the last time the entire family had sung the blessings and torn challah. But a new family would eventually grow forth from seeds that had scattered. Two parents, eight kids (including four sons and daughters-in-law), nine grandchildren, and by 2010, 17 great-grandchildren. When Sal's parents retired and moved to Miami in 1974, they carried the Zelechow Torah with them. Ending a journey that had begun 32 years before.

NOVEMBER 26, 1994

SANDY WIPED INVISIBLE schmutz off of Andy's tuxedo jacket and rested her hands on his shoulders. Already, she started crying. Sal, wearing the same navy tuxedo as his son, bent down to his mother in her wheelchair and kissed her cheek, moving aside so Andy could take his place behind his *Boobah* Perla. A melody from inside the sanctuary of Temple Emanu-El floated out through the double doors. They heard the musician strumming the guitar, the notes plucking at their heartstrings; the violin wailed through generations while the flute sang, like an angel, a prayer for a blessed union. It was almost time.

"I can't believe Robyn's getting married." Andy wore a smile that wrapped across his handsome, clean-shaven face belonging not to a little boy anymore, but a man of 25. Sal looked from his son to his daughter, now a bride, and wondered where the time had gone. It seemed like just yesterday that he had became a father — first to Andy, and then to Robyn, named after his sister Rivka.

The music grew louder as the wedding coordinator opened the door and nodded. As Andy pushed his grandmother down the aisle, Sandy peeked into the room. A white satin runner led down the red-carpeted aisle and up the bima steps to the *chuppah*, a canopy of white silk covered in orchids and lilies, birds of paradise and other colorful, tropical flora. Heads turned and 225 faces peered at the first of the bridal procession. Sandy and Sal's friends stood out in the crowd — the Gardner's, Rosenberg's, and Zucker's. Sandy saw Thea and Larry sitting towards the back with Audrey and Tommy; Marty and Sharon smiled as Andy pushed Sal's mother down the aisle. But the majority of the guests were family.

Finally it was Sal and Sandy's turn to take a walk they themselves took 29 years before. Their daughter — a stunning figure in antique white — floated down the aisle between them. Sal couldn't make out a single face in the crowd. He just beamed, accompanying Robyn to her betrothed. *Noah's not such a kid, anymore,* Sal thought to himself, walking towards his almost son-in-law. Noah had grown since he first showed up at their house seven years before as a junior in high school, a year behind Robyn. And he grew on Sal who saw him now for the mensch he was – a young man who loved his daughter, who took to Andy like a brother, treating him with the respect he deserved.

Sal's siblings were all represented in the bridal party. Alan's daughter Lori was a bridesmaid; Bernie's daughter Rena, younger than Robyn by over 10 years, a junior bridesmaid; and Sara's youngest granddaughter Leah was the flower girl. Sara's own children Sam and Rebecca were much older than Robyn and Andy, and the two of them with their spouses had brought forth eight grandchildren, with two more boys to come in just a few years.

Sandy and Sal stood under the chuppah as Robyn circled Noah seven times and Rabbi Farber recited the *sheva brachot*, the seven blessings. *Baruch atah Adonai, m'sameiach chatan v'chalah.* Blessed are you, Lord our God, who grants the joy of groom and bride. Rabbi Schiff, the same rabbi who had married Sandy and Sal, stood under the chuppah as well, contributing to the ceremony. Sandy gazed around the sanctuary, taking in the beauty of the Byzantine architectural details, the midnight blue ceiling of the rotunda that reached four stories high, the dark cherry wood. Many a Wainberg simcha had been celebrated inside these Jerusalem stone walls: Robyn and Andy's Bnai Mitzvah in 1982, Sal's parents' 50th anniversary party a year later, the weddings of Sara's kids whose devout observance enabled them to softly chant by heart the words of the seven Hebrew prayers calling for mirth, song, delight, love, harmony, peace and companionship.

But beyond the sentimentality of the location was the practicality – a huge contingent of their guests was Orthodox. And though the ceremony didn't officially start until sundown, they needed to hold the wedding near the kosher hotel on Miami Beach so that these relatives, who had traveled from all over the world, could either walk or take transportation just as Shabbos ended, without missing the events. Sal could have practically chartered a plane from Costa Rica for all the *mishpocha.* Cousin Herschel (long since Enrique) had suffered a stroke and needed round-the-clock care, but his wife Sarita and their daughter and son-in-law came, along with Bernardo (Sal's older cousin Berl), his wife and two of his six children. Uncle Simon and Aunt Pearl also made the trip, though their daughters who lived in Israel couldn't come due to financial constraints. Traveling from Israel, however, were Uncle Yehuda's son and daughter, along with their spouses.

THE BAND, ONE of Miami's top wedding performers, struck up a hora; clarinets and trumpets filled the social hall with their call of celebration. *Hava nagila, vey'nismecha* "Let us rejoice and be glad!" The accordion cheered and the violin crooned. Sandy had danced a million horas at various Bar Mitzvahs and weddings throughout the years, but this one was different. Sal's family swept onto the dance floor and formed two circles, one inside the other, separating the men from the women. The secular friends fell into place, following a tradition of modesty they'd seen only in film, the first of many differences in the evening's festivities. Before the dinner was served the religious guests davened in the corner, and by the end of the affair, the band stopped to accommodate their *benching*, or singing aloud the *Birkat Hamazon,* a prayer prescribed by Jewish law to follow a meal that included bread. But until then, they all rejoiced through dance.

Suit jackets flared, skirts twirled above stockinged knees, and hundreds of feet criss-crossed the floor in concentric circles of celebration. *Hava neranena* "Let us sing!" The passion rose with the wail of the clarinet, an organized frenzy spun as one, dipping to the left and up again. Sal watched his daughter and her husband in the center of it all, beaming at each other and clutching opposite ends of a single linen napkin as they rose into the air, the bride and groom each in a different chair held aloft by strong men, Jewish men, family. Andy, whose smile had not faded one bit; Alan's sons David and Daniel; Bernie's son Mitchell. Had Sara's grandsons David, Masha, Michael, Naftali and Noam been old enough to stay for the reception, they, too, would have wanted in on the action. With her left hand, Robyn grabbed the arm of the chair and laughed as the revelers raised and lowered her to the beat of the music. *Uru achim, b'liv sameach* "Awaken brethren with a cheerful heart!" The crowd dancing around the couple dropped their arms and clasped hands, fingers locking as men and women, separately, swooped to the center of the floor, raising joined fists into the air. Knuckles grazed, perspiration mingled through navy wool or silk, and the group stepped back again, recreating two larger circles, flinging hands out behind them as they shouted, "Mazel tov!"

Sal moved away from the crowd, watching his daughter and son-in-law dance their first dance to the Beatle's *And I Love Her*. Sal was still *kvelling* over the hors d'ourves he had savored during the cocktail hour — lamb chops, pasta stations, carving stations, all sorts of tasty morsels passed by tuxedoed waiters with white gloves and silver trays; the finest food one could ever imagine. The magnificence surrounded him, along with so many people who had touched him and Sandy in some way. He couldn't believe this was his life. Two grown, wonderful children — one on her way to becoming a pediatrician, the other following in the family's footsteps with a zeal for retail — children who had led lives of ease and happiness. A life he as a child never knew.

Sandy glided across the dance floor, her feet never touching the ground. She saw her mother-in-law sitting at a table off in the corner. If there was to be any sadness at this event, this was it; Perla was but a shell of her former self, the

Alzheimer's so advanced. But still, she was there, the last leaf on the tree. Both of Sal's Uncle Moshes had passed away, after spending their later years in New York, as had Uncle Yehuda, who they had visited on several occasions in Israel. Sandy recalled the past twenty years with Boobah Perla and Zhaida Jaime. She was never sure how Bubbe and Zayde became Boobah and Zhaida; was it Sam or Rebecca who couldn't pronounce the Yiddish words for grandparents so many years ago? Sandy thought it was too bad Robyn and Andy never learned Yiddish, or herself for that matter. Robyn had spoken of her grandmother as a loving and constant presence in her life; a squishy woman who cooked gefilte fish and kugel, who played Cats Cradle with string, and who, with whiskery lips, kissed everything she had eaten onto her grandkids' cheeks.

As faces twirled by Sal, Bernie and Alan stopped and stood by his side. "If only Pop were here." Alan put his arm around Sal and squeezed him into a bear hug, thinking about the father they had lost just two years before. "He'd be filled with such *nachas*."

"You know what he'd say, right?" Bernie thickened his Yiddish accent. "*Did you ever think ...*"

Sal smiled; he'd been thinking it too. He remembered Sara's wedding almost 30 years before, Pop dancing and grabbing Sal's arms, both for balance and a solid embrace, stopping to catch his breath. "Did you ever think," his father had panted, "when we were in Sokol's greeb..." Always the 'greeb.' Pop would often stop mid-bite during a hearty meal, or after shaking hands with a valued customer, and contemplate their good fortune. "When we were hiding in that pit, did you ever imagine we'd be living like this?"

Sal stood with his brothers and remembered, 30 years ago, holding his father's elbows and looking down into his eyes, wondering when he had become taller than the man he had always looked up to. His father had reached up that day and patted Sal's cheek, then reached around to the back of his son's neck, pulling his head down and planting a firm kiss on Sal's forehead.

The three brothers stood locked together now in an embrace of joy and reflection. A waiter interrupted offering them each a flute of champagne. Sal raised the glass, not that he'd drink it, and whispered, "*L'Chaim*."

To life.

TELLING: FALL 2009

SANDY KNOWS THIS will be the last call. For months, she and Sal have been going through this process together, finally together, and she can't help but think how healing it has been. "Miraculous" was how she described it to me when just the two of us had spoken a few weeks before. I had asked Sandy if hearing Sal tell his story in this level of detail had shaken the foundation of their marriage. "No, not at all," Sandy had said. "It strengthens it. I didn't just marry Sal; I married his history." But she did say out loud something that she'd felt all along. "I, too, am a survivor," she told me. "A survivor of this marriage."

Now, as she listens to Sal open up on the phone, she knows so much more than she ever did before, she gains a deeper understanding of just how much he lost. And she finds that there aren't enough tears.

A week ago, after one of our marathon conversations, Sandy hung up the phone and turned to Sal. "How come you never told me that?" she asked him.

Sal had shrugged. "You never asked."

Sandy was flabbergasted. He made it sound so simple, as if there had been a time in the past for questions. For Sal, it was never the right time. Their lives had been filled with Sal's career, the kids, the house – all the everyday complexities of sheer normalcy. And it had been filled with his silence; the Holocaust had been the white elephant in the room of their marriage. It's only been recently that Sal has begun to examine his past. Sandy can count on one hand the number of times he ever spoke of it before then, the first being on the plane ride to Poland. Yes, there are many things she never asked.

But I'm asking now. "Sal," I say, "I'm having a hard time reconciling this intense need to tell your story, to get it all out, with a lifetime of your reluctance and repression. Why the change?"

"It's all timing, I suppose."

Sandy remembers the Hidden Children's Conference in New York they had attended in 1991. Sal had shared his story, but in a very different way than he speaks now. There were others in attendance, Survivors who had lost their childhood as well. Sara came, too, which Sandy had thought odd since Sal's sister refused to speak in the group therapy sessions. The tension between her and Sal over what should or should not be shared was palpable, as if Sara felt violated anytime Sal opened his mouth.

"The tapes you sent me," I say, "from your video testimony. Those were from 1995. How did that come about?"

"I have a friend, Bobbi Kaufman. She was working with the Shoah Foundation collecting video testimonies and wondered if I'd be willing to sit for an interview."

"She knew you were a Survivor?" I ask.

"Yes," says Sal. "It's not that people didn't know. I just didn't talk about it. But she asked me and I thought about it for some time. Eventually, I agreed. I wanted to leave a legacy for Andy and Robyn, so they could understand my past and what I went through."

"If she had come to you, say in 1975, and asked you to speak, would you have?"

"Probably not, no. I was still worried about making a life, the office. I wouldn't have been as receptive." Sal takes a sip from his glass of water. "But if it weren't for Bobbi, I would never have begun to open up. God has his or her ways. I was fortunate that this hit me at the right time."

"Talk to me about your retirement," I say. "It sounds like that's what propelled this change."

"It was in 1999. I had time on my hands. Time to ruminate, to remember. I started reading everything I could about the Holocaust. I felt there was something unresolved within me," Sal says. "I still feel that way."

Sandy thinks back to the months leading up to Sal's retirement. She had been nervous; he didn't have any hobbies or social life, only his career. They moved from Miami to Tampa the year he retired, and then became grandparents. But Sal needed something to do. In April of that year, he saw an article in *The Tribune* that said The Florida Holocaust Museum in St. Pete needed docents. Sandy remembers the day he came home from the training. Apparently, he had been instructed to develop a timeline of his life. When the head of the museum saw that Sal was a Survivor, he approached Sal — very gently, as Sal described it — and asked if he'd be interested in talking about his experience to larger groups. Sandy had been shocked when Sal agreed.

Now she worries that he's doing too much. Interpreting for patients at the health clinic, the Guardian Ad Lightum, traveling all over Southwest Florida speaking to school groups. He can't stop. She's amazed at his desire to help the most people he can, at how he uses every spare minute to give to others.

"I'm not such a young man, but you should know I'm one of the youngest Survivors." Sal talks about the museum and what it's like speaking to students. "Some of these Survivors, when they speak before an audience, you realize that they're losing it. They've forgotten a lot of their story, or they mess up the details." *Oy,* Sal thinks. *Please God if I ever get to be that way, I should know enough to quit.* "I would like to speak as long as my body carries me. As long as I can stand up and speak coherently, I will keep going."

Sandy knows that for Sal, this has become his sacred obligation. As if he survived in order to bear witness. She recalls the book *Night* by Elie Wiesel. Sal couldn't get past the first few pages. "Too poetic," he had said years before. But Sandy couldn't put it down. *For the survivor who chooses to testify,* Wiesel wrote, *it is clear: his duty is to bear witness for the dead and for the living. He has no right to deprive future generations of a past that belongs to our collective memory. To forget would be not only dangerous but offensive; to forget the dead would be akin to killing them a second time.* Now, with his work through the museum and all of his lectures, Sal brings the dead back to life. His sister, his aunts and cousins. The entire town of Zelechow. And with each telling, more memories rise to the surface.

Earlier in the year, Sandy had sat in the rear of the museum auditorium and watched as Sal spoke to a group of schoolchildren. He looked up and stared into the crowd for a minute before continuing with his story. "One time," he said, "when Mr. Sokol was lowering the bucket of food, it fell and hit my father on the face. 'Til the day he died, my father had a black mark right here." He rubbed the bridge of his nose. Sandy's mouth dropped. She had always wondered where her father-in-law's bruise had come from.

Sal tells me about speaking on behalf of the museum. "They do something terrific when they introduce me; they do a whole *shpiel.* 'You are very lucky,' they say. 'You are the last generation to hear a real Survivor tell his story.' It makes me feel important. If I was reluctant at one time to speak, now I feel they really want me."

"You didn't think people wanted to hear your story?" I recall the few times as a teenager when I had the honor of hearing a Survivor tell his or her story. How I sobbed not only listening to the horror of it all, but thinking that soon, there wouldn't be anyone left to give a firsthand account. "How could you think no one wanted to hear it?"

"It's not that I'm such a private person," Sal tries to explain. "But the years had taught me something. In the 1950's and 60's, friends or co-workers would ask where I was from, and then not ask any more questions. Or, if I mentioned to someone that I left Poland in 1946, they'd change the subject to a golf game or some such triviality."

"Really?" I'm shocked. "Why?"

"Who knows? But after a while, I realized that maybe that's what I should do, too. I should change the subject in my head … let it go." Sal describes the mood of the country after the war. How Jews in America were purposely trying to distance themselves from their Eastern European brethren because American society wasn't as accepting of Jewish life as it is today. "I figured the Holocaust was not something people wanted to talk about or hear, so who was I to impose my story on them?"

"Do you think that maybe people felt guilty about not doing more during the war," I propose, not knowing for sure. "Maybe it was less a reaction to you and what you went through, and more a turning away from their own apathy?"

"Perhaps." Sal stops to reflect for a moment. "Looking back on it, I think I understand people's reactions a lot better now. Maybe they simply didn't want to open up new wounds. Maybe they felt I wanted to forget."

"But, you didn't even share this with Sandy," I say. I can't imagine keeping a secret like this from my husband. "Explain that to me. A co-worker is one thing, but your wife?"

"As we started dating and getting close, I assumed she wasn't interested in my past," Sal says. He still wonders what she first saw in him; in her he saw light, a smile. "And I thanked God she didn't ask because I didn't want to lie. I think that by the time we got married, I was so used to not talking about it that it became natural."

Sandy thinks about Sal's words last week. "You never asked." For 45 years, she's tried to piece together a history, stumbling over family relations. She may have probed, *Where were you at this time?* And when he said, *hiding in the cellar*, she froze, not knowing how to go on from there. It had been such a shocking response. The man she loves, the father of her children, led a life she cannot even begin to imagine.

She knows now that everything she had taken for granted, he had watched with envy, experiencing moments that had been missing from his own youth. There had been a total void, no cultural cues that would have allowed him to laugh along at a dinner party. Old songs, comic strip characters, any semblance of a typical boyhood with typical worries – the frame of reference was missing. Sandy thinks Sal is like someone without sight or hearing, an amnesiac.

"But you can never forget," I say, thinking about Sal's explanation of people's disinterest. I'm afraid to ask the next question, not sure if it's even appropriate. "What about forgiveness?"

"Would you believe I bought a Leica camera?" Sal chuckles, thinking about how his son-in-law Noah will be horrified when he finds out. Noah wouldn't let Robyn get a BMW years ago. *How could the daughter of a Holocaust Survivor buy a German car?* he had said to his wife. Sal's afraid to tell them he might actually consider buying one of those cars, too. "Many years ago I had the opportunity to purchase a Mercedes for half price; Sandy really wanted one. But there was no way I was going to support the German economy."

I've heard this sentiment, not only amongst Survivors, but many American Jews. I had been surprised when I went to Israel in 1987 and saw that all of the cabs were Mercedes, until I learned that they had been given to the country as war reparations.

"I realize now that maybe my line of thinking was wrong, especially since I see that the Germans are genuinely sorry and have genuinely tried to atone." Sal's not sure he can say this about the Polish. "I've become more tolerant of the people I used to hate. I feel like I'm 180 degrees from where I was six or eight years ago."

"What accounts for the change?" I ask. "What was the pivotal moment?"

"It's more of a slow evolution," Sal says. "Well, not slow. The change has happened in a relatively short amount of years. But it's been a lifetime leading up to it." He thinks about the time he has spent in the museum, working in the clinic, seeing all different kinds of people walk through the door with all kinds of questions and backgrounds and life experiences. "Maybe it's from all the reading I'm able to do now. I just learned that Leica, back in the late 30's and 40's found jobs for Jews in their factories and sent them to the United States. This German company that I've been boycotting all these years, they saved Jews!"

Sal is still trying to figure it all out. He doesn't have absolute conviction any more. His mind is changing all the time. "It's ironic – now that I have more time in my life for learning, I'm less sure about things than I had ever been before," he admits. "I hear one side, and I get it. And then I hear the other side, and I get that too. But maybe that's progress."

He tells me a story about a wise old rabbi. A husband and wife are having an argument and they go to their spiritual leader for advice. First the rabbi listens to the wife and says, "You are 100% correct." Then the husband speaks and he says, "You are 100% correct." The rabbi's wife, the *rebetzen* looks at him and says, "How can they both be correct?" The rabbi thinks for a minute and says, "You're right, too!"

"That's the way I feel," says Sal. "I'm still learning, still going through changes. I'll probably be doing this for the rest of my life."

Sandy knows this, in and of itself, is very new for Sal – being tolerant, changing his mind. It's not something he used to do very easily. He knew what was right, what was wrong, and no one could tell him different.

"We talk about intolerance as being something that was a German or Polish problem. But when you refuse to see in others some change, or some capacity for good, what does that make you?"

"Here's a question you may have heard," I say. "Are people inherently good, or inherently evil?"

"Four years ago, my answer would have been very different. Now, I think people are good and it takes something – an extraordinary circumstance, what have you – to cause people to become evil." Sal talks about the discussions he used to have with his father. If he had to attribute a fault to him, it'd be that his father was extremely dogmatic. *If you're Jewish, you're good,* his father had always said, implying that someone who wasn't Jewish was lesser. "I argued with my father – the only thing we argued about – I'd beg him to consider the possibility that there might be at least one honest goy in this world. 'I don't want you to agree that I am right and you are wrong,' I'd plead. 'I only want you to admit that there is a possibility that there could be another opinion.' Dad couldn't."

"And you?"

"I learned at a young age that people aren't always what they seem to be." Sal remembers being 11 years old when the Red Scare hit. It was the beginning of the Berlin Blockade and there was talk of World War III. He started hearing terrible things about the Russians, the atrocities they had committed. He had to reconcile this with what he knew of them from two years before when they were his teachers and saviors and source of income. "Seeing truths about things you remember and interpreted differently," Sal says, "it's very disturbing and quite educational."

"If you could erase anything from your memory," I ask, "what would it be?"

"Oy, you ask some incredible questions." Sal takes a moment to think. "I don't think there's anything I would erase, because then I would give up a part of me."

I ask the question in a different way. "If you had a magic wand, and could wave it and make things different, would you make it so that the Holocaust never happened?"

"Well, if it never happened, I wouldn't be talking to you. I wouldn't have been halfway around the world; I wouldn't have spoken so many languages." Sal pauses before continuing. "We were among the richest people in Zelechow, yet I couldn't even think about buying a pineapple or an orange. And that was living the best life there. I would have lived out my life in a tiny town in Poland, an old man with peyes who may never have even heard of The United States or known of the miracles of the modern world. Not even a provincial life, but a nothing life." Sal doesn't know that it's something he would have wanted.

"They always say 'be careful what you wish for.'"

"I do sometimes ask myself, 'why me?' I don't ask myself why I survived. I ask why did I have to go through what I went through. Why couldn't I have survived by being born before this all happened, or born someplace else?" Sal speaks of the question students always ask him when they hear his story. *Why did you survive?*

His answer is 'I don't know; God had to leave some people.' But he doesn't like to think about it. It carries too much responsibility, too many possibilities he's not prepared to accept. It leads to even more questions in his mind. *Did God want us to survive? Why did all of those miracles occur if God did not want us to survive? Yet, if it's true that God wanted us to survive, would we have survived no matter what, whether or not we struggled for it every moment of every day? And if he was so keen on our survival, why did we have to suffer so much? Were we chosen, or was it just dumb luck?* Sal's not sure he'll ever know the answers. "All these questions about God and our survival make me uncomfortable. Just asking them assumes that God made those choices; admits that there is in fact a God. I've not been able to get to that point yet. I'm still debating."

Sal wants to go back to discussing tolerance and forgiveness. It's something he's been grappling with for several years now. "I don't believe you *must* be able to forgive in order to be a tolerant person." He holds the phone with one hand and raises the other in the air like a scale of justice. "You must *think* of forgiveness, because otherwise, living would be impossible. If you were to think 'that's the way the world is and that's the way it's meant to be,' then what's the use of living? You must let yourself adjust to a different world, a different life."

But as he considers the notion of forgiveness, he knows that as of right now, he hasn't forgiven. It doesn't mean that if he lives long enough he won't get there. "There are many discussions among Survivors," he tells me. "In order to be a person, you must be a decent person. But will I ever be able to reconcile what happened to me … what happened to the world? I don't know. At least now, I'm open to the possibility."

Author's Notes and Acknowledgments

SAL WAINBERG LEFT this world on February 22, 2012. It's a credit to his strength, honesty, courage and trust that his story did not die with him. I will never forget the day he called asking me to write a book about his experience; I still don't know why he chose me for this monumental task, but I'm grateful that he did.

My heartfelt thanks go to Sal and Sandy both for allowing me to share in their journey; for trusting me with their memories – both painful and cherished – and for laying themselves bare, when it might have been easier to remain guarded. To Robyn Jacobson, their daughter, who offered even more insight and a different perspective.

I have strived to remain truthful to their recollections, but memory is a funny thing. If asked, would you be able to recall what you had for breakfast a week prior? Or provide a perfectly accurate transcript of a conversation from only hours before? Likely not. But you'd know what you typically eat, and where. Or the gist of the communication and how it made you feel. These are the memories I have sought to bring to life – the details of traditions observed, relationships tested, the sensations and emotions of a little boy that remained vivid even seventy years later. And so if I took any liberties in writing this book, it was in service to developing a narrative that would show how a community thrived – until it didn't any longer. Sal was adamant I not make anything up for the sake of storytelling. I didn't. The historical details of Sal's life were dramatic enough that I didn't need to embellish them.

Because of Sal's insistence on being completely truthful (and because memory lapses are entirely possible), when it came to chronology and history, I conferred with many additional sources. I am amazed at Sal's accuracy. My gratitude goes to the following people and institutions: Shulamith Berger, Curator of Special Collections at Yeshiva University for opening up their archives and helping me locate not just pictures of the orphanage run by Agudath Israel, but the picture of Sal as a young boy on the cover of this book; Misha Mitsel, JDC Senior Archivist for opening up their archives and helping me locate information on the HIAS operation that carried Jewish children (orphans or otherwise) out of Poland, as well as information about the *Jagiello* that set sail from France to Costa Rica; JewishGen, Inc., an affiliate of the Museum of Jewish Heritage – on their website, I discovered the *Yizkor* (memorial) Book of Zelechow. I had chills scrolling through the lists of names, often including occupations or family members. I wrote many of these people into the book both to provide authenticity to the minor characters in Sal's story and, in some small way, to help those who perished live on. I found photographs of Sal's relatives – both those who survived and those who were murdered – as well as some of the people who were in hiding with him. Thank you to Lance Ackerfeld who carried out the translation of the Yizkor book and sent me the higher res versions of many of the photos included on the following pages. This Yizkor Book also provided historical background and information that Sal may not have been privy to at the time, but I felt the reader needed for context. Thanks go to my brother, Ron Rosenberg, who pointed me to the Freedom of Information Act and, specifically, the U.S. Department of Homeland Security's U.S. Citizenship and Immigration Services. They sent me a disc with 35 pages of Sal's various immigration applications and certificates of naturalization. How many times did I refer to HebCal.com and make use of their Hebrew / Gregorian calendar converter? When Sal couldn't remember the exact year in which the fire occurred in his house during Pesach, I confirmed the date with HebCal. Truly an amazing resource.

I must also thank Bobbi Kaufman who conducted an interview with Sal in 1995, taking his video testimony and creating a manuscript, both of which were a tremendous resource and a springboard for a thousand more questions. And thanks to the Florida Holocaust Museum for giving Sal an audience, many audiences, when his story could not be repressed any longer.

How does one begin to express gratitude towards those who helped me on this journey? To my parents, Lydia and Bill Rosenberg, for reading a draft, and for asking how the writing was coming along *every single time* we spoke on the phone. What might have normally driven me crazy was welcomed, as I needed that outlet. To the women of my book club who have shaped me as a reader, and thus shaped me as a writer. To Cate Baily, Dionne Ford, Kristen Kemp, Maura Rhodes, and Nancy Williams for each reading a draft and offering invaluable perspective, guidance and support. And Jonathan Eig, who pushed the book past the finish line and prepared me for launch. To Ariel Cooke and Jill Hamburg who helped me find the framework in which to tell this story, and Patty Dwyer who helped format the book and design its cover. To Sarah Blaine and Andrew Gelman who offered legal advice, and Deborah Garrison and George Greenfield who provided great insight into the world of publishing. I thank you all.

To my sons Jacob, Asher and Zane for providing perspective in more ways than one. You became the perfect frame of reference as I delved into the world of another little boy, one who was not nearly as lucky as you all are. I wrote your sensory quirks and self-soothing habits into Szulim's story, and when I sought to capture the dismantling of Szulim's world through the eyes of a child, I stared into your own. On the playground, at the dentist, everywhere I turned, a little Yiddish boy with sidelocks and short pants became the doppelganger to you three.

To my husband, David – my first reader and supportive from the start. You always knew how important this was to me and you remain my biggest cheerleader to this day. Thank you for your loving encouragement of my obsession with another man, and another marriage. This book is dedicated to you.

Yom Ha'Shoah is the Day of Remembrance established to making sure the world will never forget this recent chapter of human suffering. And in Israel, when sirens sound for two minutes, the entire country comes to a halt. Literally. Cars stop on the highway and people stand in silent tribute to the perished. Yet here in America, we designate no foods, sing no songs, stop not a moment of our daily life. We have created no customs so that we will never forget. How can one even begin to ritualize a time so inconceivable?

Perhaps by continuing to absorb the history. We may think that when it comes to the Holocaust we've heard it before. In fact, we haven't. We can never hear enough. We must listen to those who survived; we must read their personal accounts. We must recognize that the collective suffering is nothing less than six million and more unique stories of struggle, determination, tradition and fate – every single one of them incredible, all of them heartbreaking.

Sal's mother Perl, center, with two of her sisters. This picture was found after Sal's death, thus the two aunts on either side of her could not be identified.

Mimeh Gitel Szyfman and Sal's younger cousin Berl; photograph taken around 1937 or '38. Both were killed by Polish bandits while hiding in Turek's farmhouse.

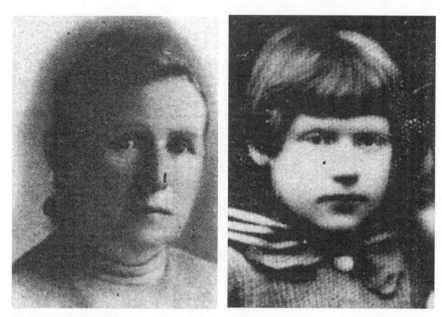

Mimeh Laicha Boruchowicz and her daughter Sara, Sal's aunt and cousin, killed on the way from the attic to the Sokol's cellar

Sal's sister Sara (left) who survived, and his sister Rivka (right) who was killed by Polish bandits when they were discovered in Sokol's cellar

Feters Moshe Boruchowicz and Moshe Szyfman, Sal's uncles, both of whom survived

Sal's mother (left) and both of his parents (right) holding the Torah that had been saved from the burning shul in Poland, and then carried across Europe, and to South America and North America, before finding its home in Israel

The shul in Zelechow

The marketplace in Zelechow

A Zelechower wearing an armband with a yellow star speaking with a droshky driver

Sal in front of his childhood home on a trip to Poland in 1973

Pela (Mr. Sokol's daughter), Mrs. Sokol and Sal in front of the armoire that hid the opening to the trap door, 1973

Mietka Sokol in the kitchen of their farmhouse

Mrs. Sokol in her yard

Made in the USA
Charleston, SC
27 April 2013